Three Men in an Omnibus

JEROME K. JEROME

Three Men
in an Omnibus

A METHUEN HUMOUR CLASSIC

His funniest writings

edited and introduced by Martin Green

with drawings by Posy Simmonds

comprising the entire text of

THREE MEN IN A BOAT

with selections from six other books

A METHUEN PAPERBACK

This selection first published in 1984
by Methuen London Ltd
11 New Fetter Lane, London EC4P 4EE
This compilation © 1984 by Methuen London Ltd
Introduction and Notes copyright © 1984 by Martin Green
Illustrations Copyright © 1984 by Posy Simmonds

Made and printed in Great Britain by
Richard Clay (The Chaucer Press) Ltd,
Bungay, Suffolk

ISBN 0 413 54250 5 (paperback)
0413 567508 (hardback)

On the Stage – and Off was first published in 1885;
Idle Thoughts of an Idle Fellow 1886; Three Men in a Boat 1889.
Novel Notes first appeared as a series in The Idler
and subsequently as a book in 1893. 'Mrs Korner Sins Her Mercies'
is from The Passing of the Third Floor Back published in 1907.
They and I was published in 1909. 'Wheels of Change' is from My Life and Times
published in 1926.

Contents

Introduction

Jerome K. Jerome is so closely associated with his great comic masterpiece *Three Men in a Boat* that it is difficult to stake a claim for him as a writer, not only of humorous books and stories, but also of other works which stand up well against those of his contemporaries. Among these were Rudyard Kipling, J. M. Barrie, Rider Haggard, Arthur Conan Doyle, W. W. Jacobs, G. B. Shaw and H. G. Wells, and many of their names appeared in *The Idler*, a monthly magazine edited by Jerome.

His other works suffer and are largely obscured by the failure of his second-best-known book, *Three Men on a Bummel*. Published in 1900, eleven years after *Three Men in a Boat*, it failed to recreate the innocent delight of its illustrious forbear. It was written at the behest of a publisher solely with profit in mind and artistically it was a failure.

Most adult, literate English people will have heard of *Three Men in a Boat* if they haven't read it at some time in their lives. A number of devotees refresh themselves by reading it at least once a year, and can sometimes quote passages from memory. Not so long ago there was a stand-up comedian whose repertoire included some of the set pieces from the book, such as Uncle Podger's attempt to hang up a picture, or the disquisition on work ('I like work; it fascinates me. I can sit and look at it for hours'). After discovering the delights of *Three Men in a Boat* enthusiasts have sometimes turned to his *Three Men on a Bummel*, only to be let down. They came to the erroneous opinion that he was simply a one-book man, and that *Three Men in a Boat* was a phenomenon, a bestseller by accident. There was also the slur that Jerome was a superficial hack from an obscure, lower-middle class background who had simply struck it lucky and would never have been heard of had it not been for *Three Men in a Boat*. But the facts of Jerome's writing career are otherwise.

Jerome K. Jerome 1859 – 1927

Jerome Klapka Jerome was born at Walsall in 1859, his father a colliery-owner and nonconformist preacher, his mother the daughter of a Swansea solicitor. The father's fortune, acquired through marriage, was lost when his pit was flooded, and the family removed to the East End of London where Jerome's father hoped to get by as an ironmonger. Jerome junior managed to get a place at the St Marylebone Grammar School which he left at the age of fourteen to become a railway clerk, just after the death of his father and a year before his mother died. After a brief spell schoolmastering, he tried his luck on the stage and finally took to journalism. A series of vignettes recounting his experiences as an actor led to his first book, *On the Stage – and Off*, published in 1885; his *Idle Thoughts of an Idle Fellow* – begun as a series commissioned by *Home Chimes* – was published as a book in 1886; and three years later came *Three Men in a Boat*.

In 1892, by now a successful author, Jerome with two others founded *The Idler*, an illustrated monthly magazine which was remarkably successful and in which his *Novel Notes* first appeared (published in 1893). He followed *The Idler* in 1893 with a twopenny weekly called *To-Day*; but a costly libel action ended his interests in both journals four years later. He was meanwhile producing other books, tales and sketches, including *Three Men on a Bummel*, *Diary of a Pilgrimage* and various dramatic works.

He had married in 1885, the year his first book was published, and he inherited a step-daughter who was shortly joined by a daughter of his own, who was later to have an ephemeral career on the stage. His first success in writing for the theatre came in 1886 when *Barbara* was produced at the Globe by Sir Charles Hawtrey, though it was not until 1908 that he won popular appeal with *The Passing of the Third Floor Back*. A number of other plays followed, as well as a semi-autobiographical memoir disguised as a novel, *They and I*, published in 1909. In 1926, just after finishing his autobiography, *My Life and Times* – his last work – even though his health wasn't good, he set out on a motoring tour of England. He was taken ill in Northampton and died in 1927 at the age of sixty-eight.

Though he had his ups and downs after the publication of *Three Men in a Boat*, Jerome on the whole must have made a very good living with his pen, both from his books and his journalism, as well as from his plays. The worst thing to befall him, as far as his finances were concerned, was the libel action. This was unwittingly attracted through some uncautious remarks in the City column of his magazine *To-Day*, questioning whether it was possible for domestic gas to be made out of water, as was claimed by a dubious Leeds company promoter called Samson Fox. The words were not written by Jerome himself, but he was the editor and was therefore liable for the costs. At the end of the day, Mr Fox the plaintiff was awarded a farthing damages, but as no order was made as to costs, each party had to pay his own, and Jerome's were £9000, which was a considerable sum in those days. It meant that he had to sell his interests in *To-Day* and *The Idler* and to face the fact that he would have to spend the next few years paying off the balance. However, with the fortitude and good humour that were typical of him, he managed to survive, and he recalls that after the action Samson Fox, whose costs were greater than Jerome's – £11,000, in fact – shook hands with him.

'He informed me,' says Jerome in his memoirs, 'that he was going back to Leeds to strangle his solicitors; and hoped I would do the same by mine.'

There are various light-heartedly disparaging references to Germany, her language and her people, in the pages of *Three Men in a Boat*. Jerome mentions learning German at school, for instance, and how painful it is, and there is the episode of the pompous Herr Slossen Boschen who is tricked by two awful young men. But Jerome had a love for Germany, particularly Dresden, where he lived for a couple of years at the turn of the century, and the Germans took to him, even going so far as to found a Jeromian Club in his honour, the aim of which was to 'read and study the writings of Jerome K. Jerome.'

A few weeks before the outbreak of the First World War, Jerome had written a play, *The Great Gamble*, that drew on his experience of, and affection for Germany, and it had begun what appeared to be a successful run in the West End. Even *The Times* didn't think it was too bad:

> On a Teutonic hill-top, amid tall pines and tall beakers of lager and flowing rivulets of Rhenish wines, and student songs exploding at regular intervals 'off' – your familiar 'Old Heidelberg' atmosphere, in fact – Mr Jerome offers you a blend, or rather a juxtaposition of sentiment and fun. . . .

But a few weeks after the play opened, war broke out and *The Great Gamble* was finished.

Though Jerome had initially welcomed the war, he could not believe the stories of the German atrocities in Belgium and he publicly disassociated himself from his friends and fellow writers Rudyard Kipling and H. G. Wells, with their atavistic talk about 'the Foe' and acclaim for 'the Holy War'; as a result he was attacked in the press and consequently became the recipient of threatening letters. In spite of his attitude, however, he was sent in a party by the British Government to America, to enlist sympathy for the British cause. He even had an interview with President Wilson, who pointed out to him that millions of American citizens were not only of German descent but of Irish descent too. He returned dispirited and, with all his misgivings, he offered to join up as he couldn't bear to be inactive. He was turned down on account of his age and through a chance encounter with a friend in Bond Street, wearing a resplendent uniform, he managed to join a French ambulance unit as a driver. (Elsewhere on the same front and serving in a similar unit was a young American poet called E. E. Cummings, though it is doubtful if they ever met.) Jerome's account of his experiences at the front would suggest that he had taken Dame Edith Cavell's last words as his guide.

Three Men in a Boat

Writing came naturally to Jerome and, with the publication of his first book, he never ceased writing until the day he died. He wrote journalism, essays, stories, novels and plays, as well as editing *The Idler* and *To-Day*; and a quick dip into his hilarious account of stage life, *On the Stage – and Off*, will show that Jerome had arrived at his inimitable style well before *Three Men in a Boat*.

It could well be that if he'd never written *Three Men in a Boat* his other work would be more widely appreciated. Nevertheless in *Three Men* he found his perfect subject and the range of his work was neglected during his lifetime. Even so, *Three Men in a Boat* was looked on by some as a work of the utmost vulgarity; indeed Jerome K. Jerome was dubbed ''Arry K. 'Arry' in the pages of *Punch* (his palindromic name being a disadvantage here). *Three Men in a Boat* is 'vulgar', in that it is a work of immense popularity and can be enjoyed by people who don't normally read books; but in this he shared a popularity comparable to that of Dickens and Shakespeare in their own time.

Even today, though, Jerome's masterpiece is often looked upon as a flawed book, of which the purple passages have to be waded through in order to get to the funny bits. Benny Green, a fellow alumnus of the St Marylebone Grammar School (now alas closed), introducing a handsomely-illustrated *Three Men in a Boat*, makes some slighting remark to this effect. However, I challenge this. The high-flown passages work beautifully in contrast to the comedy: there is a felicitous parody of Mallory concluding one chapter, followed in the next by the episode when George's shirt is dropped overboard. It is through the contrapuntal effect of the sublime and the ridiculous that Jerome gets his effects. It would be impossible to sustain the one without the other.

In a perceptive reassessment of *Three Men in a Boat* in the *New Statesman* some years back, V. S. Pritchett made the claim for the book that it was an idyll, in its purest form, and that this was the reason for its enduring popularity. And certainly it is an idyll, as is remembered pleasure – the wonderful day by the seaside in childhood when nothing went wrong: what the childhood memory doesn't recall is all the tears and organisation on the part of the adults who made the time possible, the row over the forgotten corkscrew, the missing salt. So it is with the three men. They are, by all accounts, three debonair young men untrammelled by the responsibility of family, without a care in the world, who set out to have a good time on the river. And there was of course pleasure for such freeborn Englishmen who

[xi]

had achieved sufficient education to be able to wear white collars and sit upon stools in offices. It was a different story for the submerged masses in the East End of London, where Jerome had spent his early years and from whence he had fled with such relief into a clerkship on the Great Western Railway and into a lodging house in Bloomsbury.

It was just such a lodging-house from which emerged the extraordinary story, 'The Passing of the Third Floor Back', which later became his most successful play. The desperate charade the characters play, aping the social positions they can only aspire to, is the reality of the background from which J. Harris, and George have come or escaped. Jerome must have felt this story very deeply as it was his own and, cruellest of all, one in which a family sinks from comparative affluence into genteel poverty until conditions become almost unendurable. He recalls this with devastating economy – and economy was one of Jerome's triumphs as a comic writer – in the account in *Three Men in a Boat* of the three of them coming across the body of a young woman floating in the river: 'Rather a hackneyed story', he calls it.

> Left to fight the world alone, with the millstone of her shame around her neck, she had sunk lower and lower. For a while she kept both herself and the child on the twelve shillings a week the twelve hours' drudgery a day procured for her, paying six shillings out of it for the child, and keeping her own body and soul together on the remainder.
>
> Six shillings a week does not keep body and soul together very unitedly. . . .

Jerome knew; he had seen the effects of the rise in price of coal on his mother's face, and he quoted her diary in *My Life and Times*:

> January 12th. A very severe frost set in this week. Skating by torchlight in Victoria Park. Coals have risen eight shillings a ton. It is a fearful prospect. I have asked the lord to remove it.

So behind the glitter of the sun on the River Thames, the careless young men in boaters and the pretty girls in muslin dresses and flowered hats, the life Jerome left behind him in the East End of London – Narrow Street, in fact – was still nasty, brutish and short. Yet it is this dark side of life, only hinted at in Jerome's comic writing, that gives it the buoyancy that sustains the humour.

One of the chief delights of *Three Men in a Boat* is that it is so good-humoured: there is never any malice in his pages, though the self-important are gently mocked. Even in the episode of the old man and the skulls – 'The man who loves not graves and coffins and skulls' – when J. comes very close to losing his temper, he merely tells the old man that when he (the old man) is dead and buried, he (J.) will come and see his grave. 'That is all I can do for you,' he says, before fleeing. And again, when Harris deals with the tough on the river bank who wants to know whether they know they are trespassing or not, he is seen off without even a harsh word. Mind you, Harris does go slightly overboard when saying what he would like to do to the people who put up notice-boards warning trespassers. J. has merely said of the sight of them, 'I feel I want to tear each one down, and hammer it over the head of the man who put it up, until I have killed him, and then I would bury him, and put the board up over the grave as a tombstone,' whereas Harris wanted to slaughter the man's family and burn the house down.

Another quality that shows up in everything Jerome wrote – as it did in his own life – is his human decency. So that, however mawkish some of his descriptive and mystical passages seem, they are always saved from going too far – in *Three Men in a Boat* anyway – by someone or something breaking in and bringing J. and the reader back to earth. A good example of this is when J. has been enthusing about camping under the stars and Harris rudely interrupts the flow with, 'What about when it rained?'; and while Jerome complains that there is no poetry in Harris, Harris takes Jerome by the arm and says he knows a place round the corner 'where you can get a drop of the finest Scotch whisky.'

The Man and His Range

Players and painted stage took all my love,
And not those things that they were emblems of,

[xiii]

said W. B. Yeats in a well-known poem. And so it was with Jerome: his first and lasting love was the stage. It can hardly have been otherwise, in the case of a young man who, before the turn of the century, was willing to give up a secure job on the railways as a clerk, with a few shillings a week *and* prospects, to try his luck on the stage. There was no Equity in those days, but a host of crooked theatrical-agents and rapacious managers who made a living out of the incautious ambition and vanity of aspiring actors and actresses. Jerome's journalism and his successful authorship did not get in the way of his writing plays and busying himself about the theatre. Admirers of Jerome could be forgiven today for not crediting him with any theatrical success, but even in his own day it sometimes went unnoticed. At the height of his career, he recalls in *My Life and Times*, there was a similar neglect:

A lady on one occasion, asked me why I did not write a play. 'I am sure, Mr Jerome,' she continued, with a bright engaging smile, 'that you could write a play.'

I told her that I had written nine; that six of them had been produced, that three of them had been successful both in England and America, that one of them was still running at the Comedy Theatre and approaching its two hundredth night.

Her eyebrows went up in amazement.

'Dear me,' she said. 'You do surprise me.'

This is another example of the modest decency of the man – particularly if you imagine what George Bernard Shaw's reaction might have been to the same silly question.

So his first book, *On the Stage – and Off*, was not a flash in the pan, but an account of his first-hand experiences in the theatre, the theatre with which he was to have an enduring love affair, though his initial steps were of an extremely humble nature as a bit-part player. These early experiences must have been invaluable, too, when it came to writing his own plays, as at least he knew the whole business.

One of Jerome's qualities which I hope to have demonstrated is a kind of native decency, infused with his humour and running through his comic works. It is reflected, too, in Jerome's life, manifested in his autobiography and the recollections of his friends. This decency of Jerome has a peculiarly English quality about it.

This is something utterly other than a similar quality you might look for in Kipling, an immensely popular author, and possibly the last English poet to be accessible to the ordinary English public. Kipling was British and his work appealed to the proletariat who saw themselves as British first and English second, as well as to Victoria's loyal middle-class subjects. The quality of Jerome's Englishness, however, is something to do with the countryside itself in and around the Thames valley, as well as such surviving virtues as are retained in country inns and rare City pubs. English exiles must find Jerome's England, as described in *Three Men in a Boat* or in the extract from *Novel Notes*, as appealing as the idea of sitting outside a country pub and drinking a pint of beer (the beer, that is, that would have been obtained in Jerome's England, before Pasteur and pressurisation had stolen its natural vitality).

It is an ideal England that Jerome writes about, as doubtless it was to the slightly better-off in the reign of Queen Victoria. The police were guardians of the law, on the side of the propertied classes, but also a degree lower down, as in the wonderful episode of George's early rising in *Three Men in a Boat*. The only contact with them was through some exuberant youthful behaviour that brought you before the local beak. There is all this in Wodehouse, too, in a distilled form.

Yet despite this very English decency Jerome has had little real critical attention in his native land. His books have gone into almost all European tongues, including Irish, as well as Afrikaans; and a writer that is as popular as this must surely express something about the English that foreigners find attractive, as indeed do the English themselves. But apart from Alfred Moss's *Jerome K. Jerome*, a brief and hagiographical resumé of his life published in 1928, just after his death, and Joseph Connolly's recently-published *Jerome K. Jerome: A Critical Biography*, the only other serious attention that has been paid to Jerome is – inevitably – by German scholars, Walter Gutkess and Magnus Wolfsenberger. There is also a bibliography published by Walsall Library in 1971 and an American critical thesis published by Twayne in 1974.

It is as if the taint of 'Arry K. 'Arry still clings to Jerome K. Jerome in this country and it is my hope that this volume will show the public that Jerome was more than a one-book author. If so, the reader's appreciation will be the reward for my enthusiasm.

M.G.
July 1983

Three Men in an Omnibus

from On the Stage – and Off

On the Stage – and Off, published in 1885, was Jerome's first book.
Written originally as a book,
it appeared in serial form in *The Play*,
a penny-paper edited by Aylmer Gowing, a retired actor.
It was subsequently published as originally intended
by Field & Tuer, the Leadenhall Press,
in exchange for a free gift of the copyright.
Three chapters are included here.

CHAPTER I

I Determine to Become an Actor

There comes a time in every one's life when he feels he was born to be an actor. Something within him tells him that he is the coming man, and that one day he will electrify the world. Then he burns with a desire to shew them how the thing's done, and to draw a salary of three hundred a week.

This sort of thing generally takes a man when he is about nineteen, and lasts till he is nearly twenty. But he doesn't know this at the time. He thinks he has got hold of an inspiration all to himself – a kind of solemn 'call,' which it would be wicked to disregard; and when he finds that there are obstacles in the way of his immediate appearance as Hamlet at a leading West-End theatre, he is blighted.

I myself caught it in the usual course. I was at the theatre one evening seeing *Romeo and Juliet* played, when it suddenly flashed across me that that was my vocation. I thought all acting was making love in tights to pretty women, and I determined to devote my life to it. When I communicated my heroic resolution to my friends, they reasoned with me. That is, they called me a fool; and then said that they had always thought me a sensible fellow, though that was the first I had ever heard of it.

But I was not to be turned from my purpose.

I commenced operations by studying the great British dramatists. I was practical enough to know that some sort of preparation was necessary, and I thought that, for a beginning, I could not do better than this. Accordingly, I read through every word of Shakespeare, – with notes, which made it still more unintelligible, – Ben Jonson, Beaumont and Fletcher, Sheridan, Goldsmith, and Lord Lytton. This brought me into a state of mind bordering on insanity. Another standard dramatist, and I should have gone raving mad: of that I feel sure. Thinking that a change would do me good, I went in for farces and burlesques, but found them more depressing than the tragedies, and the idea then began to force itself upon me that, taking one consideration with another, an actor's lot would not be a happy one. Just when I was getting most despondent, however, I came across a little book on the art of 'making-up,' and this resuscitated me.

I suppose the love of 'making-up' is inherent in the human race. I remember belonging, when a boy, to 'The West London United Concert and Entertainment Association.' We used to meet once a week for the purpose of regaling our relations with original songs and concertina solos, and on these occasions we regularly burnt-corked our hands and faces. There was no earthly reason for doing so, and I am even inclined to think we should have made our friends less unhappy if we had spared them this extra attraction. None of our songs had the slightest reference to Dinah. We didn't even ask each other conundrums; while, as for the jokes, they all came from the audience. And yet we daubed ourselves black with as much scrupulousness as if it had been some indispensable religious rite. It could only have been vanity.

'Making-up' certainly assists the actor to a very great degree. At least, I found it so in my case. I am naturally of mild and gentle appearance, and, at that time, was particularly so. It was no earthly use my standing in front of the glass and trying to rehearse the part of, say, a drunken costermonger. It was perfectly impossible for me to imagine myself the character. I am ashamed to have to confess it, but I looked more like a young curate than a drunken costermonger, or even a sober one, and the delusion could not be sustained for a moment. It was just the same when I tried to turn myself into a desperate villain; there was nothing of the desperate villain about me. I might, perhaps, have imagined myself going for a walk on Sunday, or saying 'bother it,' or even playing ha'penny nap, but as for ill-treating a lovely and unprotected female, or murdering my grandfather, the thing was absurd. I could not look myself in the face and do it. It was outraging every law of Lavater. My fiercest scowl was a milk-and-watery accompaniment to my blood-thirsty speeches; and, when I tried to smile sardonically, I merely looked imbecile.

[4]

But crêpe hair and the rouge pot changed all this. The character of Hamlet stood revealed to me the moment that I put on false eyebrows, and made my cheeks look hollow. With a sallow complexion, dark eyes, and long hair, I *was* Romeo, and, until I washed my face, loved Juliet to the exclusion of all my female cousins. Humour came quite natural when I had a red nose; and, with a scrubby, black beard, I felt fit for any amount of crime.

My efforts to study elocution, however, were not so successful. I have the misfortune to possess a keen sense of the ludicrous, and to have a morbid dread of appearing ridiculous. My extreme sensitiveness on this point would have been enough to prevent my ever acting well under any circumstances, and, as it was, it hampered and thwarted me at every turn: not only on the stage, but even in my own room, with the door locked. I was always in a state of terror lest any one should overhear me, and half my time was taken up in listening on one side of the keyhole, to make sure that no one was listening on the other; while the slightest creak on the stairs was sufficient to make me stop short in the middle of a passage, and commence whistling or humming in an affectedly careless manner, in order to suggest the idea that I was only amusing myself. I tried getting up early and going to Hampstead Heath, but it was no good. If I could have gone to the Desert of Sahara and assured myself, by the aid of a powerful telescope, that no living creature was within twenty miles of me, I might have come out strong, but not else. Any confidence I might have placed in Hampstead Heath was rudely dissipated on the very second morning of my visits. Buoyed up by the belief that I was far from every vestige of the madding crowd, I had become quite reckless, and, having just delivered, with great vigour, the oration of Antony over the body of Caesar, I was about starting on something else, when I heard a loud whisper come from some furze bushes close behind me: 'Ain't it proper, Liza! Joe, you run and tell 'Melia to bring Johnny.'

I did not wait for Johnny. I left that spot at the rate of six miles an hour. When I got to Camden Town I looked behind me, cautiously. No crowd appeared to be following me, and I felt relieved, but I did not practise on Hampstead Heath again.

After about two months of this kind of thing, I was satisfied that I had learned all that could possibly be required, and that I was ready to 'come out.' But here the question very naturally arose, 'How can I get out?' My first idea was to write to one of the leading managers, tell him frankly my ambition, and state my abilities in a modest but straightforward manner. To this, I argued, he would reply by requesting me to call upon him, and let him see for himself what I could do. I should then go to the theatre at the time appointed, and send up my card. He would ask me into his private room, and, after a little general conversation on the weather, and the latest murder, etc., etc., he would suggest my rehearsing some short scene before him, or reciting one or two speeches. This I should do in a way that would quite astonish him, and he would engage me on the spot at a small salary. I did not expect much at first, but fancied that five or six pounds per week would be near the mark. After that, the rest would be easy. I should go on for some months, perhaps a year, without making any marked sensation. Then my opportunity would come. A new play would be produced, in which there would be some minor part, not considered of any importance, but which in my hands (I had just read the history of 'Lord Dundreary,' and believed every word of it) would become the great thing in the play, and the talk of London.

I should take the town by storm, make the fortune of my manager, and be the leading actor of the day. I used to dwell on the picture of the night when I should first startle the world. I could see the vast house before me with its waves of wild, excited faces. I could hear their hoarse roar of applause ringing in my ears. Again and again I bowed before them, and again and again the cheers burst forth, and my name was shouted with waving of hats and with bravos.

I did not write to a manager, though, after all. A friend who knew something about the subject said he wouldn't if he were me, and I didn't.

I asked him what course he would advise, and he said: 'Go to an agent, and tell him just exactly what you want.' I went to two or three agents, and told them all just exactly what I wanted, and they were equally frank, and told me just exactly what *they* wanted, which, speaking generally, was five shillings booking fee, to begin with. To do them justice, though, I must say that none of them appeared at all anxious to have me; neither did they hold out to me much hope of making my fortune. I believe my name is still down in the books of most of the agents – at least, I have never been round to take it off – and I expect that amongst them they will obtain for me a first-class engagement one of these days, when I am Bishop of London, or editor of a society paper, or something of that sort.

It was not for want of worrying that they did not do anything for me then. I was for ever what I called 'waking them up,' a process which consisted of studying the photos in the outer office for half an hour, and then being requested to call again. I had regular days for performing this duty, on the mornings of which I would say to myself: 'Well, I must go round, and wake those agents up again to-day.' When I had said this, I felt quite important, and had some vague idea that I was over-working myself. If, on my way, I happened to meet a friend, I greeted him with 'Haven't got a minute, old man. I'm just going round to my agents,' and, scarcely stopping to shake hands, would rush off, leaving him with the impression that I had been telegraphed for.

But I never succeeded in rousing them to a full sense of their responsibilities, and after a while, we began to get mutually tired of one another; especially as about this time I managed to get hold of two or three sham agents, – or rather, they managed to get hold of me, – who were much more pleased to see me. One of these, a very promising firm (though not quite so good at performing), had its offices then in Leicester Square, and consisted of two partners, one of whom, however, was always in the country on important business, and could never be seen. I remember they got four pounds out of me, for which they undertook, in writing, to obtain me a salaried London engagement before the expiration of a month. Just when the time was nearly up, however, I received a long and sympathetic letter from the mysterious travelling partner. This hitherto rusticating individual had, it appeared, returned to town the previous day, but only to discover a state of things that had shocked him beyond all expression. His partner, the one to whom I had paid the four pounds, besides defrauding nearly all the clients by taking money for engagements which he had no possible means of obtaining, had robbed him, the writer of the letter, of upwards of seventy pounds, and had bolted, no one knew whither. My present correspondent expressed himself deeply grieved at my having been so villainously cheated, and hoped I would join him in taking proceedings against his absconding partner – when found. He concluded by stating that four pounds was an absurd sum to charge for obtaining such an engagement as had been held out to me, and that if I would give him (who really had the means of performing his promises) two pounds, he would get me one in a week, or ten days at the outside. Would I call and see him that evening? I did not go that evening, but I went the first thing the next morning. I then found the door locked, and a notice on it that all letters were to be left with the housekeeper. Coming down stairs, I met a man coming up, and asked him if he knew where either of the partners could be found. He said that he would give a sovereign to know, and that he was the landlord. I heard of the firm again the other day, and I believe it is still flourishing, though with the customary monthly change as to name and address. By the bye, I wonder if the agent nuisance will ever be stamped out. Perhaps, now that education is compulsory, the next generation of actors and managers may be able to look after their own affairs, and so dispense with the interference of these meddlers on commission.

CHAPTER 5

A Rehearsal

I hurriedly unfolded the paper, to see what kind of a part I had got. I was anxious to begin studying it immediately. I had to form my conception of the character, learn the words and business, and get up gesture and expression, all in one week. No time was therefore to be lost. I give the part in extenso:

Joe Junks.
———

Act I, scene 1
———

——————comes home.
It's a rough night.
——————if he does.
Ay. Ay.
—————— stand back.
(*Together*) 'Tis he!
Fall down as scene closes in.

Act IV, scene 2
On with rioters

I was of a sanguine disposition at that time, but I didn't exactly see how I was going to make much of a sensation with *that*. It seemed to me that my talents were being thrown away. An ordinary actor would have done for a part like that. However, if they chose to waste me, it was more their misfortune than mine. I would say nothing, but do the best I could with the thing, and throw as much feeling into the character as it would hold. In truth, I ought to have been very proud of the part, for I found out later on that it had been written specially for me by the

[9]

manager. Our low comedy, who knew the whole piece by heart, told me this. Then he added musingly, 'A very good idea, too, of the boss's. I always said the first act wanted strengthening.'

At last, everybody having been supplied with his or her part, and the leader of the band having arrived, the rehearsal really commenced. The play was one of the regular old-fashioned melodramas, and the orchestra had all its work cut out to keep up with it. Nearly all the performers had a bar of music to bring them on each time, and another to take them off; a bar when they sat down, and a bar when they got up again; while it took a small overture to get them across the stage. As for the leading lady, every mortal thing she did or said, from remarking that the snow was cold, in the first act, to fancying she saw her mother and then dying, in the last, was preceded by a regular concert. I firmly believe that if, while on the stage, she had shown signs of wanting to sneeze, the band would at once have struck up quick music. I began to think, after a while, that it must be an opera, and to be afraid that I should have to sing my part.

The first scene was between the old landlord of an old inn, some village gossips, and the villain of the piece. The stage manager (who played the villain – naturally) stood in the centre of the stage, from which the rest of the company had retired, and, from there, with the manuscript in his hand, he directed the proceedings.

'Now then, gentlemen,' cried he, 'first scene, please. Hallett, landlord, Bilikins, and Junks,' (I was Junks) 'up stage right. I shall be here,' (walking across and stamping his foot on the spot intended) 'sitting at table. All discovered at rise of curtain. You,' (turning and speaking to me, about whom he had evidently been instructed) 'you, Mr L, will be sitting at the end, smoking a pipe. Take up your cues sharply, and mind you speak up, or nobody will hear you: this is a big house. What are you going to give us for an overture, Mr P?' (I call the leader of the band Mr P.) 'Can you give us something old English, just before we ring up? Thanks, do – has a good effect. Now then, please, we will begin. Very piano all through this scene, Mr P, until near the end. I'll tell you where, when we come to it.'

Then, reading from our parts, we commenced. The speeches, with the exception of the very short ones, were not given at full length. The last two or three words, forming the cues, were clearly spoken, but the rest was, as a rule, mumbled through, skipped altogether, or else represented by a droning 'er, er, er,' interspersed with occasional disjointed phrases. A scene of any length, between only two or three of the characters, – and there were many such, – was cut out entirely, and gone through apart by the people concerned. Thus, while the main rehearsal was proceeding in the centre of the stage, a minor one was generally going on at the same time in some quiet corner – two men fighting a duel with walking sticks; a father denouncing his son, and turning him out of doors; or some dashing young gallant, in a big check ulster, making love to some sweet young damsel, whose little boy, aged seven, was sitting on her lap.

I waited eagerly for my cue, not knowing when it was coming, and, in my anxiety, made two or three false starts. I was put out of any doubt about it, when the time really did come, by a friendly nod from the gentleman who represented the landlord, and thereupon I made my observation as to the dreadful state of the weather in a loud, clear, and distinct voice, as it seemed to me. As, however, nobody appeared to have heard me, and as they were evidently waiting for me, I repeated the information in a louder, clearer, and more distinct voice, if possible; after which the stage manager spoke and said:

'Now then, Mr L, come along, let's have it.'

I explained to him that he had already had it, and he then replied, 'Oh, that will never do at all. You must speak up more than that. Why, even *we* couldn't hear you on the stage. Bawl it out. Remember this is a large place; you're not playing in a back drawing-room now.'

I thought it was impossible for me to speak louder than I had, without doing myself some serious injury, and I began to pity the gallery boys. Any one never having attempted to speak in a large public building would hardly imagine how weak and insignificant the ordinary conversational tones are, even at their loudest. To make your voice 'carry,' you have to *throw* it out, instead of letting it crawl out when you open your mouth. The art is easily acquired, and, by it, you are able to make your very whispers heard.

I was cautioned to look to this, and then we went on. The close of the scene was a bustling one, and the stage manager explained it thus:

'You' (the landlord) 'put the lantern close to my face, when you say "'Tis he!" I spring up, throwing down the table' (a stamp here, to emphasize this). 'I knock you down. You two try to seize me; I break from you, and throw you down, and cross centre' (doing so). 'I gain door, open it, and stand there, pointing revolver. You all cower down.' We were squatting on our toes, as an acknowledgement of having been all bowled over like a set of nine-pins – or rather four-pins in our case – and we now further bobbed our heads, to show that we did cower.

'Picture,' says the stage manager approvingly, as drop falls. 'Hurried music all through that, Mr P. Mind you all keep well up the stage' ('up' the stage means towards the back, and 'down' the stage, consequently, implies near the footlights), 'so as to let the drop come down. What front drops have you got? Have you got an interior? We want a cottage interior.' This latter was spoken to a stage carpenter, who was dragging some flats about. Do not be shocked, gentle reader; a stage flat is a piece of scenery. No other kind of flat is ever seen on the stage.

'I dunno,' answered the man. 'Where's Jim? Jim!'

It appeared that Jim had just stepped outside for a minute. He came back at that point, however, wiping his mouth, and greatly indignant at hearing the sound of his own name.

'All right, all right,' was his wrathful comment, as he came up the yard; 'don't sing it; he ain't dead. What the devil's the matter? Is the 'ouse a-fire? *You* never go out, do yer!'

Jim was the head carpenter, and was a sulky and disagreeable man, even for a stage carpenter. When he wasn't 'just stepped outside for a minute,' he was quarrelling inside, so that instead of anybody's objecting to his frequent temporary retirements, his absence was rather welcomed. He, in common with all stage carpenters, held actors and actresses in the greatest contempt, as people who were always in the way, and without whom the play would get on much better. The chief charm about him, however, was his dense stupidity. This trait was always brought into particular prominence whenever the question of arranging scenery was under discussion.

Fresh scenery is a very great rarity at the minor theatres. When anything very special is produced, and an unusually long run is expected, say, of a month or six weeks, one or two scenes may, perhaps, be specially painted, but, as a rule, reliance is placed upon the scenery, the gradual growth of years, already in stock, which, with a little alteration, and a good deal of make-shift, generally does duty for the 'entirely new and elaborate scenery' so minutely described in the posters. Of course, under these circumstances, slight inconsistencies must be put up with. Nobody objects to a library drop representing "tween decks of the *Sarah Jane*,' or to a back parlour being called a banqueting hall. This is to be expected. Our stage manager was not a narrow-minded man on the subject of accessories. He would have said nothing about such things as these. He himself had, on the occasion of one of his benefits, played *Hamlet* with nothing but one 'interior' and 'a garden,' and he had been a member of a fit-up company that travelled with a complete Shakespearian *repertoire* and four set scenes; so that he was not likely to be too exacting. But even *he* used to be staggered at Jim's ideas of mounting. Jim's notion of a 'distant view of Hampstead Heath by moonlight,' was either a tropical island, or the backing of an old transformation scene; and for any place in London – no matter what, whether Whitechapel or St James's Park – he invariably suggested a highly realistic representation of Waterloo Bridge in a snow-storm.

In the present instance, on being asked for the cottage interior, he let down a log cabin, with a couple of bowie knives and revolvers artistically arranged over the fire-place; anticipating any doubt upon the subject of suitableness by an assurance that, there you were, and you couldn't do better than that. The objection, that a log cabin with bowie knives and revolvers over the fire-place, though it was doubtless a common enough object in the Australian bush or the backwoods of America, was never, by any chance, found in England, and that the cottage to be represented was supposed to be within a few miles of London, he considered as too frivolous to need comment, and passed it over in silent contempt. Further argument had the effect of raising up Jim's stock authority, a certain former lessee, who had been dead these fifteen years, and about whom nobody else but Jim seemed to have the faintest recollection. It appeared that this gentleman had always used the log cabin scene for English cottages, and Jim guessed that *he* (the defunct lessee) knew what he was about, even if he (Jim) was a fool. The latter of Jim's suppositions had never been disputed, and it was a little too late then to discuss the former. All I can say is, that if Jim's Mr Harris – as this mysterious manager was generally dubbed – really did mount his productions in the manner affirmed, their effect must have been novel in the extreme.

Nothing could induce Jim to shew anything else that morning, although the manager reminded him of a cottage scene having been expressly painted for the last lessee. Jim didn't know where it was. Besides, one of the ropes was broken, and it couldn't be got at then. After which little brush with the enemy, he walked away, and took up a row with the gas man at the very point where he had dropped it twenty minutes before.

Scenery and props were not being used at this, the first, rehearsal, the chief object of which was merely to arrange music, entrances and exits, and general business; but of course it was desirable to know as soon as possible what scenery was available, and whether it required any altering or repairing.

In the second scene, the leading lady made her first appearance, an event which called forth all the energies of the orchestra. It would not do for her to burst upon the audience all at once. Great and sudden joy is dangerous. They must be gradually prepared for it. Care was exercised that the crisis should be well led up to, and that she should appear exactly at the right moment. When all was satisfactorily settled, the cue was announced to her by the stage manager. He said it was, 'Pom-pom – pom-pom – pom-pom – pom – Pom – POM.'

'That's your cue, my dear.'

On the stage, everybody calls the actresses, 'My dear.' You soon pick it up, especially in the case of the young and pretty ones.

'Where do I come on from?' asked the leading lady.

'I can't say, my dear, until I've seen the drop. There'll most likely be a door in it, and then you can come on from the back.'

Entrances from the back, it may be remarked, are the favourite ones. Indeed, some artistes will never come on from anywhere else. Of course, you make a much better impression on an audience, as regards first appearance, by facing them on your entrance and walking straight down towards them, than by coming on sideways and then turning round. Entrances from the back, however, are sometimes carried to excess, and a whole scene is rendered unnatural and absurd, merely to gratify personal vanity.

I will finish what I have to say about this rehearsal by giving a verbatim report of a small part of it; viz., the fourth scene of the first act. The actual scene is this:

STAGE MANAGER, *standing* CENTRE *with his back to the footlights. Close behind him, perched in a high chair, the* LEADER OF THE BAND *solus, representing the orchestra with a fiddle. Two or three groups of artistes, chatting at the wings.* THE HEAVY MAN, *pacing up and down at the back, conning his part in an undertone, and occasionally stopping to suit the action to the word.* LOW COMEDY *and* WALKING GENT., *going through scene by themselves in* L. 3. E. SINGING CHAMBER-MAID, *flirting with* JUVENILES (*only one of them*), R. 2. E. PROPERTY MAN, *behind, making a veal and ham pie out of an old piece of canvas and a handful of shavings.* COUPLE OF CARPENTERS, *in white jackets, hovering about, with hammers in their hands, and mischief in their eyes, evidently on the look-out for an excuse to make a noise.* CALL BOY, *all over the place, and always in the way – except when wanted.*

OUR FIRST OLD MAN (*standing* R. C., *and reading his part by the aid of a large pair of specs*): 'Er-er – wind howls – er-er-er – night as this, fifteen years ago – er – sweet child – er-r-r – stolen away – er-r-r – baby prattle – er-ears – er-r – shall I never hear her voice again?'
He looks up, and finding that nobody makes any sign of caring a hang whether he does or not, he repeats the question louder.

STAGE MANAGER (*severely, as if this was a question that really must be answered*): 'Shall I never hear her voice again?' Oh! that's a music cue, Mr P. Have you got it down? Miss – (*stage name of the manager's wife*) sings a song there, without.

MR P: No, I'll put it down now. What is it – 'hear her voice again?' (*Writes on some loose slips of paper, lying before him on the stage.*) Have you the music?

STAGE MAN.: Oh, anything dismal does. No matter what it is, so long as it gives 'em the hump. What will you have, my dear?

MANAGER'S WIFE (*who has just finished a social bottle of Bass with another lady*): Oh, the old thing, you know. 'Home, sweet home.'

JUVENILES (*in a whisper to* LOW COM): Is *she* going to *sing?*

LOW COM: Yes, always does it.

[15]

JUVENILES: Oh, my – !

MAN. WIFE AND THE FIDDLE *do first verse of 'Home, sweet home.'*

FIRST OLD MAN.: 'Ah, that voice – er-er – echo of old memories – er-er-er –houseless wanderer – dry herself' (*crossing, and opening an imaginary door*). 'Poor child – er-er-er – I'm an old man – er – my wife's out – return and –er – the homeless orphan.'

MAN. WIFE: Will there be any lime-light on here?

FIRST OLD WOMAN (*sotto voce*): Oh, let her have some limelight. She wants to let her back hair down.

STAGE MAN.: Certainly, my dear. There'll be a fire-place in this corner, and red limelight from it.

MAN. WIFE: Oh, all right; I only wanted to know. Now, what was it – 'homeless orphan'. Oh, that's my long speech, you know: 'Is this a dream that I have dreamt before – played here when a child.'

FIRST O. M.: 'Sweet child – your face recalls strange memories of – er-er-er – been just your age.'

STAGE MAN. (*interrupting*): Slow music throughout.

FIRST O. M. (*continuing*): 'Never from that night & er – golden – I can't believe she's dead.'
Scrape from the fiddle, followed by bar, to bring on FIRST OLD WOMAN.

FIRST O. W. (*without moving from her seat, and coming straight to the cue with a suddenness which startles everybody*): 'Fold you to my breast.'

MAN. WIFE.: 'Mother!' – Got the rheumatism again?

FIRST O. W.: Got it *again!* It's never gone yet, drat it – 'My child!'
Powerful scrape from the fiddle.

FIRST O. M.: Where am I?

STAGE MAN.: Left, down stage.

MAN. WIFE: We embrace, left centre. Knock heard.

STAGE MAN. (*crossing centre*): That's me.* Keep it up: it's a picture. You and Mrs – there, embracing, and the old boy down in the corner, when I open the door. – Rain and wind for this scene, mind.

HOVERING CARPENTER (*at top of his voice*): Jim! wind and rain for last scene of first act.

* That was the way he treated Lindley Murray. We were inexpressibly grieved and shocked – all of us – but what were we to do?

[16]

Husky but indignant voice from the flies, expressing an earnest desire that every one should go to the devil.

STAGE MAN. (*who always rehearsed his speeches at full length, and in a tone of voice as if he were reciting the multiplication table*): 'I am pursued. My life is at stake. Hide me from these bloodhounds who are on my track. Hark! they are here. Thank Heaven, they are past. I am safe. Ha, who is this we have here? 'Sdeath, I am in luck to-night. Sir Henry will thank me, when I bring his strayed lamb back to him. Come with me, my little runaway.' Business. 'Nay, resist not, or 'twill be the worse for all.' I catch hold of you. We struggle. 'Come, I say, with me. Come, I say.'

FIRST O. W.: 'Die together.'

Scrape from the fiddle.

STAGE MAN. (*loudly, after waiting a minute*): 'Die together.'

FIRST O. M.: I beg pardon. I didn't hear. (*Fumbles with his part, and loses his place.*)

MAN. WIFE.: He really ought to use an ear-trumpet.

FIRST O. M.: 'Er-r-r – Heaven will give me strength – er – can strike a blow.' (*Shakes his stick at* STAGE MANAGER).

Tremendous hammering suddenly begun at back, eliciting forcible expressions of disapproval from all the members of the company, with the exception of the FIRST OLD MAN, *who doesn't hear it, and goes on calmly with the rehearsal all by himself.*

STAGE MAN. (*in a rage*): Stop that noise! Stop that noise, I say!

Noise continues.

JIM (*eager for the fray*): How can we do our work without noise, I should like to know?

STAGE MAN. (*crossly*): Can't you do it at some other time?

JIM (*angrily*): No, we can't do it at some other time! Do you think we're here all night?

STAGE MAN. (*mildly*): But, my dear fellow, how can we go on with the rehearsal?

JIM (*in a rage*): *I* don't know anything about you and your rehearsal! That's not my business, is it? I do my own work; I don't do other people's work! I don't want to be told how to do my work! (*Pours forth a flood of impassioned eloquence for the next ten minutes, during which time the hammering is also continued. Complete collapse of* STAGE MANAGER, *and suspension of rehearsal. Subsequent dryness on the part of* JIM.)

[17]

MAN. WIFE (*when rehearsal is at last resumed*): Just try back that last bit, will you, for positions?

The last two or three movements gone over again. Then:

STAGE MAN.: We all three struggle towards door. 'Stand back, old man! I do not wish to harm thee!' – I push you aside. 'Back, or it will be murder!' – This must be well worked up. 'Who dares to stay me?' (*to* LOW COMEDY). There'll be a bar to bring you on. You know the business.

LOW COM. (*coming forward*): 'Shure an *I* will.'

Scrape from fiddle.

STAGE MAN.: Well, then there's our struggle.

(STAGE MANAGER *and* LOW COMEDY *take hold of each other's shoulders, and turn round*.) I'll have the book in the left-hand side.

LOW COM.: 'Ah, begorra, shure he's clane gone; but, be jabers, I've got this' (*holding up an imaginary pocket-book*), 'and it's worth a precious deal more than he is.'

STAGE MAN.: End of first act. – Tommy, go and fetch me half a pint of stout.

CHAPTER 17

I Join a 'Fit-Up'

The show which I now graced with my presence was a 'fit-up.' I didn't know this beforehand, or I should never had engaged myself. A 'fit-up' is only one grade higher than a booth, which latter branch of the profession, by the way, I have always regretted never having explored. I missed the most picturesque and romantic portion of the theatrical world by not penetrating into that time-forsaken corner. Booth life is a Bohemia within a Bohemia. So far as social and artistic position is concerned, it is at the bottom of the dramatic ladder; but for interest and adventure, it stands at the very top.

However, I never did join a booth, so there is an end of the matter. The nearest I approached to anything of the kind was this fit-up, and that I didn't like at all. We kept to the very small towns, where there was no theatre, and fitted up an apology for a stage in any hall or room we could hire for the purpose. The town hall was what we generally tried for, but we were not too particular; any large room did, and we would even put up with a conveniently situated barn. We carried our own props, scenery, and proscenium, and trusted for the woodwork to some local carpenter. A row of candles did duty for footlights, and a piano, hired in the town, represented the orchestra. We couldn't get a piano on one occasion, so the proprietor of the hall lent us his harmonium.

I will not linger over my experiences with this company; they were not pleasant ones. Short extracts from two letters, one written just after joining, and the other sent off just before I left, will be sufficient:

DEAR JIM, I find I've dropped the substance and grasped the shadow (I pride myself not so much on the originality of

[19]

this remark as on its applicability). I shall leave as soon as possible, and try my luck in London. My ambition to play Juvenile Lead vanished the moment I saw the Leading Lady, who is, as usual, the manager's wife. She is a fat, greasy old woman. She has dirty hands and finger nails, and perspires freely during the course of the performance. She is about three times my size, and if the audiences to which we play have the slightest sense of humour – which, from what I have seen of them, I think extremely doubtful – our love-making must be a rare treat to them. How a London first-night gallery would enjoy it! I'm afraid, though, it's only wasted down here. My arm, when I try to clasp her waist, reaches to about the middle of her back; and, when we embrace, the house can't see me at all. I have to carry her half-way across the stage in one part. By Jove! I'm glad we don't play that piece often.

She says I shall never make a good 'lover' unless I throw more ardour ('*harder*,' she calls it) into my acting. . . .

. . . Shall be with you on Monday next. Can't stand this any longer. It's ruining me. Seven-and-six was all I could get last week, and eleven shillings the week before. We are not doing bad business by any means. Indeed, we have very good houses. The old man has got the knack of making out good gag bills, and that pulls 'em in for the two or three nights we stay at each place. You know what I mean by a 'gag' bill: 'The Ruined Mill by Dead Man's Pool. Grace Mervin thinks to meet a friend, but finds a foe. Harry Baddun recalls old days. "Why do you not love me?" "Because you are a bad man." "Then die!" The struggle on the brink!! "Help!!" "There is none to help you here." "You lie, Harry Baddun; *I* am here." A hand from the grave!! Harry Baddun meets his doom !!!'

That's what I mean by a gag bill.

Whatever money is made, however, he takes care to keep for himself. He can always put up at the best hotel in the place, while we have to pawn our things to pay for the meanest of lodgings.

It isn't only actors who get robbed by these managers: authors also suffer pretty considerably. We have two copyright pieces in our list, both of which draw very well, but

[20]

not a penny is paid for performing them. To avoid any chance of unpleasantness, the titles of the pieces and the names of the chief characters are altered. So that even if the author or his friends (supposing it possible for an author to have any friends) were on the lookout, they would never know anything about it. And, if they did, it would be of no use. It would be throwing good money after bad to attempt to enforce payment from the men who do this sort of thing – and I hear that it is done all over the provinces, – they have no money, and none can be got out of them. Your penniless man can comfortably defy half the laws in the statute book.

What a nuisance firearms are on the stage! I thought I was blinded the other night, and my eyes are painful even now. The fellow should have fired up in the air. It is the only safe rule on a small stage, though it does look highly ridiculous to see a man drop down dead because another man fires a pistol at the moon. But there is always some mishap with them. They either don't go off at all, or else they go off in the wrong place, and, when they do go off, there is generally an accident. They can never be depended upon. You rush on to the stage, present a pistol at somebody's head, and say, 'Die!' but the pistol only goes click, and the man doesn't know whether to die or not. He waits while you have another try at him, and the thing clicks again; and then you find out that the property man hasn't put a cap on it, and you turn round to get one. But the other man, thinking it is all over, makes up his mind to die at once from nothing else but fright, and, when you come back to kill him for the last time, you find he's already dead.

We have recourse to some rum makeshifts here, to eke out our wardrobes. My old frock coat, with a little cloth cape which one of the girls has cut out for me pinned on underneath the collar, and with a bit of lace round the cuffs, does for the gallant of half the old comedies; and, when I pin the front corners back and cover them with red calico, I'm a French soldier. A pair of white thingummies does admirably for buckskin riding breeches, and, for the part of a Spanish conspirator, I generally borrow my landlady's tablecloth. . . .

It was about the end of October when I found myself one more in London. The first thing I then did was to go to my old shop on the Surreyside. Another company and another manager were there, but the latter knew me, and, as I owned a dress suit, engaged me at a salary of twelve shillings weekly to play the part of a swell. When I had been there just one week, he closed. Whether it was paying me that twelve shillings that broke him, I cannot say; but on Monday morning some men came and cut the gas off, and then he said he shouldn't go on any longer, and that we must all do the best we could for ourselves.

I, with two or three others, thereupon started off for a theatre at the East End, which was about to be opened for a limited number of nights by some great world-renowned actor. This was about the fortieth world-renowned party I had heard of for the first time within the last twelvemonth. My education in the matter of world-renowned people had evidently been shamefully neglected.

The theatre was cunningly contrived, so that one had to pass through the bar of the adjoining public house – to the landlord of which it belonged – to get to the stage. Our little party was saved from temptation, however, for I don't think we could have mustered a shilling amongst the lot of us that morning. I was getting most seriously hard up at this time. The few pounds I had had left, after purchasing my wardrobe and paying my railway fares, etc., had now dwindled down to shillings, and, unless things mended, I felt I should have to throw up the sponge and retire from the stage. I was determined not to do this though, till the very last, for I dreaded the chorus of 'I told you so's, and 'I knew very well how 'twould be's, and such like well-known and exasperating crows of triumph, which which, in these cases, our delighted friends glorify themselves and crush us.

The East End theatre proved a stop-gap for a while. I was fortunate enough to be one of those engaged out of the crowd of eager and anxious applicants, among whom I met a couple from the fit-up company I had lately left, they having come to the same conclusion as myself, viz., that it was impossible to live well and 'dress respectably on and off the stage' upon an average salary of ten shillings weekly. The engagement was only for a fortnight, and there is only one incident connected with it that I particularly remember. That was my being 'guyed' on one occasion. We were playing a melodrama, the scene of which was laid in some outlandish place or other, and the stage manager insisted on my wearing a most outrageous costume. I knew it would be laughed at, especially in that neighbourhood, and my expectations were more than fulfilled. I hadn't been on the stage five seconds before I heard a voice from the gallery hoarsely inquire: 'What is it, Bill?' And then another voice added: 'Tell us what it is, and you shall have it.'

A good deal of laughter followed these speeches. I got hot all over, and felt exceedingly uncomfortable and nervous. It was as much as I could do to recollect my part, and it was with a great effort that I began my first line. No sooner had I opened my mouth, however, than somebody in the pit exclaimed, in tones of the utmost surprise, 'Blowed if it ain't alive!'

After that, the remarks on my personal appearance fell thick and fast: 'Look well in a shop window, that bloke!' 'Nice suit to take your gal out on a Sunday in!' 'This style, thirty shillin's,' etc.; while one good-natured man sought to put me at my ease by roaring out in a stentorian voice, 'Never you mind, old man; you go on. They're jealous 'cos you've got nice clothes on.' How I managed to get through the part I don't know. I became more nervous and awkward every minute, and, of course, the more I bungled, the more the house jeered. I gained a good deal of sympathy behind, for most of them had had similar experiences of their own; but I was most intensely miserable all that evening, and for the next night or two, quite dreaded to face the audience. Making game of any one is a very amusing occupation, but the 'game' doesn't see the fun till a long while afterwards. I can't bear to hear any of the performers chaffed when I'm at a theatre. Actors are necessarily a sensitive class of people, and I don't think those who make fun of them, when any little thing goes wrong, have any idea of the pain they are inflicting. It is quite right, and quite necessary sometimes, that disapprobation should be expressed, and that unmistakably, but it should be for the purpose of correcting real faults. 'Guying' is, as a rule, indulged in only by the silliest portion of the audience, and for no other object but to display their own vulgar wit.

After my fortnight at the East End, I went as one of the chorus in a new opera-bouffe to be brought out at a West End theatre. We rehearsed for three weeks, the piece ran for one, and then I again took a provincial engagement, which, as it was now close upon Christmas, was easy enough to obtain.

My stay in London had not been very profitable to me, but it had given my friends a treat, as they had been able to come and see me act again. At least, I suppose it was a treat to them, though they did not say so. My friends are always most careful never to overdo the thing in the matter of praise. I cannot accuse them of sycophancy. They scorn to say pleasant things that they don't mean. They prefer saying unpleasant things that they do mean. There's no humbug about them; they never hesitate to tell me just exactly what they think of me. This is good of them. I respect them for saying what they think; but if they would think a little differently, I should respect them still more. I wonder if everybody's friends are as conscientious? I've heard of people having 'admiring friends,' and 'flattering friends,' and 'over-indulgent friends,' but I've never had any of that sort myself. I've often thought I should rather like to, though, and if any gentleman has more friends of that kind than he wants, and would care to have a few of the opposite stamp, I am quite ready to swop with him. I can warrant mine never to admire or flatter under any circumstances whatsoever; neither will he find them over-indulgent. To a man who really wishes to be told of his faults, they would be invaluable; on this point, they are candour itself. A conceited man would also derive much benefit from their society. I have myself.

from Idle Thoughts of an Idle Fellow

Idle Thoughts of an Idle Fellow, four of which have been selected
here, began as a series commissioned by *Home Chimes*,
on sight of the first one submitted by Jerome.
This too was published by Field & Tuer in 1886,
Jerome receiving 2½d a copy as royalty.
Pirated in America, it sold 100,000 copies.

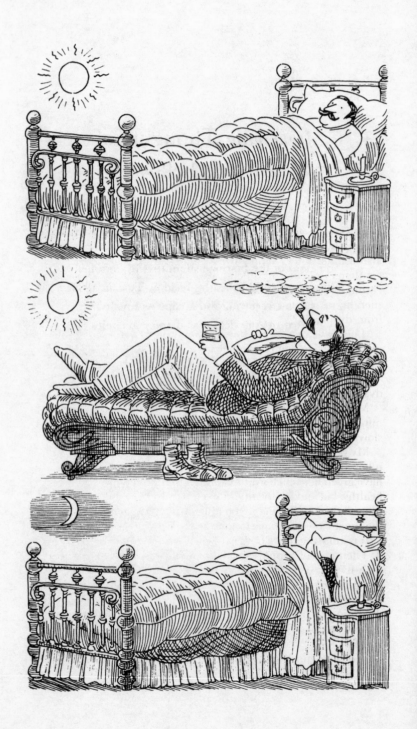

On Eating and Drinking

I always was fond of eating and drinking, even as a child – especially eating, in those early days. I had an appetite then, also a digestion. I remember a dull-eyed, livid-complexioned gentleman coming to dine at our house once. He watched me eating for about five minutes, quite fascinated, seemingly, and then he turned to my father, with, 'Does your boy ever suffer from dyspepsia?'

'I never heard him complain of anything of that kind,' replied my father. 'Do you ever suffer from dyspepsia, Collywobbles?' (They called me Collywobbles, but it was not my real name.)

'No, pa,' I answered. After which, I added, 'What is dyspepsia, pa?'

My livid-complexioned friend regarded me with a look of mingled amazement and envy. Then in a tone of infinite pity he slowly said, 'You will know – some day.'

My poor, dear mother used to say she liked to see me eat, and it has always been a pleasant reflection to me since, that I must have given her much gratification in that direction. A growing, healthy lad, taking plenty of exercise, and careful to restrain himself from indulging in too much study, can generally satisfy the most exacting expectations as regards his feeding powers.

It is amusing to see boys eat, when you have not got to pay for it. Their idea of a square meal is a pound and a half of roast beef with five or six good-sized potatoes (soapy ones preferred, as being more substantial), plenty of greens, and four thick slices of Yorkshire pudding, followed by a couple of currant dumplings, a few green apples, a pen'orth of nuts, half-a-dozen jumbles, and a bottle of ginger beer. After that, they play at horses.

How they must despise us men, who require to sit quiet for a couple of hours after dining off a spoonful of clear soup and the wing of a chicken!

But the boys have not all the advantages on their side. A boy never enjoys the luxury of being satisfied. A boy never feels full. He can never stretch out his legs, put his hands behind his head, and, closing his eyes, sink into the ethereal blissfulness that encompasses the well-dined man. A dinner makes no difference whatever to a boy. To a man, it is as a good fairy's potion, and, after it, the world appears a brighter and a better place. A man who has dined satisfactorily experiences a yearning love towards all his fellow-creatures. He strokes the cat quite gently, and calls it 'poor pussy,' in tones full of the tenderest emotion. He sympathises with the members of the German band outside, and wonders if they are cold; and, for the moment, he does not even hate his wife's relations.

A good dinner brings out all the softer side of a man. Under its genial influence, the gloomy and morose become jovial and chatty. Sour, starchy individuals, who all the rest of the day go about looking as if they lived on vinegar and Epsom salts, break out into wreathed smiles after dinner, and exhibit a tendency to pat small children on the head, and to talk to them – vaguely – about sixpences. Serious young men thaw, and become mildly cheerful; and snobbish young men, of the heavy moustache type, forget to make themselves objectionable.

I always feel sentimental myself after dinner. It is the only time when I can properly appreciate love stories. Then, when the hero clasps 'her' to his heart in one last wild embrace, and stifles a sob, I feel as sad as though I had dealt at whist, and turned up only a deuce; and, when the heroine dies in the end, I weep. If I read the same tale early in the morning, I should sneer at it. Digestion, or rather indigestion, has a marvellous effect upon the heart. If I want to write anything very pathetic – I mean, if I want to *try* to write anything very pathetic – I eat a large plateful of hot buttered muffins about an hour beforehand, and, then, by the time I sit down to my work, a feeling of unutterable melancholy has come over me. I picture heart-broken lovers parting for ever at lonely wayside stiles, while the sad twilight deepens around them, and only the tinkling of a distant sheep bell breaks the sorrow-laden silence. Old men sit and gaze at withered flowers till their sight is dimmed by the mist of tears. Little dainty maidens wait and watch at open casements; but, 'he cometh not,' and the heavy years roll by, and the sunny gold tresses wear white and thin. The babies that they dandled have become grown men and women with podgy torments of their own, and the playmates that they laughed with are lying very silent under the waving grass. But still they wait and watch, till the dark shadows of the unknown night steal up and gather round them, and the world with its childish troubles fades from their aching eyes.

I see pale corpses tossed on white-foamed waves, and death-beds stained with bitter tears, and graves in trackless deserts. I hear the wild wailing of women, the low moaning of the little children, the dry sobbing of strong men. It's all the muffins. I could not conjure up one melancholy fancy upon a mutton chop and a glass of champagne.

A full stomach is a great aid to poetry, and, indeed, no sentiment of any kind can stand upon an empty one. We have not time or inclination to indulge in fanciful troubles, until we have got rid of our real misfortunes. We do not sigh over dead dicky-birds with the bailiffs in the house; and, when we do not know where on earth to get our next shilling from we do not worry as to whether our mistress's smiles are cold, or hot, or lukewarm, or anything else about them.

Foolish people – when I say 'foolish people' in this contemptuous way, I mean people who entertain different opinions to mine. If there is one person I do despise more than another, it is the man who does not think exactly the same on all topics as I do. Foolish people, I say, then, who have never experienced much of either, will tell you that mental distress is far more agonising than bodily. Romantic and touching theory! so comforting to the love-sick young sprig who looks down patronisingly at some poor devil with a white starved face, and thinks to himself, 'Ah, how happy you are compared with me!' so soothing to fat old gentlemen who cackle about the superiority of poverty over riches. But it is all nonsense – all cant. An aching head soon makes one forget an aching heart. A broken finger will drive away all recollections of an empty chair. And when a man feels really hungry, he does not feel anything else.

We sleek, well-fed folk can hardly realise what feeling hungry

[29]

is like. We know what it is to have no appetite, and not to care
for the dainty victuals placed before us, but we do not
understand what it means to sicken for food – to die for bread
while others waste it – to gaze with famished eyes upon coarse
fare steaming behind dingy windows, longing for a pen'orth
of pease pudding, and not having the penny to buy it – to feel
that a crust would be delicious, and that a bone would be a
banquet.

Hunger is a luxury to us, a piquant, flavour-giving sauce. It is
well worth while to get hungry and thirsty, merely to discover
how much gratification can be obtained from eating and
drinking. If you wish to thoroughly enjoy your dinner, take a
thirty-mile country walk after breakfast, and don't touch
anything till you get back. How your eyes will glisten at sight of
the white table-cloth and steaming dishes then! With what a
sigh of content you will put down the empty beer tankard, and
take up your knife and fork! And how comfortable you feel
afterwards, as you push back your chair, light a cigar, and beam
round upon everybody.

Make sure, however, when adopting this plan, that the good
dinner is really to be had at the end, or the disappointment is
trying. I remember once a friend and I – dear old Joe, it was.
Ah! how we lose one another in life's mist. It must be eight years
since I last saw Joseph Taboys. How pleasant it would be to
meet his jovial face again, to clasp his strong hand, and to hear
his cheery laugh once more! He owes me fourteen shillings, too.
Well, we were on a holiday together, and one morning we had
breakfast early, and started for a tremendous long walk. We had
ordered a duck for dinner over night. We said, 'Get a big one,
because we shall come home awfully hungry:' and, as we were
going out, our landlady came up in great spirits. She said, 'I
have got you gentlemen a duck, if you like. If you get through
that, you'll do well;' and she held up a bird about the size of a
door-mat. We chuckled at the sight, and said we would try. We
said it with self-conscious pride, like men who know their own
power. Then we started.

We lost our way, of course. I always do in the country, and it
does make me so wild, because it is no use asking direction of
any of the people you meet. One might as well inquire of a
lodging-house slavey the way to make beds, as expect a country

bumpkin to know the road to the next village. You have to shout the question about three times, before the sound of your voice penetrates his skull. At the third time, he slowly raises his head, and stares blankly at you. You yell it at him then for a fourth time, and he repeats it after you. He ponders while you could count a couple of hundred, after which, speaking at the rate of three words a minute, he fancies you 'couldn't do better than –'. Here he catches sight of another idiot coming down the road, and bawls out to him the particulars, requesting his advice. The two then argue the case for a quarter of an hour or so, and finally agree that you had better go straight down the lane, round to the right, and cross by the third stile, and keep to the left by old Jimmy Milcher's cow-shed, and across the seven-acre field, and through the gate by Squire Grubbin's haystack, keeping the bridle path for a while, till you come opposite the hill where the windmill used to be – but it's gone now – and round to the right, leaving Stiggin's plantation behind you; and you say 'Thank you,' and go away with a splitting headache, but without the faintest notion of your way, the only clear idea you have on the subject being that somewhere or other there is a stile which has to be got over; and, at the next turn, you come upon four stiles, all leading in different directions.

We had undergone this ordeal two or three times. We had tramped over fields. We had waded through brooks, and scrambled over hedges and walls. We had had a row as to whose fault it was that we had first lost our way. We had got thoroughly disagreeable, footsore, and weary. But, throughout it all, the hope of that duck kept us up. A fairy-like vision, it floated before our tired eyes, and drew us onward. The thought of it was as a trumpet call to the fainting. We talked of it, and cheered each other with our recollections of it. 'Come along,' we said, 'the duck will be spoilt.'

We felt a strong temptation, at one point, to turn into a village inn we passed, and have a cheese and a few loaves between us; but we heroically restrained ourselves: we should enjoy the duck all the better for being famished.

We fancied we smelt it when we got into the town and did the last quarter of a mile in three minutes. We rushed upstairs, and washed ourselves, and changed our clothes, and came down, and pulled our chairs up to the table, and sat and rubbed our hands while the landlady removed the covers, when I seized the knife and fork and started to carve.

It seemed to want a lot of carving. I struggled with it for about five minutes without making the slightest impression, and then Joe, who had been eating potatoes, wanted to know if it wouldn't be better for someone to do the job that understood carving. I took no notice of his foolish remark, but attacked the bird again; and so vigorously this time, that the animal left the dish, and took refuge in the fender.

We soon had it out of that though, and I was prepared to make another effort. But Joe was getting unpleasant. He said that if he had thought we were to have a game of blind hockey with the dinner, we would have got a bit of bread and cheese outside.

I was too exhausted to argue. I laid down the knife and fork with dignity, and took a side seat; and Joe went for the wretched creature. He worked away, in silence for a while, and then he muttered, 'Damn the duck,' and took his coat off.

We did break the thing up at length, with the aid of a chisel; but it was perfectly impossible to eat it, and we had to make a dinner off the vegetables and an apple tart. We tried a mouthful of the duck, but it was like eating india-rubber.

It was a wicked sin to kill that drake. But there! there's no respect for old institutions in this country.

I started this paper with the idea of writing about eating and drinking, but I seem to have confined my remarks entirely to eating as yet. Well, you see, drinking is one of those subjects with which it is unadvisable to appear too well acquainted. The days are gone by when it was considered manly to go to bed intoxicated every night, and a clear head and a firm hand no longer draw down upon their owner the reproach of effeminacy. On the contrary, in these sadly degenerate days, an evil-smelling breath, a blotchy face, a reeling gait, and a husky voice are regarded as the hall-marks of the cad rather than of the gentleman.

Even nowadays, though, the thirstiness of mankind is something supernatural. We are for ever drinking on one excuse or another. A man never feels comfortable unless he has a glass before him. We drink before meals, and with meals, and after meals. We drink when we meet a friend, also when we part from a friend. We drink when we are talking, when we are reading, and when we are thinking. We drink one another's healths, and spoil our own. We drink the Queen, and the Army, and the Ladies, and everybody else that is drinkable; and, I believe, if the supply ran short, we should drink our mothers-in-law.

By the way, we never *eat* anybody's health, always *drink* it. Why should we not stand up now and then and eat a tart to somebody's success?

To me, I confess, the constant necessity of drinking under which the majority of men labour is quite unaccountable. I can understand people drinking to drown care, or to drive away maddening thoughts, well enough. I can understand the ignorant masses loving to soak themselves in drink – oh, yes, it's very shocking that they should, of course – very shocking to us who live in cosy homes, with all the graces and pleasures of life around us, that the dwellers in damp cellars and windy attics should creep from their dens of misery into the warmth and glare of the public-house bar, and seek to float for a brief space away from their dull world upon a Lethe stream of gin.

But think, before you hold up your hands in horror at their ill-living, what 'life' for these wretched creatures really means. Picture the squalid misery of their brutish existence, dragged on from year to year in the narrow, noisome room where, huddled like vermin in sewers, they welter, and sicken, and sleep; where dirt-grimed children scream and fight, and sluttish, shrill-voiced women cuff, and curse, and nag; where the street outside teems with roaring filth, and the house around is a bedlam of riot and stench.

Think what a sapless stick this fair flower of life must be to them, devoid of mind and soul. The horse in his stall scents the sweet hay, and munches the ripe corn contentedly. The watch-dog in his kennel blinks at the grateful sun, dreams of a glorious chase over the dewy fields, and wakes with a yelp of gladness to greet a caressing hand. But the clod-like life of these human logs never knows one ray of light. From the hour when they crawl from their comfortless bed to the hour when they lounge back into it again, they never live one moment of real life. Recreation, amusement, companionship, they know not the meaning of. Joy, sorrow, laughter, tears, love, friendship, longing, despair, are idle words to them. From the day when

[33]

their baby eyes first look out upon their sordid world to the day when, with an oath, they close them for ever, and their bones are shovelled out of sight, they never warm to one touch of human sympathy, never thrill to a single thought, never start to a single hope. In the name of the God of mercy let them pour the maddening liquor down their throats, and feel for one brief moment that they live!

Ah! we may talk sentiment as much as we like, but the stomach is the real seat of happiness in this world. The kitchen is the chief temple wherein we worship, its roaring fire is our vestal flame, and the cook is our great high-priest. He is a mighty magician and a kindly one. He soothes away all sorrow and care. He drives forth all enmity, gladdens all love. Our God is great, and the cook is his prophet. Let us drink, and be merry.

On the Weather

Things do go so contrary-like with me. I wanted to hit upon an especially novel, out-of-the-way subject for one of these articles. 'I will write one paper about something altogether new,' I said to myself; 'something that nobody else has ever written or talked about before; and then I can have it all my own way.' And I went about for days, trying to think of something of this kind; and I couldn't. And Mrs Cutting, our charwoman, came yesterday – I don't mind mentioning her name, because I know she will not see this book. She would not look at such a frivolous publication. She never reads anything but the Bible and *Lloyd's Weekly News*. All other literature she considers unnecessary and sinful.

She said: 'Lor', sir, you do look worried.'

I said: 'Mrs Cutting, I am trying to think of a subject, the discussion of which will come upon the world in the nature of a startler – some subject upon which no previous human being has ever said a word – some subject that will attract by its novelty, invigorate by its surprising freshness.'

She laughed, and said I was a funny gentleman.

That's my luck again. When I make serious observations, people chuckle; when I attempt a joke, nobody sees it. I had a beautiful one last week. I thought it so good, and I worked it up, and brought it in artfully at a dinner party. I forget how exactly, but we had been talking about the attitude of Shakespeare towards the Reformation, and I said something, and immediately added, 'Ah, that reminds me; such a funny thing happened the other day in Whitechapel.' 'Oh,' said they; 'what was that?' 'Oh, 'twas awfully funny,' I replied, beginning to giggle myself; 'it will make you roar;' and I told it them.

[35]

There was dead silence when I finished – it was one of those long jokes, too – and then, at last somebody said: 'And that was the joke?'

I assured them that it was, and they were very polite, and took my word for it. All but one old gentleman, at the other end of the table, who wanted to know which was the joke – what he said to her, or what she said to him; and we argued it out.

Some people are too much the other way. I knew a fellow once, whose natural tendency to laugh at everything was so strong that, if you wanted to talk seriously to him, you had to explain beforehand that what you were going to say would not be amusing. Unless you got him to clearly understand this, he would go off into fits of merriment over every word you uttered. I have known him, on being asked the time, stop short in the middle of the road, slap his leg, and burst into a roar of laughter. One never dared say anything really funny to that man. A good joke would have killed him on the spot.

In the present instance, I vehemently repudiated the accusation of frivolity, and pressed Mrs Cutting for practical ideas. She then became thoughtful and hazarded 'samplers'; saying that she never heard them spoken much of now, but that they used to be all the rage when she was a girl.

I declined samplers, and begged her to think again. She pondered a long while, with the tea tray in her hands, and at last suggested the weather, which she was sure had been most trying of late.

And ever since that idiotic suggestion, I have been unable to get the weather out of my thoughts, or anything else in.

It certainly is most wretched weather. At all events, it is so, now, at the time I am writing and if it isn't particularly unpleasant when I come to be read, it soon will be.

It always is wretched weather, according to us. The weather is like the Government, always in the wrong. In summer time we say it is stifling; in winter that it is killing; in spring and autumn we find fault with it for being neither one thing nor the other, and wish it would make up its mind. If it is fine, we say the country is being ruined for want of rain; if it does rain, we pray for fine weather. If December passes without snow, we indignantly demand to know what has become of our good old-fashioned winters, and talk as if we had been cheated out of

[36]

something we had bought and paid for; and when it does snow, our language is a disgrace to a Christian nation. We shall never be content until each man makes his own weather, and keeps it to himself.

If that cannot be arranged, we would rather do without it altogether.

Yet I think it is only to us in cities that all weather is so unwelcome. In her own home, the country, Nature is sweet in all her moods. What can be more beautiful than the snow, falling big with mystery in silent softness, decking the fields and trees with white as if for a fairy wedding! And how delightful is a walk when the frozen ground rings beneath our swinging tread – when our blood tingles in the rare keen air, and the sheep dog's distant bark and children's laughter peals faintly clear like Alpine bells across the open hills! And then skating! scudding with wings of steel across the swaying ice, waking whirring music as we fly. And oh, how dainty its spring – Nature at sweet eighteen! When the little, hopeful leaves peep out so fresh and green, so pure and bright, like young lives pushing shyly out into the bustling world; when the fruit-tree blossoms, pink and white, like village maidens in their Sunday frocks, hide each white-washed cottage in a cloud of fragile splendour; and the cuckoo's note upon the breeze is wafted through the woods! And summer, with its deep, dark green, and drowsy hum – when the raindrops whisper solemn secrets to the listening leaves, and the twilight lingers in the lanes! And autumn! ah, how sadly fair, with its golden glow, and the dying grandeur of its tinted woods – its blood-red sunsets, and its ghostly evening mists, with its busy murmur of reapers, and its laden orchards, and the calling of the gleaners, and the festivals of praise!

The very rain, and sleet, and hail, seem only Nature's useful servants, when found doing their simple duties in the country; and the East Wind himself is nothing worse than a boisterous friend, when we meet him between the hedgerows.

But in the city, where the painted stucco blisters under the smoky sun, and the sooty rain brings slush and mud, and the snow lies piled in dirty heaps, and the chill blasts whistle down dingy streets, and shriek round flaring, gas-lit corners, no face of Nature charms us. Weather in towns in like a skylark in a counting house – out of place, and in the way. Towns ought to be covered in, warmed by hot-water pipes, and lighted by electricity. The weather is a country lass, and does not appear to advantage in town. We liked well enough to flirt with her in the hayfield, but she does not seem so fascinating when we meet her in Pall Mall. There is too much of her there. The frank free laugh and hearty voice, that sounded so pleasant in the dairy, jars against the artificiality of town-bred life, and her ways become exceedingly trying.

Just lately she has been favouring us with almost incessant rain for about three weeks; and I am a demd, damp, moist, unpleasant body, as Mr Mantalini puts it.

Our next door neighbour comes out in the back garden every now and then, and says it's doing the country a world of good – not his coming out into the back garden, but the weather. He doesn't understand anything about it, but ever since he started a cucumber frame last summer, he has regarded himself in the light of an agriculturist, and talks in this absurd way with the idea of impressing the rest of the terrace with the notion that he is a retired farmer. I can only hope that, for this once, he is correct, and that the weather really is doing good to something, because it is doing *me* a considerable amount of damage. It is spoiling both my clothes and my temper. The latter I can afford, as I have a good supply of it, but it wounds me to the quick to see my dear old hats and trousers sinking, prematurely worn and aged, beneath the cold world's blasts and snows.

There is my new spring suit too. A beautiful suit it was, and now it is hanging up so bespattered with mud, I can't bear to look at it.

That was Jim's fault, that was. I should never have gone out in it that night, if it had not been for him. I was just trying it on when he came in. He threw up his arms with a wild yell, the moment he caught sight of it, and exclaimed that he had 'got 'em again!'

I said: 'Does it fit all right behind?'

'Spiffin, old man,' he replied. And then he wanted to know if I was coming out.

I said 'no,' at first, but he overruled me. He said that a man with a suit like that had no right to stop indoors. 'Every citizen,' said he, 'owes a duty to the public. Each one should contribute to the general happiness, as far as lies in his power. Come out, and give the girls a treat.'

Jim is slangy. I don't know where he picks it up. It certainly is not from me.

I said: 'Do you think it will really please 'em?'

He said it would be like a day in the country to them.

That decided me. It was a lovely evening, and I went.

When I got home, I undressed and rubbed myself down with whisky, put my feet in hot water, and a mustard plaster on my chest, had a basin of gruel and a glass of hot brandy and water, tallowed my nose, and went to bed.

These prompt and vigorous measures, aided by a naturally strong constitution, were the means of preserving my life; but as for the suit! Well, there, it isn't a suit; it's a splash board.

And I did fancy that suit too. But that's just the way. I never do get particularly fond of anything in this world, but what something dreadful happens to it. I had a tame rat when I was a boy, and I loved that animal as only a boy would love an old water rat; and, one day, it fell into a large dish of gooseberry-fool that was standing to cool in the kitchen, and nobody knew what had become of the poor creature, until the second helping.

I do hate wet weather, in town. At least, it is not so much the wet, as the mud, that I object to. Somehow or other, I seem to possess an irresistible alluring power over mud. I have only to show myself in the street on a muddy day to be half smothered by it. It all comes of being so attractive, as the old lady said when she was struck by lightning. Other people can go out on dirty days, and walk about for hours without getting a speck upon themselves; while, if I go across the road, I come back a perfect disgrace to be seen (as, in my boyish days, my poor dear mother used often to tell me). If there were only one dab of mud to be found in the whole of London, I am convinced I should carry it off from all competitors.

I wish I could return the affection, but I fear I never shall be able to. I have a horror of what they call the 'London particular.' I feel miserable and muggy all through a dirty day, and it is quite a relief to pull one's clothes off and get into bed, out of the way of it all. Everything goes wrong in wet weather. I don't know how it is, but there always seem to me to be more people, and dogs, and perambulators, and cabs, and carts,

[39]

about in wet weather than at any other time, and they all get in your way more, and everybody is so disagreeable – except myself – and it does make me so wild. And then, too, somehow, I always find myself carrying more things in wet weather than in dry; and, when you have a bag, and three parcels, and a newspaper; and it suddenly comes on to rain, you can't open your umbrella.

Which reminds me of another phase of the weather that I can't bear, and that is April weather (so-called, because it always comes in May). Poets think it very nice. As it does not know its own mind five minutes together, they liken it to a woman; and it is supposed to be very charming on that account. I don't appreciate it, myself. Such lightning change business may be all very agreeable in a girl. It is no doubt highly delightful to have to do with a person who grins one moment about nothing at all, and snivels the next for precisely the same cause, and who then giggles, and then sulks, and who is rude, and affectionate, and bad-tempered, and jolly, and boisterous, and silent, and passionate, and cold, and stand-offish, and flopping, all in one minute (mind *I* don't say this. It is those poets. And they are supposed to be connoisseurs of this sort of thing); but in the weather, the disadvantages of the system are more apparent. A woman's tears do not make one wet, but the rain does; and her coldness does not lay the foundations of asthma and rheumatism, as the east wind is apt to. I can prepare for, and put up with a regularly bad day, but these ha'porth of all sorts kind of days do not suit me, when I am walking along wet through; and there is something so exasperating about the way the sun comes out, smiling after a drenching shower, and seems to say: 'Lord, love you, you don't mean to say you're wet? Well, I am surprised. Why it was only my fun.'

They don't give you time to open or shut your umbrella in an English April, especially if it is an 'automaton' one – the umbrella I mean, not the April.

I bought an 'automaton' once in April, and I did have a time with it! I wanted an umbrella, and I went into a shop in the Strand, and told them so, and they said:

'Yessir; what sort of an umbrella would you like?'

I said I should like one that would keep the rain off, and that would not allow itself to be left behind in a railway carriage.

'Try an "automaton," ' said the shopman.

'What's an "automaton"?' said I.

'Oh, it's a beautiful arrangement,' replied the man, with a touch of enthusiasm. 'It opens and shuts itself.'

I bought one, and found that he was quite correct. It did open and shut itself. I had no control over it whatever. When it began to rain, which it did, that season, every alternate five minutes, I used to try and get the machine to open, but it would not budge; and then I used to stand and struggle with the wretched thing, and shake it, and swear at it, while the rain poured down in torrents. Then the moment the rain ceased, the absurd thing would go up suddenly with a jerk, and would not come down again; and I had to walk about under a bright blue sky, with an umbrella over my head, wishing that it would come on to rain again, so that it might not seem that I was insane.

When it did shut, it did so unexpectedly, and knocked one's hat off.

I don't know why it should be so, but it is an undeniable fact that there is nothing makes a man look so supremely ridiculous as losing his hat. The feeling of helpless misery that shoots down one's back on suddenly becoming aware that one's head is bare is among the most bitter ills that flesh is heir to. And then there is the wild chase after it, accompanied by an excitable small dog, who thinks it is a game, and in the course of which you are certain to upset three or four innocent children – to say nothing of their mothers – butt a fat old gentleman on the top of a perambulator, and cannon off a ladies' seminary into the arms of a wet sweep. After this, the idiotic hilarity of the spectators, and the disreputable appearance of the hat, when recovered, appear but of minor importance.

Altogether, what between March winds, April showers, and the entire absence of May flowers, spring is not a success in cities. It is all very well in the country, as I have said, but in towns, whose population is anything over ten thousand, it most certainly ought to be abolished. In the world's grim workshops, it is like the children – out of place. Neither show to advantage amidst the dust and din. It seems so sad to see the little dirt-grimed brats, trying to play in the noisy courts and muddy streets. Poor little uncared-for, unwanted human atoms, they are not children. Children are bright-eyed, chubby, and shy. These are dingy, screeching elves, their tiny faces seared and withered, their baby laughter cracked and hoarse.

The spring of life, and the spring of the year were alike meant to be cradled in the green lap of Nature. To us, in the town, spring brings but its cold winds and drizzling rains. We must seek it amongst the leafless woods, and the brambly lanes, on the healthy moors, and the great, still hills, if we want to feel its joyous breath, and hear its silent voices. There is a glorious freshness in the spring there. The scurrying clouds, the open bleakness, the rushing wind, and the clear bright air, thrill one with vague energies and hopes. Life, like the landscape around us, seems bigger, and wider, and freer – a rainbow road, leading to unknown ends. Through the silvery rents that bar the sky, we seem to catch a glimpse of the great hope and grandeur that lies around this little throbbing world, and a breath of its scent is wafted us on the wings of the wild March wind.

Strange thoughts we do not understand are stirring in our hearts. Voices are calling us to some great effort, to some mighty work. But we do not comprehend their meaning yet, and the hidden echoes within us that would reply are struggling, inarticulate, and dumb.

We stretch our hands like children to the light, seeking to grasp we know not what. Our thoughts, like the boys' thoughts in the Danish song, are very long, long thoughts, and very vague; we cannot see their end.

It must be so. All thoughts that peer outside this narrow world cannot be else than dim and shapeless. The thoughts that we can clearly grasp are very little thoughts – that two and two make four – that when we are hungry it is pleasant to eat – that honesty is the best policy; all greater thoughts are undefined and vast to our poor childish brains. We see but dimly through the mists that roll around our time-girt isle of life, and only hear the distant surging of the great sea beyond.

On Being Idle

Now this is a subject on which I flatter myself I really am *au fait*. The gentleman who, when I was young, bathed me at wisdom's font for nine guineas a term – no extras – used to say he never knew a boy who could do less work in more time; and I remember my poor grandmother once incidentally observing, in the course of an instruction upon the use of the prayer-book, that it was highly improbable that I should ever do much that I ought to do, but, that she felt convinced beyond a doubt that I should leave undone pretty well everything that I ought to do.

I am afraid I have somewhat belied half the dear old lady's prophecy. Heaven help me! I have done a good many things that I ought not to have done, in spite of my laziness. But I have fully confirmed the accuracy of her judgment so far as neglecting much that I ought not to have neglected is concerned. Idling always has been my strong point. I take no credit to myself in the matter – it is a gift. Few possess it. There are plenty of lazy people and plenty of slow-coaches, but a genuine idler is a rarity. He is not a man who slouches about with his hands in his pockets. On the contrary, his most startling characteristic is that he is always intensely busy.

It is impossible to enjoy idling thoroughly unless one has plenty of work to do. There is no fun in doing nothing when you have nothing to do. Wasting time is merely an occupation then, and a most exhausting one. Idleness, like kisses, to be sweet must be stolen.

Many years ago, when I was a young man, I was taken very ill – I never could see myself that much was the matter with me, except that I had a beastly cold. But I suppose it was something very serious, for the doctor said that I ought to have come to him a month before, and that if it (whatever it was) had gone on for

[43]

another week he would not have answered for the consequences. It is an extraordinary thing, but I never knew a doctor called into any case yet, but what it transpired that another day's delay would have rendered cure hopeless. Our medical guide, philosopher, and friend is like the hero in a melodrama, he always comes upon the scene just, and only just, in the nick of time. It is Providence, that is what it is.

Well, as I was saying, I was very ill, and was ordered to Buxton for a month, with strict injunctions to do nothing whatever all the while that I was there. 'Rest is what you require,' said the doctor, 'perfect rest.'

It seemed a delightful prospect. 'This man evidently understands my complaint,' said I, and I pictured to myself a glorious time – a four weeks' *dolce far niente* with a dash of illness in it. Not too much illness, but just illness enough – just sufficient to give it the flavour of suffering, and make it poetical. I should get up late, sip chocolate, and have my breakfast in slippers and a dressing-gown. I should lie out in the garden in a hammock, and read sentimental novels with a melancholy ending, until the book would fall from my listless hand, and I should recline there, dreamily gazing into the deep blue of the firmament, watching the fleecy clouds, floating like white-sailed ships, across its depths, and listening to the joyous song of the birds, and the low rustling of the trees. Or, when I became too weak to go out of doors, I should sit propped up with pillows, at the open window of the ground floor front, and look wasted and interesting, so that all the pretty girls would sigh as they passed by.

And, twice a day, I should go down in a Bath chair to the Colonnade, to drink the waters. Oh, those waters! I knew nothing about them then, and was rather taken with the idea. 'Drinking the waters' sounded fashionable and Queen Anneified, and I thought I should like them. But, ugh! after the first three or four mornings! Sam Weller's description of them, as 'having a taste of warm flat-irons,' conveys only a faint idea of their hideous nauseousness. If anything could make a sick man get well quickly, it would be the knowledge that he must drink a glassful of them every day until he was recovered. I drank them neat for six consecutive days, and they nearly killed me; but, after then, I adopted the plan of taking a stiff glass of brandy and water immediately on the top of them, and found much relief thereby. I have been informed since, by various eminent medical gentlemen, that the alcohol must have entirely counteracted the effects of the chalybeate properties contained in the water. I am glad I was lucky enough to hit upon the right thing.

But 'drinking the waters' was only a small portion of the torture I experienced during that memorable month, a month which was, without exception, the most miserable I have ever spent. During the best part of it, I religiously followed the doctor's mandate, and did nothing whatever, except moon about the house and garden, and go out for two hours a day in a Bath chair. That did break the monotony to a certain extent. There is more excitement about Bath-chairing – especially if you are not used to the exhilarating exercise – than might appear to the casual observer. A sense of danger, such as a mere outsider might not understand, is ever present to the mind of the occupant. He feels convinced every minute that the whole concern is going over, a conviction which becomes especially lively whenever a ditch or a stretch of newly macadamised road comes in sight. Every vehicle that passes he expects is going to run into him; and he never finds himself ascending or descending a hill, without immediately beginning to speculate upon his chances, supposing – as seems extremely probable – that the weak-kneed controller of his destiny should let go.

But even this diversion failed to enliven after a while, and the *ennui* became perfectly unbearable. I felt my mind giving way under it. It is not a strong mind, and I thought it would be unwise to tax it too far. So somewhere about the twentieth morning, I got up early, had a good breakfast, and walked straight to Hayfield at the foot of the Kinder Scout – a pleasant, busy, little town, reached through a lovely valley, and with two sweetly pretty women in it. At least they were sweetly pretty then; one passed me on the bridge, and I think, smiled; and the other was standing at an open door, making an unremunerative investment of kisses upon a red-faced baby. But it is years ago, and I daresay they have both grown stout and snappish since that time. Coming back, I saw an old man breaking stones, and it roused such strong longing in me to use my arms, that I offered him a drink to let me take his place. He was a kindly old man, and he humoured me. I went for those stones with the accumulated energy of three weeks, and did more work in half-an-hour than he had done all day. But it did not make him jealous.

Having taken the plunge, I went further and further into dissipation, going out for a long walk every morning, and listening to the band in the Pavilion every evening. But the days still passed slowly notwithstanding, and I was heartily glad when the last one came, and I was being whirled away from gouty, consumptive Buxton to London with its stern work and life. I looked out of the carriage as we rushed through Hendon in the evening. The lurid glare overhanging the mighty city seemed to warm my heart, and, when later on, my cab rattled out of St Pancras' station, the old familiar roar that came swelling up around me sounded the sweetest music I had heard for many a long day.

I certainly did not enjoy that month's idling. I like idling when I ought not to be idling; not when it is the only thing I have to do. That is my pig-headed nature. The time when I like best to stand with my back to the fire, calculating how much I owe, is when my desk is heaped highest with letters that must be answered by the next post. When I like to dawdle longest over my dinner, is when I have a heavy evening's work before me. And if, for some urgent reason, I ought to be up particularly early in the morning, it is then, more than at any other time, that I love to lie an extra half-hour in bed.

Ah! how delicious it is to turn over and go to sleep again: 'just for five minutes.' Is there any human being, I wonder, besides the hero of a Sunday-school 'tale for boys,' who ever gets up willingly? There are some men to whom getting up at the proper time is an utter impossibility. If eight o'clock happens to be the time that they should turn out, then they lie till half-past. If circumstances change and half-past eight becomes early enough for them, then it is nine before they can rise; they are like the statesman of whom it was said that he was always punctually half an hour late. They try all manner of schemes. They buy alarum clocks (artful contrivances that go off at the wrong time, and alarm the wrong people). They tell Sarah Jane to knock at the door and call them, and Sarah Jane does knock at the door, and does call them, and they grunt back 'awri,' and then go comfortably to sleep again. I knew one man who would actually get out, and have a cold bath; and even that was of no use, for, afterwards, he would jump into bed again to warm himself.

I think myself that I could keep out of bed all right, if I once got out. It is the wrenching away of the head from the pillow that I find so hard, and no amount of over-night determination makes it easier. I say to myself, after having wasted the whole evening, 'Well, I won't do any more work to-night; I'll get up early to-morrow morning;' and I am thoroughly resolved to do so – then. In the morning, however, I feel less enthusiastic about the idea, and reflect that it would have been much better if I had stopped up last night. And then there is the trouble of dressing, and the more one thinks about that, the more one wants to put it off.

It is a strange thing this bed, this mimic grave, where we stretch out tired limbs, and sink away so quietly into the silence and rest. 'Oh bed, oh bed, delicious bed, that heaven on earth to the weary head,' as sang poor Hood, you are a kind old nurse to us fretful boys and girls. Clever and foolish, naughty and good, you take us all in your motherly lap, and hush our wayward crying. The strong man full of care – the sick man full of pain – the little maiden, sobbing for faithless lover – like children, we lay our aching heads on your white bosom, and you gently soothe us off to by-by.

Our trouble is sore indeed, when you turn away, and will not comfort us. How long the dawn seems coming, when we cannot sleep! Oh! those hideous nights, when we toss and turn in fever and pain, when we lie, like living men among the dead, staring out into the dark hours that drift so slowly between us and the light. And oh! those still more hideous nights, when we sit by another in pain, when the low fire startles us every now and then with a falling cinder, and the tick of the clock seems a hammer, beating out the life that we are watching.

But enough of beds and bedrooms. I have kept to them too long, even for an idle fellow. Let us come out, and have a smoke. That wastes time just as well, and does not look so bad. Tobacco has been a blessing to us idlers. What the civil service clerks before Sir Walter's time found to occupy their minds with, it is hard to imagine. I attribute the quarrelsome nature of the

Middle Ages young men entirely to the want of the soothing weed. They had no work to do, and could not smoke, and the consequence was they were for ever fighting and rowing. If, by any extraordinary chance, there was no war going, then they got up a deadly family feud with the next-door neighbour, and if, in spite of this, they still had a few spare moments on their hands, they occupied them with discussions as to whose sweetheart was the best looking, the arguments employed on both sides being battle-axes, clubs, etc. Questions of taste were soon decided in those days. When a twelfth-century youth fell in love, he did not take three paces backwards, gaze into her eyes, and tell her she was too beautiful to live. He said he would step outside and see about it. And if, when he got out, he met a man and broke his head – the other man's head, I mean – then that proved that his – the first fellow's girl – was a pretty girl. But if the other fellow broke *his* head – not his own, you know, but the other fellow's – the other fellow to the second fellow, that is, because of course the other fellow would only be the other fellow to him, not the first fellow, who – well, if he broke his head, then *his* girl – not the other fellow's, but the fellow who *was* the – Look here, if A broke B's head, then A's girl was a pretty girl; but if B broke A's head, then A's girl wasn't a pretty girl, but B's girl was. That was their method of conducting art criticism.

Nowadays we light a pipe, and let the girls fight it out amongst themselves.

They do it very well. They are getting to do all our work. They are doctors, and barristers, and artists. They manage theatres, and promote swindles, and edit newspapers. I am looking forward to the time when we men shall have nothing to do but lie in bed till twelve, read two novels a day, have nice little five o'clock teas all to ourselves, and tax our brains with nothing more trying than discussions upon the latest patterns in trousers, and arguments as to what Mr Jones's coat was made of and whether it fitted him. It is a glorious prospect – for idle fellows.

On Vanity and Vanities

All is vanity, and everybody's vain. Women are terribly vain. So
are men – more so, if possible. So are children, particularly
children. One of them, at this very moment, is hammering upon
my legs. She wants to know what I think of her new shoes.
Candidly I don't think much of them. They lack symmetry and
curve, and possess an indescribable appearance of lumpiness (I
believe, too, they've put them on the wrong feet). But I don't say
this. It is not criticism, but flattery that she wants; and I gush
over them with what I feel to myself to be degrading
effusiveness. Nothing else would satisfy this self-opinionated
cherub. I tried the conscientious friend dodge with her on one
occasion, but it was not a success. She had requested my
judgment upon her general conduct and behaviour, the exact
case submitted being, 'Wot oo tink of me? Oo peased wi' me?'
and I had thought it a good opportunity to make a few salutary
remarks upon her late moral career, and said, 'No, I am not
pleased with you.' I recalled to her mind the events of that very
morning, and I put it to her how she, as a Christian child, could
expect a wise and good uncle to be satisfied with the carryings
on of an infant who that very day had roused the whole house at
5 am; had upset a water jug, and tumbled downstairs after it at
7; had endeavoured to put the cat in the bath at 8; and sat on her
own father's hat at 9.35.

What did she do? Was she grateful to me for my plain speaking? Did she ponder upon my words, and determine to profit
by them, and to lead from that hour a better and a nobler life?

No! she howled.

That done, she became abusive. She said:

'Oo naughty – oo naughty, bad unkie – oo bad man – me tell
MAR.'

[49]

And she did, too.

Since then, when my views have been called for, I have kept my real sentiments more to myself like, preferring to express unbounded admiration of this young person's actions, irrespective of their actual merits. And she nods her head approvingly, and trots off to advertise my opinion to the rest of the household. She appears to employ it as a sort of testimonial for mercenary purposes, for I subsequently hear distant sounds of 'Unkie says me dood dirl – me dot to have two bikkies.'*

There she goes, now, gazing rapturously at her own toes, and murmuring 'pittie' – two-foot-ten of conceit and vanity; to say nothing of other wickednesses.

They are all alike. I remember sitting in a garden one sunny afternoon in the suburbs of London. Suddenly, I heard a shrill, treble voice calling from a top storey window to some unseen being, presumably in one of the other gardens, 'Gamma, me dood boy, me wery dood boy, Gamma; me dot on Bob's knickie-bockies.'

Why even animals are vain. I saw a great Newfoundland dog, the other day, sitting in front of a mirror at the entrance to a shop in Regent's Circus, and examining himself with an amount of smug satisfaction that I have never seen equalled elsewhere, outside a vestry meeting.

I was at a farmhouse once, when some high holiday was being celebrated. I don't opinion goodness consists of stroking her, and patting her, and feeding her with food. I fear this narrow-minded view of virtue, though, is not confined to pussies. We are all inclined to adopt a similar standard of merit in our estimate of other people. A good man is a man who is good to us, and a bad man is a man who doesn't do what we want him to. The truth is, we each of us have an inborn conviction that the whole world, with everybody and everything in it, was created as a sort of necessary appendage to ourselves. Our fellow men and women were made to admire us, and to minister to our various requirements. You and I, dear reader, are each the centre of the universe in our respective opinions. You, as I understand it, were brought into being by a considerate Providence in order that you might read and pay

* Early English for biscuits.

me for what I write; while I, in your opinion, am an article sent into the world to write something for you to read. The stars – as we term the myriad other worlds that are rushing down beside us through the eternal silence – were put into the heavens to make the sky look interesting for us at night. And the moon, with its dark mysteries and ever hidden face, is an arrangement for us to flirt under.

I fear we are most of us like Mrs Poyser's bantam cock, who fancied the sun got up every morning to hear him crow. ' 'Tis vanity that makes the world go round.' I don't believe any man ever existed without vanity, and, if he did, he would be an extremely uncomfortable person to have anything to do with. He would, of course, be a very good man, and we should respect him very much. He would be a very admirable man – a man to be put under a glass case, and shown round as a specimen – a man to be stuck upon a pedestal, and copied, like a school exercise – a man to be reverenced, but not a man to be loved, not a human brother whose hand we should care to grip. Angels may be very excellent sort of folk in their way, but we, poor mortals, in our present state, would probably find them precious slow company. Even mere good people are rather depressing. It is in our faults and failings, not in our virtues, that we touch one another, and find sympathy. We differ widely enough in our nobler qualities. It is in our follies that we are at one. Some of us are pious, some of us are generous. Some few of us are honest, comparatively speaking; and some, fewer still, may possibly be truthful. But in vanity and kindred weaknesses we can all join hands. Vanity is one of those touches of Nature that make the whole world kin. From the Indian hunter, proud of his belt of scalps, to the European general, swelling beneath his row of stars and medals; from the Chinee, gleeful at the length of his pigtail, to the 'professional beauty,' suffering tortures in order that her waist may resemble a peg-top; from draggle-tailed little Polly Stiggins, strutting through Seven Dials with a tattered parasol over her head, to the princess, sweeping through a drawing-room, with a train of four yards long; from 'Arry, winning by vulgar chaff the loud laughter of his pals, to the statesman, whose ears are tickled by the cheers that greet his high-sounding periods; from the dark-skinned African, bartering his rare oils and ivory for a few glass beads to hang about his neck, to the Christian maiden, selling her white body for a score of tiny stones and an empty title to tack before her name – all march, and fight, and bleed, and die beneath its tawdry flag.

Ay, ay, vanity is truly the motive-power that moves Humanity, and it is flattery that greases the wheels. If you want to win affection and respect in this world, you must flatter people. Flatter high and low, and rich and poor, and silly and wise. You will get on famously. Praise this man's virtues and that man's vices. Compliment everybody upon everything, and especially upon what they haven't got. Admire guys for their beauty, fools for their wit, and boors for their breeding. Your discernment and intelligence will be extolled to the skies.

Everyone can be got over by flattery. The belted earl – 'belted earl' is the correct phrase, I believe. I don't know what it means, unless it be an earl that wears a belt instead of braces. Some men do. I don't like it myself. You have to keep the thing so tight, for it to be of any use, and that is uncomfortable. Anyhow, whatever particular kind of an earl a belted earl may be, he is, I assert, get-overable by flattery; just as every other human being is, from a duchess to a cat's-meat man, from a ploughboy to a poet – and the poet far easier than the ploughboy, for butter sinks better into wheaten bread than into oaten cakes.

As for love, flattery is its very life blood. Fill a person with love for themselves, and what runs over will be your share, says a certain witty and truthful Frenchman, whose name I can't for the life of me remember. (Confound it, I never can remember names when I want to.) Tell a girl she is an angel, only more angelic than an angel; that she is a goddess, only more graceful, queenly, and heavenly than the average goddess; that she is more fairy-like than Titania, more beautiful than Venus, more enchanting than Parthenope; more adorable, lovely, and radiant, in short, than any other woman that ever did live, does live, or could live, and you will make a very favourable impression upon her trusting little heart. Sweet innocent! she will believe every word you say. It is so easy to deceive a woman – in this way.

Dear little souls, they hate flattery, so they tell you; and, when you say, 'Ah, darling, it isn't flattery in your case, it's plain, sober truth; you really are, without exaggeration, the most beautiful, the most good, the most charming, the most divine, the most perfect human creature that ever trod this earth,' they will smile a quiet, approving smile, and, leaning against your manly shoulder, murmur that you are a dear good fellow after all.

By Jove, fancy a man trying to make love on strictly truthful principles, determining never to utter a word of mere compliment or hyperbole, but to scrupulously confine himself to exact fact! Fancy his gazing rapturously into his mistress' eyes, and whispering softly to her that she wasn't, on the whole, bad looking, as girls went! Fancy his holding up her little hand, and assuring her that it was of a light drab colour, shot with red; and telling her, as he pressed her to his heart, that her nose, for a turned-up one, seemed rather pretty; and that her eyes appeared to him, as far as he could judge, to be quite up to the average standard of such things!

A nice chance *he* would stand against the man who would tell her that her face was like a fresh blush rose, that her hair was a wandering sunbeam imprisoned by her smiles, and her eyes like two evening stars.

There are various ways of flattering, and, of course, you must adapt your style to your subject. Some people like it laid on with a trowel, and this requires very little art. With sensible persons, however, it needs to be done very delicately, and more by suggestion than actual words. A good many like it wrapped up in the form of an insult, as: 'Oh, you are a perfect fool, you are. You would give your last sixpence to the first hungry-looking beggar you met;' while others will swallow it only when administered through the medium of a third person, so that if C wishes to get at an A of this sort, he must confide to A's particular friend B that he thinks A a splendid fellow, and beg him, B, not to mention it, especially to A. Be careful that B is a reliable man, though, otherwise he won't.

Those fine, sturdy John Bulls, who 'hate flattery, sir,' 'Never let anybody get over *me* by flattery,' etc., etc., are very simply managed. Flatter them enough upon their absence of vanity, and you can do what you like with them.

After all, vanity is as much a virtue as a vice. It is easy to recite copybook maxims against its sinfulness, but it is a passion that can move us to good as well as to evil. Ambition is only vanity ennobled. We want to win praise and admiration – or Fame as we prefer to name it – and so we write great books, and paint grand pictures, and sing sweet songs; and toil with willing hands in study, loom, and laboratory.

We wish to become rich men, not in order to enjoy ease and comfort – all that any one man can taste of those may be purchased anywhere for two hundred pounds per annum – but that our houses may be bigger and more gaudily furnished than our neighbours'; that our horses and servants may be more numerous; that we may dress our wives and daughters in absurd, but expensive clothes; and that we may give costly dinners of which we ourselves individually do not eat a shilling's worth. And to do this, we aid the world's work with clear and busy brain, spreading commerce among its peoples, carrying civilisation to its remotest corners.

Do not let us abuse vanity, therefore. Rather let us use it. Honour itself is but the highest form of vanity. The instinct is not confined solely to Beau Brummells and Dolly Vardens. There is the vanity of the peacock, and the vanity of the eagle. Snobs are vain. But so, too, are heroes. Come, oh! my young brother bucks, let us be vain together. Let us join hands, and help each other to increase our vanity. Let us be vain, not of our trousers and hair, but of brave hearts and working hands, of truth, of purity, of nobility. Let us be too vain to stoop to aught that is mean or base, too vain for petty selfishness and little-minded envy, too vain to say an unkind word or do an unkind act. Let us be vain of being single-hearted, upright gentlemen in the midst of a world of knaves. Let us pride ourselves upon thinking high thoughts, achieving great deeds, living good lives.

Three Men in a Boat

To say nothing of the Dog!

Three Men in a Boat, 1889, began life originally
as 'The Story of the Thames',
which was to be enlivened by 'humorous relief'.
The editor who published it serially in *Home Chimes*
threw out the scenery and history and did not like the title.
So it became *Three Men in a Boat*. It made Jerome famous
and reaped the American pirate a fortune.

Preface to the First Edition

The chief beauty of this book lies not so much in its literary style, or in the extent and usefulness of the information it conveys, as in its simple truthfulness. Its pages form the record of events that really happened. All that has been done is to colour them; and, for this, no extra charge has been made. George and Harris and Montmorency are not poetic ideals, but things of flesh and blood – especially George, who weighs about twelve stone. Other works may excel this in depth of thought and knowledge of human nature: other books may rival it in originality and size; but, for hopeless and incurable veracity, nothing yet discovered can surpass it. This, more than all its other charms, will, it is felt, make the volume precious in the eye of the earnest reader; and will lend additional weight to the lesson that the story teaches.

London,
August 1889

CHAPTER 1

There were four of us – George, and William Samuel Harris, and myself, and Montmorency. We were sitting in my room, smoking, and talking about how bad we were – bad from a medical point of view I mean, of course.

We were all feeling seedy, and we were getting quite nervous about it. Harris said he felt such extraordinary fits of giddiness come over him at times, that he hardly knew what he was doing; and then George said that *he* had fits of giddiness too, and hardly knew what *he* was doing. With me, it was my liver that was out of order. I knew it was my liver that was out of order, because I had just been reading a patent liver-pill circular, in which were detailed various symptoms by which a man could tell when his liver was out of order. I had them all.

It is a most extraordinary thing, but I never read a patent medicine advertisement without being impelled to the conclusion that I am suffering from the particular disease therein dealt with, in its most virulent form. The diagnosis seems in every case to correspond exactly with all the sensations that I have ever felt.

I remember going to the British Museum one day to read up the treatment for some slight ailment of which I had a touch – hay fever, I fancy it was. I got down the book, and read all I came to read; and then, in an unthinking moment, I idly turned the leaves, and began to indolently study diseases, generally. I forget which was the first distemper I plunged into – some fearful, devastating scourge, I know – and, before I had glanced half down the list of 'premonitory symptoms', it was borne in upon me that I had fairly got it.

I sat for a while frozen with horror; and then in the listlessness of despair, I again turned over the pages. I came to typhoid fever – read the symptoms – discovered that I had typhoid fever, must have had it for months without knowing it – wondered what else I had got; turned up St Vitus's Dance – found, as I expected, that I had that too – began to get interested in my case, and determined to sift it to the bottom, and so started alphabetically – read up ague, and learnt that I was sickening for it, and that the acute stage would commence in about another fortnight. Bright's disease, I was relieved to find, I had only in a modified form, and so far as that was concerned, I might live for years. Cholera I had, with severe complications; and diphtheria I seemed to have been born with. I plodded conscientiously through the twenty-six letters, and the only malady I could conclude I had not got was housemaid's knee.

I felt rather hurt about this at first; it seemed somehow to be a sort of slight. Why hadn't I got housemaid's knee? Why this invidious reservation? After a while, however, less grasping feelings prevailed. I reflected that I had every other known malady in the pharmacology, and I grew less selfish, and determined to do without housemaid's knee. Gout, in its most malignant stage, it would appear, had seized me without my being aware of it; and zymosis I had evidently been suffering with from boyhood. There were no more diseases after zymosis, so I concluded there was nothing else the matter with me.

I sat and pondered. I thought what an interesting case I must be from a medical point of view, what an acquisition I should be to a class! Students would have no need 'to walk the hospitals', if they had me. I was a hospital in myself. All they need do would be to walk round me, and, after that, take their diploma.

Then I wondered how long I had to live. I tried to examine myself. I felt my pulse. I could not at first feel any pulse at all. Then, all of a sudden, it seemed to start off. I pulled out my watch and timed it. I made it a hundred and forty-seven to the minute. I tried to feel my heart. I could not feel my heart. It had stopped beating. I have since been induced to come to the opinion that it must have been there all the time, and must have been beating, but I cannot account for it. I patted myself all over my front, from what I call my waist up to my head, and I went a bit round each side, and a little way up the back. But I could not feel or hear anything. I tried to look at my tongue. I stuck it out as far as ever it would go, and I shut one eye, and

tried to examine it with the other. I could only see the tip, and
the only thing that I could gain from that was to feel more
certain than before that I had scarlet fever.

I walked into that reading-room a happy healthy man. I
crawled out a decrepit wreck.

I went to my medical man. He is an old chum of mine, and
feels my pulse, and looks at my tongue, and talks about the
weather, all for nothing, when I fancy I'm ill; so I thought I
would do him a good turn by going to him now. 'What a doctor
wants', I said, 'is practice. He shall have me. He will get more
practice out of me than out of seventeen hundred of your
ordinary, commonplace patients, with only one or two diseases
each.' So I went straight up and saw him, and he said:

'Well, what's the matter with you?'

I said:

'I will not take up your time, dear boy, with telling you what
is the matter with me. Life is brief, and you might pass away
before I had finished. But I will tell you what is *not* the matter
with me. I have not got housemaid's knee. Why I have not got
housemaid's knee, I cannot tell you; but the fact remains that I
have not got it. Everything else, however, I *have* got.'

And I told him how I came to discover it all.

Then he opened me and looked down me, and clutched hold
of my wrist, and then he hit me over the chest when I wasn't
expecting it – a cowardly thing to do, I call it – and immediately
afterwards butted me with the side of his head. After that, he sat
down and wrote out a prescription, and folded it up and gave it
me, and I put it in my pocket and went out.

I did not open it. I took it to the nearest chemist's, and
handed it in. The man read it, and then handed it back.

He said he didn't keep it.

I said:

'You are a chemist?'

He said:

'I am a chemist. If I was a co-operative stores and family
hotel combined, I might be able to oblige you. Being only a
chemist hampers me.'

I read the prescription. It ran:

1 lb beefsteak, with

1 pt bitter beer
every 6 hours.
1 ten-mile walk every morning.
1 bed at 11 sharp every night.

And don't stuff up your head with things you don't understand.

I followed the directions, with the happy result – speaking for myself – that my life was preserved, and is still going on.

In the present instance, going back to the liver-pill circular, I had the symptoms, beyond all mistake, the chief among them being 'a general disinclination to work of any kind'.

What I suffer in that way no tongue can tell. From my earliest infancy I have been a martyr to it. As a boy, the disease hardly ever left me for a day. They did not know, then, that it was my liver. Medical science was in a far less advanced state than now, and they used to put it down to laziness.

'Why, you skulking little devil, you,' they would say, 'get up and do something for your living, can't you?' – not knowing, of course, that I was ill.

And they didn't give me pills; they gave me clumps on the side of the head. And, strange as it may appear, those clumps on the head often cured me – for the time being. I have known one clump on the head have more effect upon my liver, and make me feel more anxious to go straight away then and there, and do what was wanted to be done, without further loss of time, than a whole box of pills does now.

You know, it often is so – those simple, old-fashioned remedies are sometimes more efficacious than all the dispensary stuff.

We sat there for half an hour, describing to each other our maladies. I explained to George and William Harris how I felt when I got up in the morning, and William Harris told us how he felt when he went to bed; and George stood on the hearth-rug, and gave us a clever and powerful piece of acting, illustrative of how he felt in the night.

George *fancies* he is ill: but there's never anything really the matter with him, you know.

At this point, Mrs Poppets knocked at the door to know if we were ready for supper. We smiled sadly at one another, and said we supposed we had better try to swallow a bit. Harris said a little something in one's stomach often kept the disease in check; and Mrs Poppets brought the tray in, and we drew up to the table, and toyed with a little steak and onions, and some rhubarb tart.

I must have been very weak at the time; because I know, after the first half-hour or so, I seemed to take no interest whatever in my food – an unusual thing for me – and I didn't want any cheese.

This duty done, we refilled our glasses, lit our pipes, and resumed the discussion upon our state of health. What it was that was actually the matter with us, we none of us could be sure of; but the unanimous opinion was that it – whatever it was – had been brought on by overwork.

'What we want is rest,' said Harris.

'Rest and a complete change,' said George. 'The overstrain upon our brains has produced a general depression throughout the system. Change of scene, and absence of the necessity for thought, will restore the mental equilibrium.'

George has a cousin who is usually described in the charge-sheet as a medical student, so that he naturally has a somewhat family-physicianary way of putting things.

I agreed with George, and suggested that we should seek out some retired and old-world spot, far from the madding crowd, and dream away a sunny week among its drowsy lanes – some half-forgotten nook, hidden away by the fairies, out of reach of the noisy world – some quaint-perched eyrie on the cliffs of Time, from whence the surging waves of the nineteenth-century would sound far-off and faint.

Harris said he thought it would be humpy. He said he knew the sort of place I meant; where everybody went to bed at eight o'clock, and you couldn't get a *Referee* for love or money, and had to walk ten miles to get your baccy.

'No,' said Harris, 'if you want rest and change, you can't beat a sea trip.'

I objected to the sea trip strongly. A sea trip does you good when you are going to have a couple of months of it, but, for a week, it is wicked.

You start on Monday with the idea implanted in your bosom that you are going to enjoy yourself. You wave an airy adieu to the boys on shore, light your biggest pipe, and swagger about the deck as if you were Captain Cook, Sir Francis Drake, and Christopher Columbus all rolled into one. On Tuesday, you wish you hadn't come. On Wednesday, Thursday, and Friday, you wish you were dead. On Saturday you are able to swallow a little beef tea, and to sit up on deck, and answer with a wan, sweet smile when kind-hearted people ask how you feel now. On Sunday, you begin to walk again, and take solid food. And on Monday morning, as, with your bag and umbrella in your hand, you stand by the gunwale, waiting to step ashore, you begin to thoroughly like it.

I remember my brother-in-law going for a short sea trip once for the benefit of his health. He took a return berth from London to Liverpool; and when he got to Liverpool, the only thing he was anxious about was to sell that return ticket.

It was offered round the town at a tremendous reduction, so I am told; and was eventually sold for eighteenpence to a bilious-looking youth who had just been advised by his medical men to go to the seaside, and take exercise.

'Seaside!' said my brother-in-law, pressing the ticket affectionately into his hand: 'why, you'll have enough to last you a lifetime; and as for exercise! why, you'll get more exercise, sitting down on that ship, than you would turning somersaults on dry land.'

He himself – my brother-in-law – came back by train. He said the North-Western Railway was healthy enough for him.

Another fellow I knew went for a week's voyage round the coast, and, before they started, the steward came to him to ask whether he would pay for each meal as he had it, or arrange beforehand for the whole series.

The steward recommended the latter course, as it would come so much cheaper. He said they would do him for the whole week at two-pounds-five. He said for breakfast there would be fish, followed by a grill. Lunch was at one, and consisted of four courses. Dinner at six – soup, fish, entrée, joint, poultry, salad, sweets, cheese, and dessert. And a light meat supper at ten.

My friend thought he would close on the two-pounds-five job (he is a hearty eater), and did so.

Lunch came just as they were off Sheerness. He didn't feel so hungry as he thought he should, and so contented himself with a bit of boiled beef, and some strawberries and cream. He pondered a good deal during the afternoon, and at one time it seemed to him that he had been eating nothing but boiled beef for weeks, and at other times it seemed that he must have been living on strawberries and cream for years.

Neither the beef nor the strawberries and cream seemed happy, either – seemed discontented like.

At six, they came and told him dinner was ready. The announcement aroused no enthusiasm within him, but he felt that there was some of that two-pounds-five to be worked off, and he held on to ropes and things and went down. A pleasant odour of onions and hot ham, mingled with fried fish and greens, greeted him at the bottom of the ladder; and then the steward came up with an oily smile, and said:

'What can I get you, sir?'

'Get me out of this,' was the feeble reply.

And they ran him up quick, and propped him up, over to leeward, and left him.

For the next four days he lived a simple and blameless life on thin Captain's biscuits (I mean that the biscuits were thin, not the captain) and soda-water; but, towards Saturday, he got uppish, and went in for weak tea and dry toast, and on Monday he was gorging himself on chicken broth. He left the ship on Tuesday, and as it steamed away from the landing-stage he gazed after it regretfully.

'There she goes,' he said, 'there she goes, with two pounds' worth of food on board that belongs to me, and that I haven't had.'

He said that if they had given him another day he thought he could have put it straight.

So I set my face against the sea trip. Not, as I explained, upon my own account. I was never queer. But I was afraid for George. George said he should be all right, and would rather like it, but he would advise Harris and me not to think of it, as he felt sure we should both be ill. Harris said that, to himself, it was always a mystery how people managed to get sick at sea – said he thought people must do it on purpose, from affectation – said he had often wished to be, but had never been able.

Then he told us anecdotes of how he had gone across the Channel when it was so rough that the passengers had to be tied into their berths, and he and the captain were the only two living souls on board who were not ill. Sometimes it was he and the second mate who were not ill; but it was generally he and one other man. If not he and another man, then it was he by himself.

It is a curious fact, but nobody ever is sea-sick – on land. At sea, you come across plenty of people very bad indeed, whole boat-loads of them; but I never met a man yet, on land, who had ever known at all what it was to be sea-sick. Where the thousands upon thousands of bad sailors that swarm in every ship hide themselves when they are on land is a mystery.

If most men were like a fellow I saw on the Yarmouth boat one day, I could account for the seeming enigma easily enough. It was just off Southend Pier, I recollect, and he was leaning out through one of the port-holes in a very dangerous position. I went up to him to try and save him.

'Hi! come further in,' I said, shaking him by the shoulder. 'You'll be overboard.'

'Oh my! I wish I was,' was the only answer I could get; and there I had to leave him.

Three weeks afterwards, I met him in the coffee-room of a Bath hotel, talking about his voyages, and explaining, with enthusiasm, how he loved the sea.

'Good sailor!' he replied in answer to a mild young man's envious query, 'well I did feel a little queer *once*, I confess. I was off Cape Horn. The vessel was wrecked the next morning.'

I said:

'Weren't you a little shaky by Southend Pier one day, and wanted to be thrown overboard?'

'Southend Pier!' he replied, with a puzzled expression.

'Yes; going down to Yarmouth, last Friday three weeks.'

'Oh, ah – yes,' he answered, brightening up; 'I remember now. I did have a headache that afternoon. It was the pickles, you know. They were the most disgraceful pickles I ever tasted in a respectable boat. Did *you* have any?'

For myself, I have discovered an excellent preventive against sea-sickness, in balancing myself. You stand in the centre of the deck, and, as the ship heaves and pitches, you move your body about, so as to keep it always straight. When the front of the ship rises, you lean forward, till the deck almost touches your nose;

and when its back end gets up, you lean backwards. This is all very well for an hour or two; but you can't balance yourself for a week.

George said:

'Let's go up the river.'

He said we should have fresh air, exercise, and quiet; the constant change of scene would occupy our minds (including what there was of Harris's); and the hard work would give us a good appetite, and make us sleep well.

Harris said he didn't think George ought to do anything that would have a tendency to make him sleepier than he always was, as it might be dangerous. He said he didn't very well understand how George was going to sleep any more than he did now, seeing that there were only twenty-four hours in each day, summer and winter alike; but thought that if he *did* sleep any more he might just as well be dead, and so save his board and lodging.

Harris said, however, that the river would suit him to a 'T'. I don't know what a 'T' is (except a sixpenny one, which includes bread-and-butter and cake *ad lib.*, and is cheap at the price, if you haven't had any dinner). It seems to suit everybody, however, which is greatly to its credit.

It suited me to a 'T', too, and Harris and I both said it was a good idea of George's and we said it in a tone that seemed to somehow imply that we were surprised that George should have come out so sensible.

The only one who was not struck with the suggestion was Montmorency. He never did care for the river, did Montmorency.

'It's all very well for you fellows,' he says; 'you like it, but *I* don't. There's nothing for me to do. Scenery is not in my line, and I don't smoke. If I see a rat, you won't stop; and if I go to sleep, you get fooling about with the boat, and slop me overboard. If you ask me, I call the whole thing bally foolishness.'

We were three to one, however, and the motion was carried.

CHAPTER 2

We pulled out the maps, and discussed plans.

We arranged to start on the following Saturday from Kingston. Harris and I would go down in the morning, and take the boat up to Chertsey, and George, who would not be able to get away from the City till the afternoon (George goes to sleep at a bank from ten to four each day, except Saturdays, when they wake him up and put him outside at two), would meet us there.

Should we 'camp out' or sleep at inns?

George and I were for camping out. We said it would be so wild and free, so patriarchal like.

Slowly the golden memory of the dead sun fades from the hearts of the cold, sad clouds. Silent, like sorrowing children, the birds have ceased their song, and only the moorhen's plaintive cry and the harsh croak of the corncrake stirs the awed hush around the couch of waters, where the dying day breathes out her last.

From the dim woods on either bank, Night's ghostly army, the grey shadows, creep out with noiseless tread to chase away the lingering rearguard of the light, and pass, with noiseless, unseen feet, above the waving river-grass, and through the sighing rushes; and Night, upon her sombre throne, folds her black wings above the darkening world, and, from her phantom palace, lit by the pale stars, reigns in stillness.

Then we run our little boat into some quiet nook, and the tent is pitched, and the frugal supper cooked and eaten. Then the big pipes are filled and lighted, and the pleasant chat goes round in musical undertone; while, in the pauses of our talk, the river, playing round the boat, prattles strange old tales and secrets, sings low the old child's song that it has sung so many thousand years – will sing so many thousand years to come, before its voice grows harsh and old – a song that we, who have learnt to love its changing face, who have so often nestled on its yielding bosom, think, somehow, we understand, though we could not tell you in mere words the story that we listen to.

And we sit there, by its margin, while the moon, who loves it too, stoops down to kiss it with a sister's kiss, and throws her silver arms around it clingingly; and we watch it as it flows, ever singing, ever whispering, out to meet its king, the sea – till our voices die away in silence, and the pipes go out – till we, commonplace, everyday young men enough, feel strangely full of thoughts, half sad, half sweet, and do not care or want to speak – till we laugh, and rising, knock the ashes from our burnt-out pipes, and say 'Good night', and, lulled by the lapping water and the rustling trees, we fall asleep beneath the great, still stars, and dream that the world is young again – young and sweet as she used to be ere the centuries of fret and care had furrowed her fair face, ere her children's sins and follies had made old her loving heart – sweet as she was in those bygone days when, a new-made mother, she nursed us, her children, upon her own deep breast – ere the wiles of painted civilization had lured us away from her fond arms, and the poisoned sneers of artificiality had made us ashamed of the simple life we led with her, and the simple, stately home where mankind was born so many thousands of years ago.

Harris said:

'How about when it rained?'

You can never rouse Harris. There is no poetry about Harris – no wild yearning for the unattainable. Harris never 'weeps, he knows not why'. If Harris's eyes fill with tears, you can bet it is because Harris has been eating raw onions, or has put too much Worcester over his chop.

If you were to stand at night by the seashore with Harris, and say:

'Hark! Do you not hear? Is it but the mermaids singing deep below the waving waters; or sad spirits, chanting dirges for white corpses, held by seaweed?'

Harris would take you by the arm, and say:

'I know what it is, old man; you've got a chill. Now, you come along with me. I know a place round the corner here, where you can get a drop of the finest Scotch whisky you ever tasted – put you right in less than no time.'

Harris always does know a place round the corner where you can get something brilliant in the drinking line. I believe that if you met Harris up in Paradise (supposing such a thing likely), he would immediately greet you with:

'So glad you've come, old fellow; I've found a nice place round the corner here, where you can get some really first-class nectar.'

In the present instance, however, as regarded the camping out, his practical view of the matter came as a very timely hint. Camping out in rainy weather is not pleasant.

It is evening. You are wet through, and there is a good two inches of water in the boat, and all the things are damp. You find a place on the banks that is not quite so puddly as other places you have seen, and you land and lug out the tent, and two of you proceed to fix it.

It is soaked and heavy, and it flops about, and tumbles down on you, and clings round your head and makes you mad. The rain is pouring steadily down all the time. It is difficult enough to fix a tent in dry weather; in wet, the task becomes herculean. Instead of helping you, it seems to you that the other man is simply playing the fool. Just as you get your side beautifully fixed, he gives it a hoist from his end, and spoils it all.

'Here! What are you up to?' you call out.

'What are *you* up to?' he retorts. 'Leggo, can't you?'

'Don't pull it; you've got it all wrong, you stupid ass!' you shout.

'No, I haven't,' he yells back; 'let go your side!'

'I tell you you've got it all wrong!' you roar, wishing that you could get at him; and you give your ropes a lug that pulls all his pegs out.

'Ah, the bally idiot!' you hear him mutter to himself; and then comes a savage haul, and away goes your side. You lay down the mallet and start to go round and tell him what you think about the whole business, and, at the same time, he starts round in the same direction to come and explain his views to you. And you follow each other round and round, swearing at one another, until the tent tumbles down in a heap, and leaves you looking at each other across its ruins, then you both indignantly exclaim, in the same breath:

'There you are! What did I tell you?'

Meanwhile the third man, who has been baling out the boat, and who has spilled the water down his sleeve, and has been cursing away to himself steadily for the last ten minutes, wants to know what the thundering blazes you're playing at, and why the blarmed tent isn't up yet.

At last, somehow or other, it does get up, and you land the things. It is hopeless attempting to make a wood fire, so you light the methylated spirit stove, and crowd round that.

Rainwater is the chief article of diet at supper. The bread is two-thirds rainwater, the beefsteak-pie is exceedingly rich in it, and the jam, and the butter, and the salt, and the coffee have all combined with it to make soup.

After supper, you find your tobacco is damp, and you cannot smoke. Luckily you have a bottle of the stuff that cheers and inebriates, if taken in proper quantity, and this restores to you sufficient interest in life to induce you to go to bed.

There you dream that an elephant has suddenly sat down on your chest, and that the volcano has exploded and thrown you down to the bottom of the sea – the elephant still sleeping peacefully on your bosom. You wake up and grasp the idea that something terrible really has happened. Your first impression is that the end of the world has come; and then you think that this cannot be, and that it is thieves and murderers, or else fire, and this opinion you express in the usual method. No help comes, however, and all you know is that thousands of people are kicking you, and you are being smothered.

Somebody else seems in trouble, too. You can hear his faint cries coming from underneath your bed. Determining, at all events, to sell your life dearly, you struggle frantically, hitting out right and left with your arms and legs, and yelling lustily the while, and at last something gives way, and you find your head in the fresh air. Two feet off, you dimly observe a half-dressed ruffian, waiting to kill you, and you are preparing for a life-and-death struggle with him, when it begins to dawn on you that it's Jim.

'Oh, it's you, is it?' he says, recognizing you at the same moment.

'Yes,' you answer, rubbing your eyes; 'what's happened?'

'Bally tent's blown down, I think,' he says. 'Where's Bill?'

Then you both raise up your voices and shout for 'Bill!' and

the ground beneath you heaves and rocks, and the muffled voice
that you heard before replies from out of the ruin:

'Get off my head, can't you?'

And Bill struggles out, a muddy, trampled wreck, and in an
unnecessarily aggressive mood – he being under the evident
belief that the whole thing has been done on purpose.

In the morning you are all three speechless, owing to having
caught severe colds in the night; you also feel very quarrelsome,
and you swear at each other in hoarse whispers during the
whole of breakfast time.

We therefore decided that we would sleep out on fine nights;
and hotel it, and inn it, and pub it, like respectable folks, when it
was wet, or when we felt inclined for a change.

Montmorency hailed this compromise with much approval.
He does not revel in romantic solitude. Give him something
noisy; and if a trifle low, so much the jollier. To look at
Montmorency you would imagine that he was an angel sent
upon the earth, for some reason withheld from mankind, in the
shape of a small fox-terrier. There is a sort of Oh-what-a-
wicked-world-this-is-and-how-I-wish-I-could-do-something-
to-make-it-better-and-nobler expression about Montmorency
that has been known to bring the tears into the eyes of pious old
ladies and gentlemen.

When first he came to live at my expense, I never thought I
should be able to get him to stop long. I used to sit down and
look at him, as he sat on the rug and looked up at me, and think:
'Oh, that dog will never live. He will be snatched up to the
bright skies in a chariot, that is what will happen to him.'

But, when I had paid for about a dozen chickens that he had
killed; and had dragged him, growling and kicking, by the scruff
of his neck, out of a hundred and fourteen street fights; and had
had a dead cat brought round for my inspection by an irate
female, who called me a murderer; and had been summoned by
the man next door but one for having a ferocious dog at large,
that had kept him pinned up in his own tool-shed, afraid to
venture his nose outside the door, for over two hours on a cold
night; and had learned that the gardener, unknown to myself,
had won thirty shillings by backing him to kill rats against time,
then I began to think that maybe they'd let him remain on earth
for a bit longer, after all.

To hang about a stable, and collect a gang of the most disreputable dogs to be found in the town, and lead them out to march round the slums to fight other disreputable dogs, is Montmorency's idea of 'life'; and so, as I before observed, he gave to the suggestion of inns, and pubs, and hotels his most emphatic approbation.

Having thus settled the sleeping arrangements to the satisfaction of all four of us, the only thing left to discuss was what we should take with us; and this we had begun to argue, when Harris said he'd had enough oratory for one night, and proposed that we should go out and have a smile, saying that he had found a place, round by the square, where you could really get a drop of Irish worth drinking.

George said he felt thirsty (I never knew George when he didn't); and, as I had a presentiment that a little whisky, warm, with a slice of lemon, would do my complaint good, the debate was, by common assent, adjourned to the following night; and the assembly put on its hats and went out.

CHAPTER 3

Arrangements settled – Harris's method of doing work – How the elderly family-man puts up a picture – George makes a sensible remark – Delights of early morning bathing – Provisions for getting upset.

So, on the following evening, we again assembled, to discuss and arrange our plans. Harris said:

'Now, the first thing to settle is what to take with us. Now, you get a bit of paper and write down, J., and you get the grocery catalogue, George, and somebody give me a bit of pencil, and then I'll make out a list.'

That's Harris all over – so ready to take the burden of everything himself, and put it on the backs of other people.

He always reminds me of my poor Uncle Podger. You never saw such a commotion up and down a house in all your life, as when my Uncle Podger undertook to do a job. A picture would have come home from the frame-maker's, and be standing in the dining-room, waiting to be put up; and Aunt Podger would ask what was to be done with it, and Uncle Podger would say:

'Oh, you leave that to *me*. Don't you, any of you, worry yourselves about that. *I'll* do all that.'

And then he would take off his coat, and begin. He would send the girl out for sixpenn'orth of nails, and then one of the boys after her to tell her what size to get; and, from that, he would gradually work down, and start the whole house.

'Now you go and get me my hammer, Will,' he would shout; 'and bring me the rule, Tom; and I shall want the step-ladder, and I had better have a kitchen chair, too; and Jim! you run round to Mr Goggles, and tell him, "Pa's kind regards and hopes his leg's better; and will he lend him his spirit-level?" And don't you go, Maria, because I shall want somebody to hold me the light; and when the girl comes back she must go out again for a bit of picture-cord; and Tom! – where's Tom? – Tom, you come here; I shall want you to hand me up the picture.'

And then he would lift up the picture, and drop it, and it

would come out of the frame, and he would try to save the glass, and cut himself; and then he would spring round the room, looking for his handkerchief. He could not find his hankerchief, because it was in the pocket of the coat he had taken off, and he did not know where he had put the coat, and all the house had to leave off looking for his tools, and start looking for his coat; while he would dance round and hinder them.

'Doesn't anybody in the whole house know where my coat is? I never came across such a set in all my life – upon my word I didn't. Six of you! – and you can't find a coat that I put down not five minutes ago! Well, of all the –'

Then he'd get up, and find that he had been sitting on it, and would call out:

'Oh, you can give it up! I've found it myself now. Might just as well ask the cat to find anything as expect you people to find it.'

And when half an hour had been spent in tying up his finger, and a new glass had been got, and the tools, and the ladder, and the chair, and the candle had been brought, he would have another go, the whole family, including the girl, and the charwoman, standing round in a semi-circle, ready to help. Two people would have to hold the chair, and a third would help him up on it, and hold him there, and a fourth would hand him a nail, and a fifth would pass him up the hammer, and he would take hold of the nail, and drop it.

'There!' he would say, in an injured tone, 'now the nail's gone.'

And we would all have to go down on our knees and grovel for it, while he would stand on the chair, and grunt, and want to know if he was to be kept there all the evening.

The nail would be found at last, but by that time he would have lost the hammer.

'Where's the hammer? What did I do with the hammer? Great heavens! Seven of you, gaping round there, and you don't know what I did with the hammer!'

We would find the hammer for him, and then he would have lost sight of the mark he had made on the wall, where the nail was to go in, and each of us had to get up on the chair beside him, and see if we could find it; and we would each discover it in a different place, and he would call us all fools, one after another, and tell us to get down. And he would take the rule, and remeasure, and find that he wanted half thirty-one and three-eighths inches from the corner and would try to do it in his head, and go mad.

And we would all try to do it in our heads, and all arrive at different results, and sneer at one another. And in the general row, the original number would be forgotten, and Uncle Podger would have to measure it again.

He would use a bit of string this time, and at the critical moment, when the old fool was leaning over the chair at an angle of forty-five, and trying to reach a point three inches beyond what was possible for him to reach, the string would slip, and down he would slide on to the piano, a really fine musical effect being produced by the suddenness with which his head and body struck all the notes at the same time.

And Aunt Maria would say that she would not allow the children to stand round and hear such language.

At last, Uncle Podger would get the spot fixed again, and put the point of the nail on it with his left hand, and take the hammer in his right hand. And, with the first blow, he would smash his thumb, and drop the hammer, with a yell, on somebody's toes.

Aunt Maria would mildly observe that, next time Uncle Podger was going to hammer a nail into the wall, she hoped he'd let her know in time, so that she could make arrangements to go and spend a week with her mother while it was being done.

'Oh! you women, you make such a fuss over everything,' Uncle Podger would reply, picking himself up. 'Why, I *like* doing a little job of this sort.'

And then he would have another try, and, at the second blow, the nail would go clean through the plaster, and half the hammer after it, and Uncle Podger be precipitated against the wall with force nearly sufficient to flatten his nose.

Then we had to find the rule and the string again, and a new hole was made; and, about midnight, the picture would be up – very crooked and insecure, the wall for yards round looking as if it had been smoothed down with a rake, and everybody dead beat and wretched – except Uncle Podger.

'There you are,' he would say, stepping heavily off the chair on to the charwoman's corns, and surveying the mess he had made with evident pride. 'Why, some people would have had a man in to do a little thing like that!'

Harris will be just that sort of man when he grows up, I know, and I told him so. I said I could not permit him to take so much labour upon himself. I said:

'No, you get the paper, and the pencil, and the catalogue, and George write down, and I'll do the work.'

The first list we made out had to be discarded. It was clear that the upper reaches of the Thames would not allow of the navigation of a boat sufficiently large to take the things we had set down as indispensable; so we tore the list up, and looked at one another.

George said:

'You know we are on the wrong track altogether. We must not think of the things we could do with, but only of the things that we can't do without.'

George comes out really quite sensible at times. You'd be surprised. I call that downright wisdom, not merely as regards the present case, but with reference to our trip up the river of life generally. How many people, on that voyage, load up the boat till it is in danger of swamping with a store of foolish things which they think essential to the pleasure and comfort of the trip, but which are really only useless lumber.

How they pile the poor little craft mast-high with fine clothes and big houses; with useless servants, and a host of swell friends that do not care twopence for them, and that they do not care three ha'pence for; with expensive entertainments that nobody enjoys, with formalities and fashions, with pretence and ostentation, and with – oh, heaviest, maddest lumber of all! – the dread of what will my neighbour think, with luxuries that only cloy, with pleasures that bore, with empty show that, like the criminal's iron crown of yore, makes to bleed and swoon the aching head that wears it!

It is lumber, man – all lumber! Throw it overboard. It makes the boat so heavy to pull, you nearly faint at the oars. It makes it so cumbersome and dangerous to manage, you never know a moment's freedom from anxiety and care, never gain a moment's rest for dreamy laziness – no time to watch the windy shadows skimming lightly o'er the shallows, or the glittering sunbeams flitting in and out among the ripples, or the great trees by the margin looking down at their own image, or the woods all green and golden, or the lilies white and yellow, or the sombre-waving rushes, or the sedges, or the orchis, or the blue forget-me-nots.

Throw the lumber over, man! Let your boat of life be light, packed with only what you need – a homely home and simple pleasures, one or two friends, worth the name, someone to love and someone to love you, a cat, a dog, and a pipe or two, enough to eat and enough to wear, and a little more than enough to drink; for thirst is a dangerous thing.

You will find the boat easier to pull then, and it will not be so liable to upset, and it will not matter so much if it does upset; good, plain merchandise will stand water. You will have time to think as well as to work. Time to drink in life's sunshine – time to listen to the Aeolian music that the wind of God draws from the human heart-strings around us – time to –

I beg your pardon, really. I quite forgot.

Well, we left the list to George, and he began it.

'We won't take a tent,' suggested George; 'we will have a boat with a cover. It is ever so much simpler, and more comfortable.'

It seemed a good thought, and we adopted it. I do not know whether you have ever seen the thing I mean. You fix iron hoops up over the boat, and stretch a huge canvas over them, and fasten it down all round, from stem to stern, and it converts the boat into a sort of little house, and it is beautifully cosy, though a trifle stuffy; but there, everything has its drawbacks, as the man said when his mother-in-law died, and they came down upon him for the funeral expenses.

George said that in that case we must take a rug each, a lamp, some soap, a brush and comb (between us), a toothbrush (each), a basin, some tooth-powder, some shaving tackle (sounds like a French exercise doesn't it?), and a couple of big towels for bathing. I notice that people always make gigantic arrangements for bathing when they are going anywhere near the water, but that they don't bathe much when they are there.

It is the same when you go to the seaside. I always determine – when thinking over the matter in London – that I'll get up early every morning, and go and have a dip before breakfast, and I religiously pack up a pair of drawers and a bath towel. I always get red bathing drawers. I rather fancy myself in red drawers. They suit my complexion so. But when I get to the sea I don't feel somehow that I want that early morning bathe nearly so much as I did when I was in town.

On the contrary, I feel more that I want to stop in bed till the last moment, and then come down and have my breakfast. Once or twice virtue has triumphed, and I have got out at six and half-dressed myself, and have taken my drawers and towel, and stumbled dismally off. But I haven't enjoyed it. They seem to keep a specially cutting east wind waiting for me when I go to bathe in the early morning; and they pick out all the three-cornered stones, and put them on the top, and they sharpen up the rocks and cover the points over with a bit of sand so that I can't see them, and they take the sea and put it two miles out, so that I have to huddle myself up in my arms and hop, shivering, through six inches of water. And when I do get to the sea, it is rough and quite insulting.

One huge wave catches me up and chucks me in a sitting posture as hard as ever it can, down on to a rock which has been put there for me. And, before I've said 'Oh! Ugh!' and found out what has gone, the wave comes back and carries me out to mid-ocean. I begin to strike out frantically for the shore, and wonder if I shall ever see home and friends again, and wish I'd been kinder to my little sister when a boy (when *I* was a boy, I mean). Just when I have given up all hope, a wave retires and leaves me sprawling like a star-fish on the sand, and I get up and look back and find that I've been swimming for my life in two feet of water. I hop back and dress and crawl home, where I have to pretend I liked it.

In the present instance, we all talked as if we were going to have a long swim every morning. George said it was so pleasant to wake up in the boat in the fresh morning, and plunge into the limpid river. Harris said there was nothing like a swim before breakfast to give you an appetite. He said it always gave him an appetite. George said that if it was going to make Harris eat more than Harris ordinarily ate, then he should protest against Harris having a bath at all.

He said there would be quite enough hard work in towing sufficient food for Harris up against stream, as it was.

I urged upon George, however, how much pleasanter it would be to have Harris clean and fresh about the boat, even if we did have to take a few more hundredweight of provisions; and he got to see it in my light, and withdrew his opposition to Harris's bath. Agreed, finally, that we should take *three* bath towels, so as not to keep each other waiting.

For clothes, George said two suits of flannel would be sufficient as we could wash them ourselves, in the river, when they got dirty. We asked him if he had ever tried washing flannels in the river, and he replied: 'No, not exactly himself like, but he knew some fellows who had, and it was easy enough'; and Harris and I were weak enough to fancy he knew what he was talking about, and that three respectable young men, without position or influence, and with no experience in washing, could really clean their own shirts and trousers in the River Thames with a bit of soap.

We were to learn in the days to come, when it was too late, that George was a miserable impostor, who could evidently have known nothing whatever about the matter. If you had seen these clothes after – but, as the shilling shockers say, we anticipate.

George impressed upon us to take a change of underthings and plenty of socks, in case we got upset and wanted a change; also plenty of handkerchiefs, as they would do to wipe things, and a pair of leather boots as well as our boating shoes, as we should want them if we got upset.

CHAPTER 4

Then we discussed the food question. George said:

'Begin with breakfast.' (George is so practical.) 'Now for breakfast we shall want a frying-pan' – (Harris said it was indigestible; but we merely urged him not to be an ass, and George went on) – 'a teapot and a kettle, and a methylated spirit stove.'

'No oil,' said George, with a significant look; and Harris and I agreed.

We had taken up an oil stove once, but 'never again'. It had been like living in an oil shop that week. It oozed. I never saw such a thing as paraffin oil is to ooze. We kept it in the nose of the boat, and, from there, it oozed down to the rudder, impregnating the whole boat and everything in it on its way, and it oozed over the river, and saturated the scenery and spoilt the atmosphere. Sometimes a westerly oily wind blew, and at other times an easterly oily wind, and sometimes it blew a northerly oily wind, and maybe a southerly oily wind; but whether it came from the Arctic snows, or was raised in the waste of the desert sands, it came alike to us laden with the fragrance of paraffin oil.

And that oil oozed up and ruined the sunset; and as for the moonbeams, they positively reeked of paraffin.

We tried to get away from it at Marlow. We left the boat by the bridge, and took a walk through the town to escape it, but it followed us. The whole town was full of oil. We passed through the churchyard, and it seemed as if the people had been buried in oil. The High Street stank of oil; we wondered how people could live in it. And we walked miles upon miles out Birmingham way; but it was no use, the country was steeped in oil.

At the end of that trip we met together at midnight in a lonely field, under a blasted oak, and took an awful oath (we had been swearing for a whole week about the thing in an ordinary, middle-class way, but this was a swell affair) – an awful oath never to take paraffin oil with us in a boat again – except, of course, in case of sickness.

Therefore, in the present instance, we confined ourselves to methylated spirit. Even that is bad enough. You get methylated pie and methylated cake. But methylated spirit is more wholesome when taken into the system in large quantities than paraffin oil.

For other breakfast things, George suggested eggs and bacon which were easy to cook, cold meat, tea, bread and butter, and jam. For lunch, he said, we could have biscuits, cold meat, bread and butter, and jam – but *no cheese*. Cheese, like oil, makes too much of itself. It wants the whole boat to itself. It goes through the hamper, and gives a cheesy flavour to everything else there. You can't tell whether you are eating apple pie, or German sausage, or strawberries and cream. It all seems cheese. There is too much odour about cheese.

I remember a friend of mine buying a couple of cheeses at Liverpool. Splendid cheeses they were, ripe and mellow, and with a two hundred horse-power scent about them that might have been warranted to carry three miles, and knock a man over at two hundred yards. I was in Liverpool at the time, and my friend said that if I didn't mind he would get me to take them back with me to London, as he should not be coming up for a day or two himself, and he did not think the cheeses ought to be kept much longer.

'Oh, with pleasure, dear boy,' I replied, 'with pleasure.'

I called for the cheeses, and took them away in a cab. It was a ramshackle affair, dragged along by a knock-kneed, broken-winded somnambulist, which his owner, in a moment of enthusiasm, during conversation, referred to as a horse. I put the cheeses on the top, and we started off at a shamble that would have done credit to the swiftest steam-roller ever built, and all went merry as a funeral bell, until we turned a corner. There, the wind carried a whiff from the cheeses full on our steed. It woke him up, and, with a snort of terror, he dashed off at three miles an hour. The wind still blew in his direction, and before we reached the end of the street he was laying himself out at the rate of nearly four miles an hour, leaving the cripples and stout old ladies simply nowhere.

It took two porters as well as the driver to hold him in at the station; and I do not think they would have done it, even then, had not one of the men had the presence of mind to put a handkerchief over his nose, and to light a bit of brown paper.

I took my ticket, and marched proudly up the platform, with my cheeses, the people falling back respectfully on either side. The train was crowded, and I had to get into a carriage where there were already seven other people. One crusty old gentleman objected, but I got in, notwithstanding; and, putting my cheeses upon the rack, squeezed down with a pleasant smile, and said it was a warm day. A few moments passed, and then the old gentleman began to fidget.

'Very close in here,' he said.

'Quite oppressive,' said the man next to him.

And then they both began sniffing, and, at the third sniff, they caught it right on the chest, and rose up without another word and went out. And then a stout lady got up, and said it was disgraceful that a respectable married woman should be harried about in this way, and gathered up a bag and eight parcels and went. The remaining four passengers sat on for a while, until a solemn-looking man in the corner who, from his dress and general appearance, seemed to belong to the undertaker class, said it put him in mind of a dead baby; and the other three passengers tried to get out of the door at the same time, and hurt themselves.

I smiled at the black gentleman, and said I thought we were going to have the carriage to ourselves; and he laughed pleasantly and said that some people made such a fuss over a little thing. But even he grew strangely depressed after we had started, and so, when we reached Crewe, I asked him to come and have a drink. He accepted, and we forced our way into the buffet, where we yelled, and stamped, and waved our umbrellas for a quarter of an hour; and then a young lady came and asked us if we wanted anything.

'What's yours?' I said, turning to my friend.

'I'll have half-a-crown's worth of brandy, neat, if you please miss,' he responded.

[83]

And he went off quietly after he had drunk it and got into another carriage, which I thought mean.

From Crewe I had the compartment to myself, though the train was crowded. As we drew up at the different stations, the people, seeing my empty carriage, would rush for it. 'Here y' are, Maria; come along, plenty of room.' 'All right, Tom; we'll get in here,' they would shout. And they would run along, carrying heavy bags, and fight round the door to get in first. And one would open the door and mount the steps and stagger back into the arms of the man behind him; and they would all come and have a sniff, and then drop off and squeeze into other carriages, or pay the difference and go first.

From Euston I took the cheeses down to my friend's house. When his wife came into the room, she smelt round for an instant. Then she said:

'What is it? Tell me the worst.'

I said:

'It's cheeses. Tom bought them in Liverpool, and asked me to bring them up with me.'

And I added that I hoped she understood that it had nothing to do with me; and she said that she was sure of that, but that she would speak to Tom about it when he came back.

My friend was detained in Liverpool longer than he expected; and three days later, as he hadn't returned hom, his wife called on me. She said:

'What did Tom say about those cheeses?'

I replied that he had directed they were to be kept in a moist place, and that nobody was to touch them.

She said:

'Nobody's likely to touch them. Had he smelt them?'

I thought he had, and added that he seemed greatly attached to them.

'You think he would be upset,' she queried, 'if I gave a man a sovereign to take them away and bury them?'

I answered that I thought he would never smile again.

An idea struck her. She said:

'Do you mind keeping them for him? Let me send them round to you.'

'Madam,' I replied, 'for myself I like the smell of cheese, and the journey the other day with them from Liverpool I shall ever look back upon as a happy ending to a pleasant holiday. But, in this world, we must consider others. The lady under whose roof I have the honour of residing is a widow, and, for all I know, possibly an orphan too. She has a strong, I may say an eloquent, objection to being what she terms "put upon". The presence of your husband's cheese in her house she would, I instinctively feel, regard as a "put upon"; and it shall never be said that I put upon the widow and the orphan.'

'Very well, then,' said my friend's wife, rising, 'all I have to say is, that I shall take the children and go to an hotel until those cheeses are eaten. I decline to live any longer in the same house with them.'

She kept her word, leaving the place in charge of the charwoman, who, when asked if she could stand the smell, replied: 'What smell?' and who, when taken close to the cheese and told to sniff hard, said she could detect a faint odour of melons. It was argued from this that little injury could result to the woman from the atmosphere, and she was left.

The hotel bill came to fifteen guineas; and my friend, after reckoning everything up, found that the cheeses had cost him eight-and-sixpence a pound. He said he dearly loved a bit of cheese, but it was beyond his means; so he determined to get rid of them. He threw them into the canal; but had to fish them out again, as the bargemen complained. They said it made them feel quite faint. And, after that, he took them one dark night and left them in the parish mortuary. But the coroner discovered them, and made a fearful fuss.

He said it was a plot to deprive him of his living by waking up the corpses.

My friend got rid of them, at last, by taking them down to a seaside town, and burying them on the beach. It gained the place quite a reputation. Visitors said they had never noticed before how strong the air was, and weak-chested and consumptive people used to throng there for years afterwards.

Fond as I am of cheese, therefore, I hold that George was right in declining to take any.

'We shan't want any tea,' said George (Harris's face fell at this); 'but we'll have a good round, square, slap-up meal at seven – dinner, tea, and supper combined.'

Harris grew more cheerful. George suggested meat and fruit

pies, cold meat, tomatoes, fruit, and green stuff. For drink, we took some wonderful sticky concoction of Harris's, which you mixed with water and called lemonade, plenty of tea, and a bottle of whisky, in case, as George said, we got upset.

It seemed to me that George harped too much on the getting-upset idea. It seemed to me the wrong spirit to go about the trip in.

But I'm glad we took the whisky.

We didn't take beer or wine. They are a mistake up the river. They make you feel sleepy and heavy. A glass in the evening when you are doing a mooch round the town and looking at the girls is all right enough; but don't drink when the sun is blazing down on your head, and you've got hard work to do.

We made a list of the things to be taken, and a pretty lengthy one it was before we parted that evening. The next day, which was Friday, we got them all together, and met in the evening to pack. We got a big Gladstone for the clothes, and a couple of hampers for the victuals and the cooking utensils. We moved the table up against the window, piled everything in a heap in the middle of the floor, and sat round and looked at it.

I said I'd pack.

I rather pride myself on my packing. Packing is one of those many things that I feel I know more about than any other person living. (It surprises me myself, sometimes, how many of these subjects there are.) I impressed the fact upon George and Harris and told them that they had better leave the whole matter entirely to me. They fell into the suggestion with a readiness that had something uncanny about it. George put on a pipe and spread himself over the easy-chair, and Harris cocked his legs on the table and lit a cigar.

This was hardly what I intended. What I had meant, of course, was, that I should boss the job, and that Harris and George should potter about under my directions, I pushing them aside every now and then with, 'Oh, you – !' 'Here, let me do it.' 'There you are, simple enough!' – really teaching them, as you might say. Their taking it in the way they did irritated me. There is nothing does irritate me more than seeing other people sitting about doing nothing when I'm working.

I lived with a man once who used to make me mad that way. He would loll on the sofa and watch me doing things by the hour together, following me round the room with his eyes, wherever I went. He said it did him real good to look on at me messing about. He said it made him feel that life was not an idle dream to be gaped and yawned through, but a noble task, full of duty and stern work. He said he often wondered now how he could have gone on before he met me, never having anybody to look at while they worked.

Now, I'm not like that. I can't sit still and see another man slaving and working. I want to get up and superintend, and walk round with my hands in my pockets, and tell him what to do. It is my energetic nature. I can't help it.

However, I did not say anything, but started the packing. It seemed a longer job than I had thought it was going to be; but I got the bag finished at last, and I sat on it and strapped it.

'Ain't you going to put the boots in?' said Harris.

And I looked round, and found I had forgotten them. That's just like Harris. He couldn't have said a word until I'd got the bag shut and strapped, of course. And George laughed – one of those irritating, senseless, chuckle-headed, crack-jawed laughs of his. They do make me so wild.

I opened the bag and packed the boots in; and then, just as I was going to close it, a horrible idea occurred to me. Had I packed my tooth-brush? I don't know how it is, but I never do know whether I've packed my tooth-brush.

My tooth-brush is a thing that haunts me when I'm travelling, and makes my life a misery. I dream that I haven't packed it, and wake up in a cold perspiration, and get out of bed and hunt for it. And, in the morning, I pack it before I have used it, and have to unpack again to get it, and it is always the last thing I turn out of the bag; and then I repack and forget it, and have to rush upstairs for it at the last moment and carry it to the railway station wrapped up in my pocket-handkerchief.

Of course I had to turn every mortal thing out now, and, of course, I could not find it. I rummaged the things up into much the same state that they must have been before the world was created, and when chaos reigned. Of course, I found George's and Harris's eighteen times over, but I couldn't find my own. I put the things back one by one, and held everything up and shook it. Then I found it inside a boot. I repacked once more.

When I had finished, George asked if the soap was in. I said I didn't care a hang whether the soap was in or whether it wasn't; and I slammed the bag to and strapped it, and found that I had packed my tobacco pouch in it, and had to reopen it. It got shut up finally at 10.5 p.m., and then there remained the hampers to do. Harris said that we should be wanting to start in less than twelve hours' time and thought that he and George had better do the rest; and I agreed and sat down, and they had a go.

They began in a light-hearted spirit, evidently intending to show me how to do it. I made no comment; I only waited. When George is hanged Harris will be the worst packer in this world; and I looked at the piles of plates and cups, and kettles, and bottles, and jars, and pies, and stoves, and cakes, and tomatoes, etc., and felt that the thing would soon become exciting.

It did. They started with breaking a cup. That was the first thing they did. They did that just to show you what they *could* do, and to get you interested.

Then Harris packed the strawberry jam on top of a tomato and squashed it, and they had to pick out the tomato with a teaspoon.

And then it was George's turn, and he trod on the butter. I didn't say anything, but I came over and sat on the edge of the table and watched them. It irritated them more than anything I could have said. I felt that. It made them nervous and excited, and they stepped on things, and put things behind them, and then couldn't find them when they wanted them; and they packed the pies at the bottom, and put heavy things on top, and smashed the pies in.

They upset salt over everything, and as for the butter! I never saw two men do more with one-and-twopence worth of butter in my whole life than they did. After George had got it off his slipper, they tried to put it in the kettle. It wouldn't go in, and what *was* in wouldn't come out. They did scrape it out at last, and put it down on a chair, and Harris sat on it, and it stuck to him, and they went looking for it all over the room.

'I'll take my oath I put it down on that chair,' said George, staring at the empty seat.

'I saw you do it myself, not a minute ago,' said Harris.

Then they started round the room again looking for it; and then they met again in the centre and stared at one another.

'Most extraordinary thing I ever heard of,' said George. 'So mysterious!' said Harris.

Then George got round at the back of Harris and saw it.

'Why, here it is all the time,' he exclaimed, indignantly.

'Where?' cried Harris, spinning round.

'Stand still, can't you?' roared George, flying after him.

And they got it off, and packed it in the teapot.

Montmorency was in it all, of course. Montmorency's ambition in life is to get in the way and be sworn at. If he can squirm in anywhere where he particularly is not wanted, and be a perfect nuisance, and make people mad, and have things thrown at his head, then he feels his day has not been wasted.

To get somebody to stumble over him, and curse him steadily for an hour, is his highest aim and object; and, when he has succeeded in accomplishing this, his conceit becomes quite unbearable.

He came and sat down on things, just when they were wanted to be packed; and he laboured under the fixed belief that, whenever Harris or George reached out their hand for anything, it was his cold damp nose that they wanted. He put his leg into the jam, and he worried the teaspoons, and he pretended that the lemons were rats, and got into the hamper and killed three of them before Harris could land him with the frying-pan.

Harris said I encouraged him. I didn't encourage him. A dog like that don't want any encouragement. It's the natural, original sin that is born in him that makes him do things like that.

The packing was done at 12.50; and Harris sat on the big hamper, and said he hoped nothing would be found broken. George said that if anything was broken it *was* broken, which reflection seemed to comfort him. He also said he was ready for bed. We were all ready for bed. Harris was to sleep with us that night, and we went upstairs.

We tossed for bed, and Harris had to sleep with me. He said:

'Do you prefer the inside or the outside, J.?'

I said I generally preferred to sleep *inside* a bed.

Harris said it was old.

George said:

'What time shall I wake you fellows?'

Harris said:

'Seven.'

I said:

'No – six,' because I wanted to write some letters.

Harris and I had a bit of a row over it, but at last split the difference, and said half past six.

'Wake us at 6.30, George,' we said.

George made no answer, and we found, on going over, that he had been asleep for some time; so we placed the bath where he could tumble into it on getting out in the morning, and went to bed ourselves.

CHAPTER 5

Mrs P. arrouses us – George, the sluggard – The 'weather forecast' swindle – Our luggage – Depravity of the small boy – The people gather around us – We drive off in great style, and arrive at Waterloo – Innocence of South Western Officials concerning such worldly things as trains – We are afloat, afloat in an open boat.

It was Mrs Poppets that woke me up next morning.

She said:

'Do you know that it's nearly nine o'clock, sir?'

'Nine o' what?' I cried, starting up.

'Nine o'clock,' she replied, through the keyhole. 'I thought you was a-oversleeping yourselves.'

I woke Harris, and told him. He said:

'I thought you wanted me to get up at six?'

'So I did,' I answered. 'Why didn't you wake me?' he retorted. 'Now we shan't get on the water till after twelve. I wonder you take the trouble to get up at all.'

'Um,' I replied, 'lucky for you that I do. If I hadn't woke you, you'd have lain there for the whole fortnight.'

We snarled at one another in this strain for the next few minutes, when we were interrupted by a defiant snore from George. It reminded us, for the first time since our being called, of his existence. There he lay – the man who had wanted to know what time he should wake us – on his back, with his mouth wide open, and his knees stuck up.

I don't know why it should be, I am sure, but the sight of another man asleep in bed when I am up maddens me. It seems to me so shocking to see the precious hours of a man's life – the priceless moments that will never come back to him again – being wasted in mere brutish sleep.

There was George, throwing away in hideous sloth the inestimable gift of time; his valuable life, every second of which he would have to account for hereafter, passing away from him, unused. He might have been up stuffing himself with eggs and bacon, irritating the dog, or flirting with the slavey, instead of sprawling there, sunk in soul-clogging oblivion.

It was a terrible thought. Harris and I appeared to be struck by it at the same instant. We determined to save him, and, in this noble resolve, our own dispute was forgotten. We flew across and slung the clothes off him, and Harris landed him one with a slipper, and I shouted in his ear, and he awoke.

'Wassermarrer?' he observed, sitting up.

'Get up, you fat-headed chunk!' roared Harris. 'It's quarter to ten.'

'What!' he shrieked, jumping out of bed into the bath; '– Who the thunder put this thing here?'

We told him he must have been a fool not to see the bath.

We finished dressing, and, when it came to the extras, we remembered that we had packed the tooth-brushes and the brush and comb (that tooth-brush of mine will be the death of me, I know), and we had to go downstairs, and fish them out of the bag. And when we had done that, George wanted the shaving tackle. We told him that he would have to go without shaving that morning, as we weren't going to unpack that bag again for him, nor for anyone like him.

He said:

'Don't be absurd. How can I go into the City like this?'

It was certainly rather tough on the City, but what cared we for human suffering? As Harris said, in his common, vulgar way, the City would have to lump it.

We went downstairs to breakfast. Montmorency had invited two other dogs to come and see him off, and they were whiling away the time by fighting on the doorstep. We calmed them with an umbrella, and sat down to chops and cold beef.

Harris said:

'The great thing is to make a good breakfast,' and he started with a couple of chops, saying that he would take these while they were hot, as the beef could wait.

George got hold of the paper, and read us out the boating fatalities, and the weather forecast, which latter prophesied 'rain, cold, wet to fine' (whatever more than usually ghastly thing in weather that may be), 'occasional local thunderstorms, east wind, with general depression over the Midland Counties (London and Channel). Bar. falling.'

I do think that of all the silly, irritating tomfoolishness by which we are plagued, this 'weather-forecast' fraud is about the most aggravating. It 'forecasts' precisely what happened yesterday or the day before, and precisely the opposite of what is going to happen today.

I remember a holiday of mine being completely ruined one late autumn by our paying attention to the weather report of the local newspaper. 'Heavy showers, with thunderstorms, may be expected today', it would say on Monday, and so we would give up our picnic, and stop indoors all day, waiting for the rain. And people would pass the house, going off in wagonettes and coaches as jolly and merry as could be, the sun shining out, and not a cloud to be seen.

'Ah!' we said, as we stood looking out at them through the window, 'won't they come home soaked!'

And we chuckled to think how wet they were going to get, and came back and stirred the fire, and got our books, and arranged our specimens of seaweed and cockleshells. By twelve o'clock with the sun pouring into the room, the heat became quite oppressive, and we wondered when those heavy showers and occasional thunderstorms were going to begin.

'Ah! They'll come in the afternoon, you'll find,' we said to each other. 'Oh, *won't* those people get wet. What a lark!'

At one o'clock the landlady would come in to ask if we weren't going out, as it seemed such a lovely day.

'No, no,' we replied, with a knowing chuckle, 'not we. *We* don't mean to get wet – no, no.'

And when the afternoon was nearly gone, and still there was no sign of rain, we tried to cheer ourselves up with the idea that it would come down all at once, just as people had started for home, and were out of the reach of any shelter, and that they would thus get more drenched than ever. But not a drop ever fell, and it finished a grand day, and a lovely night after it.

The next morning we would read that it was going to be a 'warm, fine to set-fair day; much heat'; and we would dress ourselves in flimsy things, and go out, and, half an hour after we had started, it would commence to rain hard, and a bitterly cold wind would spring up, and both would keep on steadily for the whole day, and we would come home with colds and rheumatism all over us, and go to bed.

The weather is a thing that is beyond me altogether. I never can understand it. The barometer is useless; it is as misleading as the newspaper forecast.

There was one hanging up in a hotel at Oxford at which I was staying last spring, and, when I got there, it was pointing to 'set fair'. It was simply pouring with rain outside, and had been all day; and I couldn't quite make matters out. I tapped the barometer, and it jumped up and pointed to 'very dry'. The Boots stopped as he was passing and said he expected it meant tomorrow. I fancied that maybe it was thinking of the week before last, but Boots said, No, he thought not.

I tapped it again the next morning, and it went up still higher, and the rain came down faster than ever. On Wednesday I went and hit it again, and the pointer went round towards 'set fair', 'very dry', and 'much heat', until it was stopped by the peg, and couldn't go any further. It tried its best, but the instrument was built so that it couldn't prophesy fine weather any harder than it did without breaking itself. It evidently wanted to go on, and prognosticate drought, and water famine, and sunstroke, and simooms, and such things, but the peg prevented it, and it had to be content with pointing to the mere commonplace 'very dry'.

Meanwhile, the rain came down in a steady torrent, and the lower part of the town was under water, owing to the river having overflowed.

Boots said it was evident that we were going to have a prolonged spell of grand weather *some time*, and read out a poem which was printed over the top of the oracle, about

> Long foretold, long past;
> Short notice, soon past.

The fine weather never came that summer. I expect that machine must have been referring to the following spring.

Then there are those new style of barometers, the long straight ones. I never can make head or tail of those. There is one side for 10 a.m. yesterday, and one side for 10 a.m. today; but you can't always get there as early as ten, you know. It rises or falls for rain and fine, with much or less wind, and one end is 'Nly' and the other 'Ely' (what's Ely got to do with it?), and if you tap it, it doesn't tell you anything. And you've got to correct it to sea-level and reduce it to Fahrenheit, and even then I don't know the answer.

But who wants to be foretold the weather? It is bad enough when it comes, without our having the misery of knowing about it beforehand. The prophet we like is the old man who, on the particularly gloomy-looking morning of some day when we particularly want it to be fine, looks round the horizon with a particularly knowing eye, and says:

'Oh, no, sir, I think it will clear up all right. It will break all right enough, sir.'

'Ah, he knows,' we say, as we wish him good-morning, and start off; 'wonderful how these old fellows can tell!'

And we feel an affection for that man which is not at all lessened by the circumstance of its *not* clearing up, but continuing to rain steadily all day.

'Ah, well,' we feel, 'he did his best.'

For the man that prophesies us bad weather, on the contrary, we entertain only bitter and revengeful thoughts.

'Going to clear up, d'ye think?' we shout, cheerily, as we pass.

'Well, no, sir; I'm afraid it's settled down for the day,' he replies, shaking his head.

'Stupid old fool!' we mutter, 'what's *he* know about it?' And, if his portent proves correct, we come back feeling still more angry against him, and with a vague notion that, somehow or other, he has had something to do with it.

It was too bright and sunny on this especial morning for George's blood-curdling readings about 'Bar. falling', 'atmospheric disturbance, passing in an oblique line over Southern Europe', and 'pressure increasing', to very much upset us; and so, finding that he could not make us wretched, and was only wasting his time, he sneaked the cigarette that I had carefully rolled up for myself, and went.

Then Harris and I, having finished up the few things left on the table, carted out our luggage on to the doorstep, and waited for a cab.

There seemed a good deal of luggage, when we put it all together. There was the Gladstone and the small hand-bag, and the two hampers, and a large roll of rugs, and some four or five overcoats and mackintoshes, and a few umbrellas, and then there was a melon by itself in a bag, because it was too bulky to go in anywhere, and a couple of pounds of grapes in another bag, and a Japanese paper umbrella, and a frying-pan, which, being too long to pack, we had wrapped round with brown paper.

It did look a lot, and Harris and I began to feel rather ashamed of it, though why we should be, I can't see. No cab came by, but the street boys did, and got interested in the show, apparently, and stopped.

Biggs's boy was the first to come round. Biggs is our greengrocer, and his chief talent lies in securing the services of the most abandoned and unprincipled errand-boys that civilization has as yet produced. If anything more than usually villainous in the boy-line crops up in our neighbourhood, we know that it is Biggs's latest. I was told that, at the time of the Great Coram Street murder, it was promptly concluded by our street that Biggs's boy (for that period) was at the bottom of it, and had he not been able, in reply to the severe cross-examination to which he was subjected by No. 19, when he called there for orders the morning after the crime (assisted by No. 21, who happened to be on the step at the time), to prove a complete alibi, it would have gone hard with him. I didn't know Biggs's boy at that time, but, from what I have seen of them since, I should not have attached much importance to that alibi myself.

Biggs's boy, as I have said, came round the corner. He was evidently in a great hurry when he first dawned upon the vision, but, on catching sight of Harris and me, and Montmorency, and the things, he eased up and stared. Harris and I frowned at him. This might have wounded a more sensitive nature, but Biggs's boys are not, as a rule, touchy. He came to a dead stop, a yard from our step, and, leaning up against the railing, and selecting a straw to chew, fixed us with his eye. He evidently meant to see this thing out.

In another moment, the grocer's boy passed on the opposite side of the street. Biggs's boy hailed him:

'Hi! ground floor o' 42's a-moving.'

The grocer's boy came across, and took up a position on the other side of the step. Then the young gentleman from the boot-shop stopped, and joined Biggs's boy; while the empty-can superintendent from 'The Blue Posts' took up an independent position on the kerb.

'They ain't a-going to starve, are they?' said the gentleman from the boot-shop.

'Ah! you'd want to take a thing or two with *you*,' retorted 'The Blue Posts', 'if you was a-going to cross the Atlantic in a small boat.'

'They ain't a-going to cross the Atlantic,' struck in Biggs's boy; 'they're a-going to find Stanley.'

By this time, quite a small crowd had collected, and people were asking each other what was the matter. One party (the young and giddy portion of the crowd) held that it was a wedding, and pointed out Harris as the bridegroom; while the elder and more thoughtful among the populace inclined to the idea that it was a funeral, and that I was probably the corpse's brother.

At last, an empty cab turned up (it is a street where, as a rule, and when they are not wanted, empty cabs pass at the rate of three a minute, and hang about, and get in your way), and packing ourselves and our belongings into it, and shooting out a couple of Montmorency's friends, who had evidently sworn never to forsake him, we drove away amidst the cheers of the crowd, Biggs's boy shying a carrot after us for luck.

We got to Waterloo at eleven, and asked where the eleven-five started from. Of course nobody knew; nobody at Waterloo ever does know where a train is going to start from, or where a train when it does start is going to, or anything about it. The porter who took our things thought it would go from number two platform, while another porter, with whom he discussed the question, had heard a rumour that it would go from number one. The stationmaster, on the other hand, was convinced it would start from the local.

To put an end to the matter we went upstairs and asked the traffic superintendent, and he told us that he had just met a man who said he had seen it at number three platform. We went to number three platform, but the authorities there said that they rather thought that train was the Southampton express, or else the Windsor loop. But they were sure it wasn't the Kingston train, though why they were sure it wasn't they couldn't say.

Then our porter said he thought that it must be it on the high-level platform; said he thought he knew the train. So we went to the high-level platform and saw the engine-driver, and asked him if he was going to Kingston. He said he couldn't say for certain of course, but that he rather thought he was. Anyhow, if he wasn't the 11.5 for Kingston, he said he was pretty confident he was the 9.32 for Virginia Water, or the 10 a.m. express for the Isle of Wight, or somewhere in that direction, and we should all know when we got there. We slipped half-a-crown into his hand, and begged him to be the 11.5 for Kingston.

'Nobody will ever know, on this line,' we said, 'what you are, or where you're going. You know the way, you slip off quietly and go to Kingston.'

'Well, I don't know, gents,' replied the noble fellow, 'but I suppose *some* trains's got to go to Kingston; and I'll do it. Gimme the half-crown.'

Thus we got to Kingston by the London and South-Western Railway.

We learnt afterwards that the train we had come by was really the Exeter mail, and that they had spent hours at Waterloo looking for it, and nobody knew what had become of it.

Our boat was waiting for us at Kingston just below the bridge, and to it we wended our way, and round it we stored our luggage, and into it we stepped.

'Are you all right, sir?' said the man.

'Right it is,' we answered; and with Harris at the sculls and I at the tiller-lines, and Montmorency, unhappy and deeply suspicious, in the prow, out we shot on to the waters which, for a fortnight, were to be our home.

CHAPTER 6

Kingston – Instructive remarks on early English history – Instructive observations on carved oak and life in general – Sad case of Stivvings, junior – Musings on antiquity – I forget that I am steering – Interesting result – Hampton Court Maze – Harris as a guide.

It was a glorious morning, late spring or early summer, as you care to take it, when the dainty sheen of grass and leaf is blushing to a deeper green; and the year seems like a fair young maid, trembling with strange, wakening pulses on the brink of womanhood.

The quaint back-streets of Kingston, where they came down to the water's edge, looked quite picturesque in the flashing sunlight, the glinting river with its drifting barges, the wooded towpath, the trim-kept villas on the other side, Harris, in a red and orange blazer, grunting away at the sculls, the distant glimpses of the grey old palace of the Tudors, all made a sunny picture, so bright but calm, so full of life, and yet so peaceful, that, early in the day though it was, I felt myself being dreamily lulled off into a musing fit.

I mused on Kingston, or 'Kyningestun', as it was once called in the days when Saxon 'kinges' were crowned there. Great Caesar crossed the river there, and the Roman legions camped upon its sloping uplands. Caesar, like, in later years, Elizabeth, seems to have stopped everywhere: only he was more respectable than good Queen Bess; he didn't put up at the public-houses.

She was nuts on public-houses, was England's Virgin Queen. There's scarcely a pub of any attractions within ten miles of London that she does not seem to have looked in at, or stopped at, or slept at, some time or other. I wonder now, supposing Harris, say, turned over a new leaf, and became a great and good man, and got to be Prime Minister, and died, if they would put up signs over the public-houses that he had patronized: 'Harris had a glass of bitter in this house'; 'Harris had two of Scotch cold here in the summer of '88'; 'Harris was chucked from here in December 1886'.

No, there would be too many of them! It would be the houses
that he had never entered that would become famous. 'Only
house in South London that Harris never had a drink in!' The
people would flock to it to see what could have been the matter
with it.

How poor weak-minded King Edwy must have hated
Kyningestun! The coronation feast had been too much for him.
Maybe boar's head stuffed with sugar-plums did not agree with
him (it wouldn't with me, I know), and he had had enough of
sack and mead; so he slipped from the noisy revel to steal a quiet
moonlight hour with his beloved Elgiva.

Perhaps from the casement, standing hand-in-hand, they
were watching the calm moonlight on the river, while from the
distant halls the boisterous revelry floated in broken bursts of
faint-heard din and tumult.

Then brutal Odo and St Dunstan force their rude way into
the quiet room, and hurl coarse insults at the sweet-faced
Queen, and drag poor Edwy back to the loud clamour of the
drunken brawl.

Years later, to the crash of battle-music, Saxon kings and
Saxon revelry were buried side by side, and Kingston's
greatness passed away for a time, to rise once more when
Hampton Court became the palace of the Tudors and the
Stuarts, and the royal barges strained at their moorings on the
river's bank, and bright-cloaked gallants swaggered down the
water-steps to cry: 'What Ferry, ho! Gadzooks, gramercy.'

Many of the old houses, round about, speak very plainly of
those days when Kingston was a royal borough, and nobles and
courtiers lived there, near their King, and the long road to the
palace gates was gay all day with clanking steel and prancing
palfreys and rustling silks and velvets, and fair faces. The large
and spacious houses, with their oriel, latticed windows, their
huge fireplaces, and their gabled roofs, breathe of the days of
hose and doublet, of pearl-embroidered stomachers, and
complicated oaths. They were upraised in the days 'when men
knew how to build'. The hard red bricks have only grown more
firmly set with time, and their oak stairs do not creak and grunt
when you try to go down them quietly.

Speaking of oak staircases reminds me that there is a
magnificent carved oak staircase in one of the houses in

Kingston. It is a shop now, in the market-place, but it was evidently once the mansion of some great personage. A friend of mine, who lives at Kingston, went in there to buy a hat one day, and, in a thoughtless moment, put his hand in his pocket and paid for it then and there.

The shopman (he knows my friend) was naturally a little staggered at first; but, quickly recovering himself, and feeling that something ought to be done to encourage this sort of thing, asked our hero if he would like to see some fine old carved oak. My friend said he would, and the shopman, thereupon, took him through the shop, and up the staircase of the house. The balusters were a superb piece of workmanship and the wall all the way up was oak-panelled, with carving that would have done credit to a palace.

From the stairs they went into the drawing-room, which was a large, bright room, decorated with a somewhat startling though cheerful paper of a blue ground. There was nothing, however, remarkable about the apartment, and my friend wondered why he had been brought there. The proprietor went up to the paper, and tapped it. It gave forth a wooden sound.

'Oak,' he explained, 'All carved oak, right up to the ceiling, just the same as you saw on the staircase.'

'But, great Caesar! man,' expostulated my friend; 'you don't mean to say you have covered over the carved oak with blue wall-paper?'

'Yes,' was the reply: 'it was expensive work. Had to match-board it all over first, of course. But the room looks cheerful now. It was awful gloomy before.'

I can't say I altogether blame the man (which is doubtless a great relief to his mind). From his point of view, which would be that of the average householder, desiring to take life as lightly as possible, and not that of the old curiosity-shop maniac, there is reason on his side. Carved oak is very pleasant to look at, and to have a little of, but it is no doubt somewhat depressing to live in, for those whose fancy does not lie that way. It would be like living in a church.

No, what was sad in his case was that he, who didn't care for carved oak, should have his drawing-room panelled with it, while people who do care for it have to pay enormous prices to get it. It seems to be the rule of this world. Each person has what he doesn't want, and other people have what he does want.

Married men have wives, and don't seem to want them; and young single fellows cry out that they can't get them. Poor people who can hardly keep themselves have eight hearty children. Rich old couples, with no one to leave their money to, die childless.

Then there are girls with lovers. The girls that have lovers never want them. They say they would rather be without them, that they bother them, and why don't they go and make love to Miss Smith and Miss Brown, who are plain and elderly, and haven't got any lovers? They themselves don't want lovers. They never mean to marry.

It does not do to dwell on these things; it makes one so sad.

There was a boy at our school, we used to call him Sandford and Merton. His real name was Stivvings. He was the most extraordinary lad I ever came across. I believe he really liked study. He used to get into awful rows for sitting up in bed and reading Greek; and as for French irregular verbs, there was simply no keeping him away from them. He was full of weird and unnatural notions about being a credit to his parents and an honour to the school; and he yearned to win prizes, and grow up and be a clever man, and had all those sort of weak-minded ideas. I never knew such a strange creature, yet harmless, mind you, as the babe unborn.

Well, that boy used to get ill about twice a week, so that he couldn't go to school. There never was such a boy to get ill as that Sandford and Merton. If there was any known disease going within ten miles of him, he had it, and had it badly. He would take bronchitis in the dog-days, and have hayfever at Christmas. After a six weeks' period of drought, he would be stricken down with rheumatic fever; and he would go out in a November fog and come home with a sunstroke.

They put him under laughing-gas one year, poor lad, and drew all his teeth, and gave him a false set, because he suffered so terribly with toothache; and then it turned to neuralgia and ear-ache. He was never without a cold, except once for nine weeks while he had scarlet fever; and he always had chilblains. During the great cholera scare of 1871, our neighbourhood was singularly free from it. There was only one reputed case in the whole parish: that case was young Stivvings.

He had to stop in bed when he was ill, and eat chicken and custards and hot-house grapes; and he would lie there and sob, because they wouldn't let him do Latin exercises, and took his German grammar away from him.

And we other boys, who would have sacrificed ten terms of our school life for the sake of being ill for a day, and had no desire whatever to give our parents any excuse for being stuck-up about us, couldn't catch so much as a stiff neck. We fooled about in draughts, and it did us good, and freshened us up; and we took things to make us sick, and they made us fat, and gave us an appetite. Nothing we could think of seemed to make us ill until the holidays began. Then, on the breaking-up day, we caught colds, and whooping cough, and all kinds of disorders, which lasted till the term recommenced; when, in spite of everything we could manoeuvre to the contrary, we would get suddenly well again, and be better than ever.

Such is life; and we are but as grass that is cut down, and put into the oven and baked.

To go back to the carved oak question, they must have had very fair notions of the artistic and the beautiful, our great-great grandfathers. Why, all our art treasures of today are only the dug-up commonplaces of three of four hundred years ago. I wonder if there is any real intrinsic beauty in the old soup-plates, beer-mugs, and candle-snuffers that we prize so now, or if it is only the halo of age glowing around them that gives them their charms in our eyes. The 'old blue' that we hang about our walls as ornaments were the common every-day household utensils of a few centuries ago; and the pink shepherds and the yellow shepherdesses that we hand round now for all our friends to gush over, and pretend they understand, were the unvalued mantel-ornaments that the mother of the eighteenth-century would have given the baby to suck when he cried.

Will it be the same in the future? Will the prized treasures of today always be the cheap trifles of the day before? Will rows of our willow-pattern dinner-plates be ranged above the chimney-pieces of the great in the years 2000 and odd? Will the white cups with the gold rim and the beautiful gold flower inside (species unknown), that our Sarah Janes now break in sheer light-heartedness of spirit, be carefully mended, and stood upon a bracket, and dusted only by the lady of the house?

That china dog that ornaments the bedroom of my furnished lodgings. It is a white dog. Its eyes are blue. Its nose is a delicate red, with black spots. Its head is painfully erect, and its expression is amiability carried to the verge of imbecility. I do not admire it myself. Considered as a work of art, I may say it irritates me. Thoughtless friends jeer at it, and even my landlady herself has no admiration for it, and excuses its presence by the circumstance that her aunt gave it to her.

But in 200 years' time it is more than probable that that dog will be dug up from somewhere or other, minus its legs, and with its tail broken, and will be sold for old china, and put in a glass cabinet. And people will pass it round and admire it. They will be struck by the wonderful depth of the colour on the nose, and speculate as to how beautiful the bit of the tail that is lost no doubt was.

We, in this age, do not see the beauty of that dog. We are too familiar with it. It is like the sunset and the stars: we are not awed by their loveliness because they are common to our eyes. So it is with that china dog. In 2288 people will gush over it. The making of such dogs will have become a lost art. Our descendants will wonder how we did it, and say how clever we were. We shall be referred to lovingly as 'those grand old artists that flourished in the nineteenth century, and produced those china dogs'.

The 'sampler' that the eldest daughter did at school will be spoken of as 'tapestry of the Victorian era', and be almost priceless. The blue-and-white mugs of the present-day roadside inn will be hunted up, all cracked and chipped, and sold for their weight in gold, and rich people will use them for claret cups; and travellers from Japan will buy up the 'Presents from Ramsgate', and 'Souvenirs of Margate', that may have escaped destruction, and take them back to Jedo as ancient English curios.

At this point, Harris threw away the sculls, got up and left his seat, and sat on his back, and stuck his legs in the air. Montmorency howled, and turned a somersault, and the top hamper jumped up, and all the things came out.

I was somewhat surprised, but I did not lose my temper. I said, pleasantly enough:

'Hulloa! what's that for?'

'What's that for? Why –'

No, on second thoughts, I will not repeat what Harris said. I may have been to blame, I admit it; but nothing excuses violence of language and coarseness of expression, especially in a man who has been carefully brought up, as I know Harris has been. I was thinking of other things, and forgot, as anyone might easily understand, that I was steering, and the consequence was that we had got mixed up a good deal with the tow-path. It was difficult to say, for the moment, which was us and which was the Middlesex bank of the river, but we found out after a while, and separated ourselves.

Harris, however, said he had done enough for a bit, and proposed that I should take a turn; so as we were in, I got out and took the tow-line, and ran the boat on past Hampton Court. What a dear old wall that is that runs along by the river there! I never pass it without feeling better for the sight of it. Such a mellow, bright, sweet old wall; what a charming picture it would make, with the lichen creeping here and the moss growing there, a shy young vine peeping over the top at this spot, to see what is going on upon the busy river, and the sober old ivy clustering a little farther down! There are fifty shades and tints and hues in every ten yards of that old wall. If I could only draw, and knew how to paint, I could make a lovely sketch of that old wall, I'm sure. I've often thought I should like to live at Hampton Court. It looks so peaceful and so quiet, and it is such a dear old place to ramble round in the early morning before many people are about.

But, there, I don't suppose I should really care for it when it came to actual practice. It would be so ghastly dull and depressing in the evening, when your lamp cast uncanny shadows on the panelled walls, and the echo of distant feet rang through the cold stone corridors, and now drew nearer, and now died away, and all was death-like silence, save the beating of one's own heart.

We are creatures of the sun, we men and women. We love light and life. That is why we crowd into the towns and cities, and the country grows more and more deserted every year. In the sunlight – in the daytime, when Nature is alive and busy all around us, we like the open hillsides and the deep woods well enough: but in the night, when our Mother Earth has gone to sleep, and left us waking, oh! the world seems so lonesome, and we get frightened, like children in a silent house. Then we sit and sob, and long for the gas-lit streets, and the sound of human voices, and the answering throb of human life. We feel so helpless and so little in the great stillness, when the dark trees rustle in the night-wind. There are so many ghosts about, and their silent sighs make us feel so sad. Let us gather together in the great cities, and light huge bonfires of a million gas-jets, and shout and sing together and feel brave.

Harris asked me if I'd ever been in the maze at Hampton Court. He said he went in once to show somebody else the way. He had studied it up in a map, and it was so simple that it seemed foolish – hardly worth the twopence charged for admission. Harris said he thought the map must have been got up as a practical joke, because it wasn't a bit like the real thing, and only misleading. It was a country cousin that Harris took in. He said:

'We'll just go in here, so that you can say you've been, but it's very simple. It's absurd to call it a maze. You keep on taking the first turning to the right. We'll just walk round for ten minutes, and then go and get some lunch.'

They met some people soon after they had got inside, who said they had been there for three quarters of an hour, and had had about enough of it. Harris told them they could follow him if they liked; he was just going in, and then should turn round and come out again. They said it was very kind of him, and fell behind, and followed.

They picked up various other people who wanted to get it over, as they went along, until they absorbed all the persons in the maze. People who had given up all hopes of ever getting either in or out, or of ever seeing their home and friends again, plucked up courage at the sight of Harris and his party, and joined the procession, blessing him. Harris said he should judge there must have been twenty people following him, in all; and one woman with a baby, who had been there all the morning, insisted on taking his arm, for fear of losing him.

Harris kept on turning to the right, but it seemed a long way, and his cousin said he supposed it was a very big maze.

'Oh, one of the largest in Europe,' said Harris.

'Yes, it must be,' replied the cousin, 'because we've walked a good two miles already.'

Harris began to think it rather strange himself, but he held on until, at last, they passed the half a penny bun on the ground that Harris's cousin swore he had noticed there seven minutes ago. Harris said: 'Oh, impossible!' but the woman with the baby said, 'Not at all,' as she herself had taken it from the child, and thrown it down there, just before she met Harris. She also added that she wished she never had met Harris, and expressed an opinion that he was an impostor. That made Harris mad, and he produced his map, and explained his theory.

'That map may be all right enough,' said one of the party, 'if you know whereabouts in it we are now.'

Harris didn't know, and suggested that the best thing to do would be to go back to the entrance, and begin again. For the beginning again part of it there was not much enthusiasm; but with regard to the advisability of going back to the entrance there was complete unanimity, and so they turned, and trailed after Harris again, in the opposite direction. About ten minutes more passed, and then they found themselves in the centre.

Harris thought at first of pretending that that was what he had been aiming at; but the crowd looked dangerous, and he decided to treat it as an accident.

Anyhow, they had got something to start from then. They did know where they were, and the map was once more consulted, and the thing seemed simpler than ever, and off they started for the third time.

And three minutes later they were back in the centre again.

After that they simply couldn't get anywhere else. Whatever way they turned brought them back to the middle. It became so regular at length, that some of the people stopped there, and waited for the others to take a walk round, and come back to them. Harris drew out his map again, after a while, but the sight of it only infuriated the mob, and they told him to go and curl his hair with it. Harris said that he couldn't help feeling that, to a certain extent, he had become unpopular.

They all got crazy at last, and sang out for the keeper, and the man came and climbed up the ladder outside, and shouted out directions to them. But all their heads were, by this time, in such a confused whirl that they were incapable of grasping anything, and so the man told them to stop where they were, and he would come to them. They huddled together, and waited; and he climbed down, and came in.

He was a young keeper, as luck would have it, and new to the business; and when he got in, he couldn't get to them, and then *he* got lost. They caught sight of him, every now and then, rushing about the other side of the hedge, and he would see them, and rush to get to them, and they would wait there for about five minutes, and then he would reappear again in exactly the same spot, and ask them where they had been.

They had to wait until one of the old keepers came back from his dinner before they got out.

Harris said he thought it was a very fine maze, so far as he was a judge; and we agreed that we would try to get George to go into it, on our way back.

CHAPTER 7

It was while passing through Moulsey lock that Harris told me about his maze experience. It took us some time to pass through, as we were the only boat, and it is a big lock. I don't think I ever remember to have seen Moulsey lock, before, with only one boat in it. It is, I suppose, Boulter's not even excepted, the busiest lock on the river.

I have stood and watched it sometimes, when you could not see any water at all, but only a brilliant tangle of bright blazers, and gay caps, and saucy hats, and many-coloured parasols, and silken rugs, and cloaks, and streaming ribbons, and dainty whites; when looking down into the lock from the quay, you might fancy it was a huge box into which flowers of every hue and shade had been thrown pell-mell and lay piled up in a rainbow heap that covered every corner.

On a fine Sunday it presents this appearance nearly all day long, while, up the stream, and down the stream, lie, waiting their turn, outside the gates, long lines of still more boats; and boats are drawing near and passing away, so that the sunny river, from the Palace up to Hampton Church, is dotted and decked with yellow, and blue, and orange, and white, and red, and pink. All the inhabitants of Hampton and Moulsey dress themselves up in boating costume, and come and mooch round the lock with their dogs, and flirt, and smoke, and watch the boats, and altogether, what with the caps and jackets of the men, the pretty coloured dresses of the women, the excited dogs, the moving boats, the white sails, the pleasant landscape, and the sparkling water, it is one of the gayest sights I know of near this dull old London town.

The river affords a good opportunity for dress. For once in a way, we men are able to show *our* taste in colours, and I think we come out very natty, if you ask me. I always like a little red in my things – red and black. You know my hair is a sort of golden brown, rather a pretty shade I've been told, and a dark red matches it beautifully; and then I always think a light-blue necktie goes so well with it, and a pair of those Russian-leather shoes and a red silk handkerchief round the waist – a handkerchief looks so much better than a belt.

Harris always keeps to shades or mixtures of orange or yellow, but I don't think he is at all wise in this. His complexion is too dark for yellows. Yellows don't suit him; there can be no question about it. I want him to take a blue as a background, with white or cream for relief; but, there! the less taste a person has in dress, the more obstinate he always seems to be. It is a great pity, because he will never be a success as it is, while there are one or two colours in which he might not really look so bad, with his hat on.

George has bought some new things for this trip, and I'm rather vexed about them. The blazer is loud. I should not like George to know that I thought so, but there really is no other word for it. He brought it home and showed it to us on Thursday evening. We asked him what colour he called it, and he said he didn't know. He didn't think there was a name for the colour. The man had told him it was an Oriental design. George put it on, and asked us what we thought of it. Harris said that, as an object to hang over a flower-bed in early spring to frighten the birds away, he should respect it; but that, considered as an article of dress for a human being, except a Margate nigger, it made him ill. George got quite huffy; but, as Harris said, if he didn't want his opinion, why did he ask for it?

What troubles Harris and myself, with regard to it, is that we are afraid it will attract attention to the boat.

Girls, also, don't look half bad in a boat, if prettily dressed. Nothing is more fetching, to my thinking, than a tasteful boating costume. But a 'boating costume', it would be as well if all ladies would understand, ought to be a costume that can be worn in a boat, and not merely under a glass case. It utterly spoils an excursion if you have folk in the boat who are thinking all the time a good deal more of their dress than of the trip. It was my misfortune once to go for a water picnic with two ladies of this kind. We did have a lively time!

Beg your pardon,
I'm sure....

They were both beautifully got up – all lace and silky stuff, and flowers, and ribbons, and dainty shoes, and light gloves. But they were dressed for a photographic studio, not for a river picnic. They were the 'boating costumes' of a French fashion plate. It was ridiculous, fooling about in them anywhere near real earth, air, and water.

The first thing was that they thought the boat was not clean. We dusted all the seats for them, and then assured them that it was, but they didn't believe us. One of them rubbed the cushion with the forefinger of her glove, and showed the result to the other, and they both sighed, and sat down, with the air of early Christian martyrs trying to make themselves comfortable up against the stake. You are liable to occasionally splash a little when sculling, and it appeared that a drop of water ruined those costumes. The mark never came out, and a stain was left on the dress for ever.

I was stroke. I did my best. I feathered some two feet high, and I paused at the end of each stroke to let the blades drip before returning them, and I picked out a smooth bit of water to drop them into again each time. (Bow said, after a while, that he did not feel himself a sufficiently accomplished oarsman to pull with me, but that he would sit still, if I would allow him, and study my stroke. He said it interested him.) But notwithstanding all this, and try as I would, I could not help an occasional flicker of water from going over those dresses.

The girls did not complain, but they huddled up close together, and set their lips firm, and every time a drop touched them, they visibly shrank and shuddered. It was a noble sight to see them suffering thus in silence, but it unnerved me altogether. I am too sensitive. I got wild and fitful in my rowing, and splashed more and more, the harder I tried not to.

I gave it up at last; I said I'd row bow. Bow thought the arrangement would be better too, and we changed places. The ladies gave an involuntary sigh of relief when they saw me go, and quite brightened up for a moment. Poor girls! they had better have put up with me. The man they had got now was a jolly, light-hearted, thick-headed sort of chap with about as much sensitiveness in him as there might be in a Newfoundland puppy. You might look daggers at him for an hour and he would not notice it, and it would not trouble him if he did. He set a good, rollicking, dashing stroke that sent the spray playing all over the boat like a fountain, and made the whole crowd sit up straight in no time. When he spread more than a pint of water over one of those dresses, he would give a pleasant little laugh, and say:

'I beg your pardon, I'm sure'; and offer them his handkerchief to wipe it off with.

'Oh, it's of no consequence,' the poor girls would murmur in reply, and covertly draw rugs and coats over themselves, and try and protect themselves with their lace parasols.

At lunch they had a very bad time of it. People wanted them to sit on the grass, and the grass was dusty; and the tree-trunks, against which they were invited to lean, did not appear to have been brushed for weeks; so they spread their handkerchiefs on the ground, and sat on those, bolt upright. Somebody, in walking about with a plate of beef-steak pie, tripped up over a root, and sent the pie flying. None of it went over them, fortunately, but the accident suggested a fresh danger to them, and agitated them; and, whenever anybody moved about, after that, with anything in his hand that could fall and make a mess, they watched that person with growing anxiety until he sat down again.

'Now then, you girls,' said our friend bow to them, cheerily, after it was all over, 'come along, you've got to wash up!'

They didn't understand him at first. When they grasped the idea, they said they feared they did not know how to wash up.

'Oh, I'll soon show you,' he cried; 'it's rare fun! You lie down on your – I mean you lean over the bank, you know, and slush the things about in the water.'

The elder sister said that she was afraid that they hadn't got on dresses suited to the work.

'Oh, they'll be all right,' said he lightheartedly; 'tuck 'em up.'

And he made them do it, too. He told them that that sort of thing was half the fun of a picnic. They said it was very interesting.

Now I come to think it over, was that young man as dense-headed as we thought? or was he – no, impossible! there was such a simple, child-like expression about him!

Harris wanted to get out at Hampton Church, to go and see Mrs Thomas's tomb.

'Who is Mrs Thomas?' I asked.

'How should I know?' replied Harris. 'She's a lady that's got a funny tomb, and I want to see it.'

I objected. I don't know whether it is that I am built wrong, but I never did seem to hanker after tombstones myself. I know that the proper thing to do, when you get to a village or town, is to rush off to the churchyard, and enjoy the graves; but it is a recreation that I always deny myself. I take no interest in creeping round dim and chilly churches behind wheezy old men, and reading epitaphs. Not even the sight of a bit of cracked brass let into a stone affords me what I call real happiness.

I shock respectable sextons by the imperturbability I am able to assume before exciting inscriptions, and by my lack of enthusiasm for the local family history, while my ill-concealed anxiety to get outside wounds their feelings.

One golden morning of a sunny day, I leant against the low stone wall that guarded a little village church, and I smoked, and drank in deep, calm gladness from the sweet, restful scene – the grey old church with its clustering ivy and its quaint carved wooden porch, the white lane winding down the hill between tall rows of elms, the thatched-roof cottages peeping above their trim-kept hedges, the silver river in the hollow, the wooded hills beyond!

It was a lovely landscape. It was idyllic, poetical, and it inspired me. I felt good and noble. I felt I didn't want to be sinful and wicked any more. I would come and live here, and never do any more wrong, and lead a blameless, beautiful life, and have silver hair when I got old, and all that sort of thing.

In that moment I forgave all my friends and relations for their wickedness and cussedness, and I blessed them. They did not know that I blessed them. They went their abandoned way all unconscious of what I, far away in that peaceful village, was doing for them; but I did it, and I wished that I could let them know that I had done it, because I wanted to make them happy. I was going on thinking away all these grand, tender thoughts, when my reverie was broken in upon by a shrill piping voice crying out:

'All right, sur; I'm a-coming, I'm a-coming. It's all right, sur; don't you be in a hurry.'

I looked up, and saw an old bald-headed man hobbling

across the churchyard towards me, carrying a huge bunch of keys in his hand that shook and jingled at every step.

I motioned him away with silent dignity, but he still advanced, screeching out the while:

'I'm a-coming, sur, I'm a-coming, I'm a little lame. I ain't as spry as I used to be. This way, sur.'

'Go away, you miserable old man,' I said.

'I've come as soon as I could, sur,' he replied. 'My missis never see you till just this minute. You follow me, sur.'

'Go away,' I repeated; 'leave me before I get over the wall, and slay you.'

He seemed surprised.

'Don't you want to see the tombs?' he said.

'No,' I answered. 'I don't. I want to stop here, leaning up against this gritty old wall. Go away, and don't disturb me. I am chock full of beautiful and noble thoughts, and I want to stop like it, because it feels nice and good. Don't you come fooling about, making me mad, chivvying away all my better feelings with this silly tombstone nonsense of yours. Go away, and get somebody to bury you cheap, and I'll pay half the expense.'

He was bewildered for a moment. He rubbed his eyes, and looked hard at me. I seemed human enough on the outside: he couldn't make it out.

He said:

'Yuise a stranger in these parts? You don't live here?'

'No,' I said. 'I don't. *You* wouldn't if *I* did.'

'Well then,' he said, 'you want to see the tombs – graves – folks been buried, you know – coffins!'

'You are an untruther,' I replied, getting roused; 'I do not want to see tombs – not your tombs. Why should I? We have graves of our own, our family has. Why my Uncle Podger has a tomb in Kensal Green Cemetery, that is the pride of all that countryside; and my grandfather's vault at Bow is capable of accommodating eight visitors, while my great-aunt Susan has a brick grave in Finchley Churchyard, with a headstone with a coffee-pot sort of thing in bas-relief upon it, and a six-inch best white stone coping all the way round, that cost pounds. When I want graves, it is to those places that I go and revel. I do not want other folk's. When you yourself are buried, I will come and see yours. That is all I can do for you.'

He burst into tears. He said that one of the tombs had a bit of stone upon the top of it that had been said by some to be probably part of the remains of the figure of a man, and that another had some words carved upon it that nobody had ever been able to decipher.

I still remained obdurate, and, in broken-hearted tones, he said:

'Well, won't you come and see the memorial window?'

I would not even see that, so he fired his last shot. He drew near, and whispered hoarsely:

'I've got a couple of skulls down in the crypt,' he said; 'come and see those. Oh, do come and see the skulls! You are a young man out for a holiday, and you want to enjoy yourself. Come and see the skulls!'

Then I turned and fled, and as I sped I heard him calling to me:

'Oh, come and see the skulls; come back and see the skulls!'

Harris, however, revels in tombs, and graves, and epitaphs, and monumental inscriptions, and the thought of not seeing Mrs Thomas's grave made him crazy. He said he had looked forward to seeing Mrs Thomas's grave from the first moment that the trip was proposed – said he wouldn't have joined if it hadn't been for the idea of seeing Mrs Thomas's tomb.

I reminded him of George, and how we had to get the boat up to Shepperton by five o'clock to meet him, and then he went for George. Why was George to fool about all day, and leave us to lug this lumbering old top-heavy barge up and down the river by ourselves to meet him? Why couldn't George come and do some work? Why couldn't he have got the day off, and come down with us? Bank be blowed! What good was he at the bank?

'I never see him doing any work there,' continued Harris, 'whenever I go in. He sits behind a bit of glass all day, trying to look as if he was doing something. What's the good of a man behind a bit of glass? I have to work for my living. Why can't he work? They take your money, and then, when you draw a cheque, they send it back smeared all over with "No effects", "Refer to drawer". What's the good of that? That's the sort of trick they served me twice last week. I'm not going to stand it much longer. I shall withdraw my account. If he was here we could go and see that tomb. I don't believe he's at the bank at all. He's larking about somewhere, that's what he's doing, leaving us to do all the work. I'm going to get out, and have a drink.'

I pointed out to him that we were miles away from a pub; and then he went on about the river, and what was the good of the river, and was everyone who came on the river to die of thirst?

It is always best to let Harris have his head when he gets like this. Then he pumps himself out, and is quiet afterwards.

I reminded him that there was concentrated lemonade in the hamper, and a gallon jar of water in the nose of the boat, and that the two only wanted mixing to make a cool and refreshing beverage.

Then he flew off about lemonade, and 'such-like Sunday-school slops', as he termed them, ginger-beer, raspberry syrup, etc., etc. He said they all produced dyspepsia, and ruined body and soul alike, and were the cause of half the crime in England.

He said he must drink something, however, and climbed upon the seat, and leant over to get the bottle. It was right at the bottom of the hamper, and seemed difficult to find, and he had to lean over farther and farther, and, in trying to steer at the same time, from a topsy-turvy point of view, he pulled the wrong line, and sent the boat into the bank, and the shock upset him, and he dived down right into the hamper, and stood there on his head, holding on to the sides of the boat like grim death, his legs sticking up into the air. He dared not move for fear of going over, and had to stay there till I could get hold of his legs, and haul him back, and that made him madder than ever.

CHAPTER 8

We stopped under the willows by Kempton Park, and lunched. It is a pretty little spot there; a pleasant grass plateau, running along by the water's edge, and overhung by willows. We had just commenced the third course – the bread and jam – when a gentleman in shirt sleeves and a short pipe came along, and wanted to know if we knew that we were trespassing. We said we hadn't given the matter sufficient consideration as yet to enable us to arrive at a definite conclusion on that point, but that, if he assured us on his word as a gentleman that we *were* trespassing, we would, without further hesitation, believe it.

He gave us the required assurance, and we thanked him, but he still hung about, and seemed to be dissatisfied, so we asked him if there was anything further that we could do for him; and Harris, who is of a chummy disposition, offered him a bit of bread and jam.

I fancy he must have belonged to some society sworn to abstain from bread and jam; for he declined it quite gruffly, as if he were vexed at being tempted with it, and he added that it was his duty to turn us off.

Harris said that if it was a duty it ought to be done, and asked the man what was his idea with regard to the best means for accomplishing it. Harris is what you would call a well-made man of about number one size, and looks hard and bony, and the man measured him up and down, and said he would go and consult his master, and then come back and chuck us both into the river.

Of course, we never saw him any more, and, of course, all he really wanted was a shilling. There are a certain number of riverside roughs who make quite an income during the summer, by slouching about the banks and blackmailing weak-minded noodles in this way. They represent themselves as sent by the proprietor. The proper course to pursue is to offer your name and address, and leave the owner, if he really has anything to do with the matter, to summon you, and prove what damage you have done to his land by sitting down on a bit of it. But the majority of people are so intensely lazy and timid, that they prefer to encourage the imposition by giving in to it rather than put an end to it by the exertion of a little firmness.

Where it is really the owners that are to blame, they ought to be shown up. The selfishness of the riparian proprietor grows with every year. If these men had their way they would close the River Thames altogether. They actually do this along the minor tributary streams and in the backwaters. They drive posts in the bed of the stream, and draw chains across from bank to bank, and nail huge notice-boards on every tree. The sight of those notice-boards rouses every evil instinct in my nature. I feel I want to tear each one down, and hammer it over the head of the man who put it up, until I have killed him, and then I would bury him, and put the board up over the grave as a tombstone.

I mentioned these feelings of mine to Harris, and he said he had them worse than that. He said he not only felt he wanted to kill the man who caused the board to be put up, but that he should like to slaughter the whole of his family and all his friends and relations, and then burn down his house. This seemed to me to be going too far, and I said so to Harris; but he answered: 'Not a bit of it. Serve 'em all jolly well right, and I'd go and sing comic songs on the ruins.'

I was vexed to hear Harris go on in this bloodthirsty strain. We never ought to allow our instincts of justice to degenerate into mere vindictiveness. It was a long while before I could get Harris to take a more Christian view of the subject, but I succeeded at last, and he promised me that he would spare the friends and relations at all events, and would not sing comic songs on the ruins.

You have never heard Harris sing a comic song, or you would understand the service I had rendered to mankind. It is one of Harris's fixed ideas that he *can* sing a comic song; the fixed idea, on the contrary, among those of Harris's friends who have heard him try, is that he *can't*, and never will be able to, and that he ought not to be allowed to try.

When Harris is at a party, and is asked to sing, he replies: 'Well, I can only sing a *comic* song, you know'; and he says it in a tone that implies that his singing of *that*, however, is a thing that you ought to hear once, and then die.

'Oh, that *is* nice,' says the hostess. 'Do sing one, Mr Harris'; and Harris gets up, and makes for the piano, with the beaming cheeriness of a generous-minded man who is just about to give somebody something.

'Now, silence, please, everybody,' says the hostess, turning round, 'Mr Harris is going to sing a comic song!'

'Oh, how jolly!' they murmur; and they hurry in from the conservatory, and come up from the stairs, and go and fetch each other from all over the house, and crowd into the drawing-room, and sit round, all smirking in anticipation.

Then Harris begins.

Well, you don't look for much of a voice in a comic song. You don't expect correct phrasing or vocalization. You don't mind if a man does find out, when in the middle of a note, that he is too high, and comes down with a jerk. You don't bother about time. You don't mind a man being two bars in front of the accompaniment, and easing up in the middle of a line to argue it out with the pianist, and then starting the verse afresh. But you do expect the words.

You don't expect a man to never remember more than the first three lines of the first verse, and to keep on repeating these until it is time to begin the chorus. You don't expect a man to break off in the middle of a line, and snigger, and say, it's very funny, but he's blest if he can think of the rest of it, and then try and make it up for himself, and, afterwards, suddenly recollect it, when he has got to an entirely different part of the song, and break off without a word of warning, to go back and let you have it then and there. You don't – well, I will just give you an idea of Harris's comic singing, and then you can judge for yourself.

HARRIS (*standing up in front of piano and addressing the expectant mob*):
I'm afraid it's a very old thing, you know. I expect you all know it, you know. But it's the only thing I know. It's the Judge's song out of *Pinafore* – no, I don't mean *Pinafore* – I mean – you know what I mean – the other thing, you know. You must all join in the chorus, you know.

Murmurs of delight and anxiety to join in the chorus. Brilliant performance of prelude to the Judge's song in 'Trial by Jury' by nervous pianist. Moment arrives for Harris to join in. Harris takes no notice of it. Nervous pianist commences prelude over again, and Harris, commencing singing at the same time, dashes off the first two lines of the First Lord's song out of 'Pinafore'. Nervous pianist tries to push on with prelude, gives it up, and tries to follow Harris with accompaniment to Judge's song out of 'Trial by Jury', finds that doesn't answer, and tries to recollect what he is doing, and where he is, feels his mind giving way, and stops short.

HARRIS (*with kindly encouragement*): It's all right. You're doing it very well, indeed – go on.

NERVOUS PIANIST: I'm afraid there's a mistake somewhere. What are you singing?

HARRIS (*promptly*): Why the Judge's song out of *Trial by Jury*. Don't you know it?

SOME FRIEND OF HARRIS'S (*from the back of the room*): No, you're not, you chuckle-head, you're singing the Admiral's song from *Pinafore*.

Long argument between Harris and Harris's friend as to what Harris is really singing. Friend finally suggests that it doesn't matter what Harris is singing so long as Harris gets on and sings it, and Harris with an evident sense of injustice rankling inside him, requests pianist to begin again. Pianist, thereupon, starts prelude to the Admiral's song, and Harris, seizing what he considers to be a favourable opening in the music, begins.

HARRIS:

When I was young and called to the Bar.

General roar of laughter, taken by Harris as a compliment. Pianist, thinking of his wife and family, gives up the unequal contest and retires; his place being taken by a stronger-nerved man.

THE NEW PIANIST (*cheerily*): Now then, old man, you start off, and I'll follow. We won't bother about any prelude.

HARRIS (*upon whom the explanation of matters has slowly dawned – laughing*): By Jove! I beg your pardon. Of course – I've been mixing up the two songs. It was Jenkins who confused me, you know. Now then.

Singing; his voice appearing to come from the cellar, and suggesting the first low warnings of an approaching earthquake.

When I was young I served a term
As office-boy to an attorney's firm.

(*Aside to pianist*): It is too low, old man; we'll have that over again, if you don't mind.

Sings first two lines over again, in a high falsetto this time. Great surprise on the part of the audience. Nervous old lady near the fire begins to cry, and has to be led out.

HARRIS (*continuing*):

I swept the windows and I swept the door,
And I –

No – no, I cleaned the windows of the big front door. And I polished up the floor – no, dash it – I beg your pardon – funny thing, I can't think of that line. And I – and I – Oh, well, we'll get on to the chorus, and chance it (*sings*):

And I diddle-diddle-diddle-diddle-diddle-diddle-de,
Till now I am ruler of the Queen's navee.

Now then, chorus – it's the last two lines repeated, you know.
GENERAL CHORUS:

And he diddle-diddle-diddle-diddle-diddle-diddle-dēē'd,
Till now he is ruler of the Queen's navēē.

And Harris never sees what an ass he is making of himself, and how he is annoying a lot of people who never did him any harm. He honestly imagines that he has given them a treat, and says he will sing another comic song after supper.

Speaking of comic songs and parties reminds me of a rather curious incident at which I once assisted; which, as it throws much light upon the inner mental working of human nature in general, ought, I think, to be recorded in these pages.

We were a fashionable and highly cultured party. We had on our best clothes, and we talked pretty, and were very happy – all except two young fellows, students, just returned from Germany, commonplace young men, who seemed restless and uncomfortable, as if they found the proceedings slow. The truth was, we were too clever for them. Our brilliant but polished conversation, and our high-class tastes were beyond them.

They were out of place, among us. They never ought to have been there at all. Everybody agreed upon that, later on.

We played *morceaux* from the old German masters. We discussed philosophy and ethics. We flirted with graceful dignity. We were even humorous – in a high-class way.

Somebody recited a French poem after supper, and we said it was beautiful; and then a lady sang a sentimental ballad in Spanish, and it made one or two of us weep – it was so pathetic.

And then those two young men got up, and asked us if we had ever heard Herr Slossenn Boschen (who had just arrived, and was then down in the supper-room) sing his great German comic song.

None of us had heard it, that we could remember.

The young man said it was the funniest song that had ever been written, and that, if we liked, they would get Herr Slossenn Boschen, whom they knew very well, to sing it. They said it was so funny that, when Herr Slossenn Boschen had sung it once before the German Emperor, he (the German Emperor) had had to be carried off to bed.

They said nobody could sing it like Herr Slossenn Boschen; he was so intensely serious all through it that you might fancy he was reciting a tragedy, and that, of course, made it all the funnier. They said he never once suggested by his tone or manner that he was singing anything funny – that would spoil it. It was his air of seriousness, almost of pathos, that made it so irresistibly amusing.

We said we yearned to hear it, that we wanted a good laugh; and they went downstairs, and fetched Herr Slossenn Boschen.

He appeared to be quite pleased to sing it, for he came up at once, and sat down to the piano without another word.

'Oh, it will amuse you. You will laugh,' whispered the two young men, as they passed through the room, and took up an unobtrusive position behind the Professor's back.

Herr Slossenn Boschen accompanied himself. The prelude did not suggest a comic song exactly. It was a weird, soulful air. It quite made one's flesh creep; but we murmured to one another that it was the German method, and prepared to enjoy it.

I don't understand German myself. I learned it at school, but forgot every word of it two years after I had left, and have felt

much better ever since. Still I did not want the people there to guess my ignorance; so I hit upon what I thought to be rather a good idea. I kept my eye on the two young students, and followed them. When they tittered, I tittered; when they roared, I roared; and I also threw in a little snigger all by myself now and then, as if I had seen a bit of humour that had escaped the others. I considered this particularly artful on my part.

I noticed, as the song progressed, that a good many other people seemed to have their eye fixed on the two young men, as well as myself. These other people also tittered when the young men tittered, and roared when the young men roared; and, as the two young men tittered and roared and exploded with laughter pretty continuously all through the song, it went exceedingly well.

And yet that German professor did not seem happy. At first, when we began to laugh the expression on his face was one of intense surprise, as if laughter were the very last thing he had expected to be greeted with. We thought this very funny: we said his earnest manner was half the humour. The slightest hint on his part that he knew how funny he was would have completely ruined it all. As we continued to laugh, his surprise gave way to an air of annoyance and indignation, and he scowled fiercely round upon us all (except upon the two young men who, being behind him, he could not see). That sent us into convulsions. We told each other that it would be the death of us, this thing. The words alone, we said, were enough to send us into fits, but added to his mock seriousness – oh, it was too much!

In the last verse, he surpassed himself. He glowered round upon us with a look of such concentrated ferocity that, but for our being forewarned as to the German method of comic singing, we should have been nervous; and he threw such a wailing note of agony into the weird music that, if we had not known it was a funny song, we might have wept.

He finished amid a perfect shriek of laughter. We said it was the funniest thing we had ever heard in all our lives. We said how strange it was that, in the face of things like these, there should be a popular notion that the Germans hadn't any sense of humour. And we asked the Professor why he didn't translate the song into English, so that the common people could understand it, and hear what a real comic song was like.

Then Herr Slossenn Boschen got up, and went on awful. He swore at us in German (which I should judge to be a singularly effective language for that purpose), and he danced, and shook his fists, and called us all the English he knew. He said he had never been so insulted in all his life.

It appeared that the song was not a comic song at all. It was about a young girl who lived in the Hartz Mountains, and who had given up her life to save her lover's soul; and he died, and met her spirit in the air; and then, in the last verse, he jilted her spirit and went off with another spirit – I'm not quite sure of the details, but it was something very sad, I know. Herr Boschen said he had sung it once before the German Emperor, and he (the German Emperor) had sobbed like a little child. He (Herr Boschen) said it was generally acknowledged to be one of the most tragic and pathetic songs in the German language.

It was a trying situation for us – very trying. There seemed to be no answer. We looked round for the two young men who had done this thing, but they had left the house in an unostentatious manner immediately after the end of the song.

That was the end of that party. I never saw a party break up so quietly, and with so little fuss. We never said good night even to one another. We came downstairs one at a time, walking softly, and keeping the shady side. We asked the servant for our hats and coats in whispers, and opened the door for ourselves, and slipped out, and got round the corner quickly, avoiding each other as much as possible.

I have never taken much interest in German songs since then.

We reached Sunbury lock at half past three. The river is sweetly pretty just there before you come to the gates, and the backwater is charming; but don't attempt to row up it.

I tried to do so once. I was sculling, and asked the fellows who were steering if they thought it could be done, and they said, oh, yes, they thought so, if I pulled hard. We were just under the little footbridge that crosses it between two weirs, when they said this, and I bent down over the sculls, and set myself up and pulled.

I pulled splendidly. I got well into a steady rhythmical swing. I put my arms, and my legs, and my back into it. I set myself a good, quick, dashing stroke, and worked in really grand style.

My two friends said it was a pleasure to watch me. At the end of five minutes, I thought we ought to be pretty near the weir, and I looked up. We were under the bridge, in exactly the same spot that we were when I began, and there were those two idiots, injuring themselves by violent laughing. I had been grinding away like mad to keep that boat stuck still under that bridge. I let other people pull up backwaters against strong streams now.

We sculled up to Walton, a rather large place for a riverside town. As with all riverside places, only the tiniest corner of it comes down to the water, so that from the boat you might fancy it was a village of some half-dozen houses, all told. Windsor and Abingdon are the only towns between London and Oxford that you can really see anything of from the stream. All the others hide round corners and merely peep at the river down one street; my thanks to them for being so considerate, and leaving the river banks to woods and fields and waterworks.

Even Reading, though it does its best to spoil and sully and make hideous as much of the river as it can reach, is good-natured enough to keep its ugly face a good deal out of sight.

Caesar, of course, had a little place at Walton – a camp, or entrenchment, or something of that sort. Caesar was a regular up-river man. Also Queen Elizabeth, she was there, too. You can never get away from that woman, go where you will. Cromwell and Bradshaw (not the guide man, but the King Charles's head man) likewise sojourned here. They must have been quite a pleasant little party, altogether.

There is an iron 'scold's bridle' in Walton Church. They used these things in ancient days for curbing women's tongues. They have given up the attempt now. I suppose iron was getting scarce, and nothing else would be strong enough.

There are also tombs of note in the church, and I was afraid I should never get Harris past them; but he didn't seem to think of them, and we went on. Above the bridge the river winds tremendously. This makes it look picturesque; but it irritates you from a towing or sculling point of view, and causes argument between the man who is pulling and the man who is steering.

You pass Oatlands Park on the right bank here. It is a famous old place. Henry VIII stole it from someone or the other, I forget whom now, and lived in it. There is a grotto in the park which you can see for a fee, and which is supposed to be very wonderful; but I cannot see much in it myself. The late Duchess of York, who lived at Oatlands, was very fond of dogs, and kept an immense number. She had a special graveyard made, in which to bury them when they died, and there they lie, about fifty of them, with a tombstone over each, and an epitaph inscribed thereon.

Well, I dare say they deserve it quite as much as the average Christian does.

At 'Corway Stakes' – the first bend above Walton Bridge – was fought a battle between Caesar and Cassivelaunus. Cassivelaunus had prepared the river for Caesar, by planting it full of stakes (and had, no doubt, put up a notice-board). But Caesar crossed in spite of this. You couldn't choke Caesar off that river. He is the sort of man we want round the backwaters now.

Halliford and Shepperton are both pretty little spots where they touch the river; but there is nothing remarkable about either of them. There is a tomb in Shepperton churchyard, however, with a poem on it, and I was nervous lest Harris should want to get out and fool round it. I saw him fix a longing eye on the landing-stage as we drew near it, so I managed, by an adroit movement, to jerk his cap into the water, and in the excitement of recovering that, and his indignation at my clumsiness, he forgot all about his beloved graves.

At Weybridge, the Wey (a pretty little stream, navigable for small boats up to Guildford, and one which I have always been making up my mind to explore, and never have), the Bourne, and the Basingstoke Canal all enter the Thames together. The lock is just opposite the town, and the first thing that we saw, when we came in view of it, was George's blazer on one of the lock gates, closer inspection showing that George was inside it.

Montmorency set up a furious barking, I shrieked, Harris roared; George waved his hat, and yelled back. The lock-keeper rushed out with a drag, under the impression that somebody had fallen into the lock, and appeared annoyed at finding that no one had.

George had rather a curious oilskin-covered parcel in his

hand. It was round and flat at one end, with a long straight handle sticking out of it.

'What's that?' said Harris – 'a frying-pan?'

'No,' said George, with a strange, wild look glittering in his eyes, 'they are all the rage this season; everybody has got them up the river. It's a banjo.'

'I never knew you played the banjo!' cried Harris and I, in one breath.

'Not exactly,' replied George; 'but it's very easy, they tell me; and I've got the instruction book!'

CHAPTER 9

George is introduced to work – Heathenish instincts of tow-lines – Ungrateful conduct of a double-sculling skiff – Towers and towed – A use discovered for lovers – Strange disappearance of an elderly lady – Much haste, less speed – Being towed by girls: exciting sensation – The missing lock or the haunted river – Music – Saved!

We made George work, now we had got him. He did not want to work, of course; that goes without saying. He had had a hard time in the City, so he explained. Harris, who is callous in his nature, and not prone to pity, said:

'Ah! and now you are going to have a hard time on the river for a change; change is good for everyone. Out you get!'

He could not in conscience – not even George's conscience – object, though he did suggest that, perhaps, it would be better for him to stop in the boat, and get tea ready, while Harris and I towed, because getting tea was such a worrying work, and Harris and I looked tired. The only reply we made to this, however, was to pass him over the tow-line, and he took it, and stepped out.

There is something very strange and unaccountable about a tow-line. You roll it up with as much patience and care as you would take to fold up a new pair of trousers, and five minutes afterwards, when you pick it up, it is one ghastly, soul-revolting tangle.

I do not wish to be insulting, but I firmly believe that if you took an average tow-line, and stretched it out straight across the middle of a field, and then turned your back on it for thirty seconds, that, when you looked round again, you would find that it had got itself altogether in a heap in the middle of the field, and had twisted itself up, and tied itself into knots, and lost its two ends, and become all loops; and it would take a good half-hour, sitting down there on the grass and swearing all the while, to disentangle it again.

That is my opinion of tow-lines in general. Of course, there may be honourable exceptions; I do not say that there are not. There may be tow-lines that are a credit to their profession –

conscientious, respectable tow-lines – tow-lines that do not imagine they are crotchet-work, and try to knit themselves up into antimacassars the instant they are left to themselves. I say there *may* be such tow-lines; I sincerely hope there are. But I have not met with them.

This tow-line I had taken in myself just before we had got to the lock. I would not let Harris touch it, because he is careless. I had looped it round slowly and cautiously, and tied it up in the middle, and folded it in two, and laid it down gently at the bottom of the boat. Harris had lifted it up scientifically, and had put it into George's hand. George had taken it firmly and held it away from him, and had begun to unravel it as if he were taking the swaddling clothes off a new-born infant; and, before he had unwound a dozen yards, the thing was more like a badly made doormat than anything else.

It is always the same, and the same sort of thing always goes on in connexion with it. The man on the bank, who is trying to disentangle it, thinks all the fault lies with the man who rolled it up; and when a man up the river thinks a thing, he says it.

'What have you been trying to do with it, make a fishing-net of it? You've made a nice mess you have; why couldn't you wind it up properly, you silly dummy?' he grunts from time to time as he struggles wildly with it, and lays it out flat on the tow-path, and runs round and round it, trying to find the end.

On the other hand, the man who wound it up thinks the whole cause of the muddle rests with the man who is trying to unwind it.

'It was all right when you took it!' he exclaims indignantly. 'Why don't you think what you are doing? You go about things in such a slap-dash style. You'd get a scaffolding pole entangled, *you* would!'

And they feel so angry with one another that they would like to hang each other with the thing. Ten minutes go by, and the first man gives a yell and goes mad, and dances on the rope, and tries to pull it straight by seizing hold of the first piece that comes to his hand and hauling at it. Of course, this only gets it into a tighter tangle than ever. Then the second man climbs out of the boat and comes to help him, and they get in each other's way, and hinder one another. They both get hold of the same bit of line, and pull at it in opposite directions, and wonder where it is caught. In the end, they do get it clear, and then turn round and find that the boat has drifted off, and is making straight for the weir.

This really happened once to my own knowledge. It was up by Boveney, one rather windy morning. We were pulling down-stream, and, as we came round the bend, we noticed a couple of men on the bank. They were looking at each other with as bewildered and helplessly miserable expressions as I have ever witnessed on any human countenance before or since, and they held a long tow-line between them. It was clear that something had happened, so we eased up and asked them what was the matter.

'Why, our boat's gone off!' they replied in an indignant tone. 'We just got out to disentangle the tow-line, and when we looked round, it was gone!'

And they seemed hurt at what they evidently regarded as a mean and ungrateful act on the part of the boat.

We found the truant for them half a mile further down, held by some rushes, and we brought it back to them. I bet they did not give that boat another chance for a week.

I shall never forget the picture of those two men walking up and down the bank with a tow-line, looking for their boat.

One sees a good many funny incidents up the river in connexion with towing. One of the most common is the sight of a couple of towers, walking briskly along, deep in an animated discussion, while the man in the boat, a hundred yards behind them, is vainly shrieking to them to stop, and making frantic signs of distress with a scull. Something has gone wrong; the rudder has come off, or the boathook has slipped overboard, or his hat has dropped into the water, and is floating rapidly down-stream. He calls to them to stop, quite gently and politely at first.

'Hi! Stop a minute, will you?' he shouts cheerily. 'I've dropped my hat overboard.'

Then: 'Hi! Tom – Dick! Can't you hear?' not quite so affably this time.

Then: 'Hi! Confound you, you dunder-headed idiots! Hi! stop! Oh you – !'

After that he springs up, and dances about, and roars himself red in the face, and curses everything he knows. And the small boys on the bank stop and jeer at him, and pitch stones at him as he is pulled along past them, at the rate of four miles an hour, and can't get out.

Much of this sort of trouble would be saved if those who are towing would keep remembering that they *are* towing, and give a pretty frequent look round to see how their man is getting on. It is best to let one person tow. When two are doing it, they get chattering, and forget, and the boat itself, offering, as it does, but little resistance, is of no real service in reminding them of the fact.

As an example of how utterly oblivious a pair of towers can be to their work, George told us, later on in the evening, when we were discussing the subject after supper, of a very curious instance.

He and three other men, so he said, were sculling a very heavily laden boat up from Maidenhead one evening, and a little above Cookham lock they noticed a fellow and a girl, walking along the tow-path, both deep in an apparently interesting and absorbing conversation. They were carrying a boathook between them, and attached to the boathook was a tow-line, which trailed behind them, its end in the water. No boat was near, no boat was in sight. There must have been a boat attached to that tow-line at some time or other, that was certain; but what had become of it, what ghastly fate had overtaken it, and those who had been left in it, was buried in mystery. Whatever the accident may have been, however, it had in no way disturbed the young lady and gentleman who were towing. They had the boathook, and they had the line, and that seemed to be all that they thought necessary to their work.

George was about to call out and wake them up, but, at that moment, a bright idea flashed across him, and he didn't. He got the hitcher instead and reached over, and drew in the end of the tow-line; and they made a loop in it, and put it over their mast, and then they tidied up the sculls, and went and sat down in the stern, and lit their pipes.

And that young man and young woman towed those four hulking chaps and a heavy boat up to Marlow.

George said he never saw so much thoughtful sadness concentrated into one glance before, as when, at the lock, that young couple grasped the idea that, for the last two miles, they had been towing the wrong boat. George fancied that, if it had not been for the restraining influence of the sweet woman at his side, the young man might have given way to violent language.

The maiden was the first to recover her surprise, and, when she did, she clasped her hands and said, wildly:

'Oh, Henry, then *where* is auntie?'

'Did they ever recover the old lady?' asked Harris.

George replied he did not know.

Another example of the dangerous want of sympathy between tower and towed was witnessed by George and myself once up near Walton. It was where the tow-path shelves gently down into the water, and we were camping on the opposite bank, noticing things in general. By and by a small boat came in sight, towed through the water at a tremendous pace by a powerful barge horse, on which sat a very small boy. Scattered about the boat, in dreamy and reposeful attitudes, lay five fellows, the man who was steering having a particularly restful appearance.

'I should like to see him pull the wrong line,' murmured George, as they passed. And at that precise moment the man did it, and the boat rushed up the bank with a noise like the ripping up of forty thousand linen sheets. Two men, a hamper, and three oars immediately left the boat on the larboard side, and reclined on the bank, and one and a half moments afterwards, two other men disembarked from the starboard, and sat down among boat-hooks and sails and carpet-bags and bottles. The last man went on twenty yards farther, and then got out on his head.

This seemed to sort of lighten the boat, and it went on much easier, the small boy shouting at the top of his voice, and urging his steed into a gallop. The fellows sat up and stared at one another. It was some seconds before they realized what had happened to them, but, when they did, they began to shout lustily for the boy to stop. He, however, was too much occupied with the horse to hear them, and we watched them flying after him, until the distance hid them from view.

I cannot say I was sorry at their mishap. Indeed, I only wish that all the young fools who have their boats towed in this fashion – and plenty do – could meet with similar misfortunes. Besides the risk they run themselves, they become a danger and an annoyance to every other boat they pass. Going at the pace they do, it is impossible for them to get out of anybody else's way, or for anybody else to get out of theirs. Their line gets hitched across your mast and overturns you, or it catches somebody in the boat, and either throws them into the water, or cuts their face open. The best plan is to stand your ground, and be prepared to keep them off with the butt-end of a mast.

Of all experience in connexion with towing, the most exciting is being towed by girls. It is a sensation that nobody ought to miss. It takes three girls to tow always; two hold the rope, and the other one runs round and round and giggles. They generally begin by getting themselves tied up. They get the line round their legs, and have to sit down on the path and undo each other, and then they twist it round their necks, and are nearly strangled. They fix it straight, however, at last, and start off at a run, pulling the boat along at quite a dangerous pace. At the end of a hundred yards they are naturally breathless, and suddenly stop, and all sit down on the grass and laugh, and your boat drifts out to mid-stream and turns round, before you know what has happened, or can get hold of a scull. Then they stand up, and are surprised.

'Oh, look!' they say; 'he's gone right out into the middle.'

They pull on pretty steadily for a bit, after this, and then it all at once occurs to one of them that she will pin up her frock and they ease up for the purpose, and the boat runs aground.

You jump up and push it off, and you shout to them not to stop.

'Yes. What's the matter?' they shout back.

'Don't stop,' you roar.

'Don't what?'

'Don't stop – go on – go on!'

'Go back, Emily, and see what it is they want,' says one; and Emily comes back, and asks what it is.

'What do you want?' she says; 'anything happened?'

'No,' you reply, 'it's all right; only go on, you know – don't stop.'

'Why not?'

'Why, we can't steer, if you keep stopping. You must keep some way on the boat.'

'Keep some what?'

'Some way – you must keep the boat moving.'

'Oh, all right, I'll tell 'em. Are we doing it all right?'

'Oh, yes, very nicely, indeed, only don't stop.'

'It doesn't seem difficult at all. I thought it was so hard.'

'Oh, no, it's simple enough. You want to keep on steady at it, that's all.'

'I see. Give me out my red shawl, it's under the cushion.'

You find the shawl, and hand it out, and by this time another has come back and thinks she will have hers too, and they take Mary's on chance, and Mary does not want it, so they bring it back and have a pocket-comb instead. It is about twenty minutes before they get off again, and, at the next corner, they see a cow, and you have to leave the boat to chivvy the cow out of their way.

There is never a dull moment in the boat while girls are towing it.

George got the line right after a while, and towed us steadily on to Penton Hook. There we discussed the important question of camping. We had decided to sleep on board that night, and we had either to lay up just about there, or go on past Staines. It seemed early to think about shutting up then, however, with the sun still in the heavens, and we settled to push straight on for Runnymede, three and a half miles farther, a quite wooded part of the river, and where there is good shelter.

We all wished, however, afterward, that we had stopped at Penton Hook. Three or four miles up-stream is a trifle, early in the morning, but it is a weary pull at the end of a long day. You take no interest in the scenery during these last few miles. You do not chat and laugh. Every half-mile you cover seems like two. You can hardly believe you are only where you are, and you are convinced that the map must be wrong; and, when you have trudged along for what seems to you at least ten miles, and still the lock is not in sight, you begin to seriously fear that somebody must have sneaked it and run off with it.

I remember being terribly upset once up the river (in a figurative sense, I mean). I was out with a young lady – cousin on my mother's side – and we were pulling down to Goring. It was rather late, and we were anxious to get in – at least *she* was anxious to get in. It was half past six when we reached Benson's lock, and dusk was drawing on, and she began to get excited then. She said she must be in to supper. I said it was a thing I felt I wanted to be in at, too; and I drew out a map I had with me to see exactly how far it was. I saw it was just a mile and a half to the next lock – Wallingford – and five on from there to Cleeve.

'Oh, it's all right!' I said. 'We'll be through the next lock before seven, and then there is only one more'; and I settled down and pulled steadily away.

We passed the bridge, and soon after that I asked if she saw the lock. She said no, she did not see any lock; and I said, 'Oh'! and pulled on. Another five minutes went by, and then I asked her to look again.

'No,' she said; 'I can't see any signs of a lock.'

'You – you are sure you know a lock, when you do see one?' I asked hesitatingly, not wishing to offend her.

The question did not offend her, however, and she suggested that I had better look for myself; so I laid down the sculls, and took a view. The river stretched out straight before us in the twilight for about a mile; not a ghost of a lock was to be seen.

'You don't think we have lost our way, do you?' asked my companion.

I did not see how that was possible; though, as I suggested, we might have somehow got into the weir stream, and be making for the falls.

This idea did not comfort her in the least, and she began to cry. She said we should both be drowned, and that it was a judgment on her for coming out with me.

It seemed an excessive punishment, I thought; but my cousin thought not, and hoped it would all soon be over.

I tried to reassure her, and to make light of the whole affair. I said that the fact evidently was that I was not rowing as fast as I fancied I was, but that we should soon reach the lock now; and I pulled on for another mile.

Then I began to get nervous myself. I looked again at the map. There was Wallingford lock, clearly marked, a mile and a half below Benson's. It was a good, reliable map; and, besides, I recollected the lock myself. I had been through it twice. Where were we? What had happened to us? I began to think it must be all a dream, and that I was really asleep in bed, and should wake up in a minute, and be told it was past ten.

I asked my cousin if she thought it could be a dream, and she replied that she was just about to ask me the same question; and then we both wondered if we were both asleep, and if so, who was the real one that was dreaming, and who was the one that was only a dream; it got quite interesting.

I still went on pulling, however, and still no lock came in sight, and the river grew more and more gloomy and mysterious under the gathering shadows of night, and things seemed to be getting weird and uncanny. I thought of hob-goblins and banshees, and will-o'-the-wisps, and those wicked girls who sit up all night on rocks, and lure people into whirlpools and things; and I wished I had been a better man, and knew more hymns; and in the middle of these reflections I heard the blessed strains of 'He's got 'em on', played badly on a concertina, and knew that we were saved.

I do not admire the tones of a concertina, as a rule; but oh! how beautiful the music seemed to us both then – far, far more beautiful than the voice of Orpheus or the lute of Apollo, or anything of that sort could have sounded. Heavenly melody, in our then state of mind, would only have still further harrowed us. A soul-moving harmony, correctly, performed, we should have taken as a spirit-warning, and have given up all hope. But about the strains of 'He's got 'em on', jerked spasmodically, and with involuntary variations, out of a wheezy accordion, there was something singularly human and reassuring.

The sweet sounds drew nearer, and soon the boat from which they were worked came alongside us.

It contained a party of provincial 'Arrys and 'Arriets, out for a moonlight sail. (There was not any moon, but that was not their fault.) I never saw more attractive, lovable people in all my life. I hailed them, and asked if they could tell me the way to Wallingford lock; and I explained that I had been looking for it for the last two hours.

'Wallingford lock!' they answered. 'Lor' love you, sir, that's been done away with for over a year. There ain't no Wallingford lock now, sir. You're close to Cleeve now. Blow me tight if 'ere ain't a gentleman been looking for Wallingford lock, Bill!'

I had never thought of that. I wanted to fall upon all their necks and bless them; but the stream was running too strong just there to allow of this, so I had to content myself with mere cold-sounding words of gratitude.

We thanked them over and over again, and we said it was a lovely night, and we wished them a pleasant trip, and, I think, I invited them all to come and spend a week with me, and my cousin said her mother would be so pleased to see them. And we sang the 'Soldiers' Chorus' out of *Faust*, and got home in time for supper after all.

CHAPTER 10

Harris and I began to think that Bell Weir lock must have been done away with after the same manner. George had towed us up to Staines, and we had taken the boat from there, and it seemed that we were dragging fifty tons after us, and were walking forty miles. It was half past seven when we were through, and we all got in, and sculled up close to the left bank, looking out for a spot to haul up in.

We had originally intended to go on to Magna Charta Island, a sweetly pretty part of the river, where it winds through a soft, green valley, and to camp in one of the many picturesque inlets to be found round that tiny shore. But, somehow, we did not feel that we yearned for the picturesque nearly so much now as we had earlier in the day. A bit of water between a coal barge and a gasworks would have quite satisfied us for that night. We did not want scenery. We wanted to have our supper and go to bed. However, we did pull up to the point – 'Picnic Point', it is called – and dropped in a very pleasant nook under a great elm tree, to the spreading roots of which we fastened the boat.

Then we thought we were going to have supper (we had dispensed with tea, so as to save time), but George said no; that we had better get the canvas up first, before it got quite dark, and while we could see what we were doing. Then, he said, all our work would be done, and we could sit down to eat with an easy mind.

That canvas wanted more putting up than I think any of us had bargained for. It looked so simple in the abstract. You took five iron arches, like gigantic croquet hoops, and fitted them up over the boat, and then stretched the canvas over them, and fastened it down; it would take quite ten minutes, we thought.

That was an underestimate.

We took up the hoops, and began to drop them into the
sockets placed for them. You would not imagine this to be
dangerous work; but, looking back now, the wonder to me is
that any of us are alive to tell the tale. They were not hoops, they
were demons. First they would not fit into their sockets at all,
and we had to jump on them, and kick them, and hammer at
them with the boat-hook; and, when they were in, it turned out
that they were the wrong hoops for those particular sockets, and
they had to come out again.

But they would not come out, until two of us had gone and
struggled with them for five minutes, when they would jump up
suddenly, and try and throw us into the water and drown us.
They had hinges in the middle, and, when we were not looking,
they nipped us with these hinges in delicate parts of the body;
and endeavouring to persuade it to do its duty, the other side
would come behind us in a cowardly manner, and hit us over
the head.

We got them fixed at last, and then all that was to be done was
to arrange the covering over them. George unrolled it, and
fastened one end over the nose of the boat. Harris stood in the
middle to take it from George and roll it on to me, and I kept by
the stern to receive it. It was a long time coming down to me.
George did his part all right, but it was new work to Harris, and
he bungled it.

How he managed it I do not know, he could not explain
himself; but by some mysterious process or other he succeeded,
after ten minutes of superhuman effort, in getting himself
completely rolled up in it. He was so firmly wrapped round and
tucked in and folded over, that he could not get out. He, of
course, made frantic struggles for freedom – the birthright of
every Englishman – and in doing so (I learned this afterwards),
knocked over George; and then George, swearing at Harris,
began to struggle too, and got *himself* entangled and rolled up.

I knew nothing about all this at the time. I did not
understand the business at all myself. I had been told to stand
where I was, and wait till the canvas came to me, and
Montmorency and I stood there and waited both as good as
gold. We could see the canvas being violently jerked and tossed
about, pretty considerably; but we supposed this was part of the
method, and did not interfere.

We also heard much smothered language coming from underneath it, and we guessed that they were finding the job rather troublesome, and concluded that we would wait until things had got a little simpler before we joined in.

We waited some time, but matters seemed to get only more and more involved, until, at last, George's head came wriggling out over the side of the boat, and spoke up.

It said:

'Give us a hand here, can't you, you cuckoo; standing there like a stuffed mummy, when you see we are both being suffocated, you dummy!'

I never could withstand an appeal for help, so I went and undid them; not before it was time, either, for Harris was nearly black in the face.

It took us half an hour's hard labour, after that, before it was properly up, and then we cleared the decks, and got out supper. We put the kettle on to boil, up in the nose of the boat, and went down to the stern and pretended to take no notice of it, but set to work to get the other things out.

That is the only way to get a kettle to boil up the river. If it sees that you are waiting for it and are anxious, it will never even sing. You have to go away and begin your meal, as if you were not going to have any tea at all. You must not even look round at it. Then you will soon hear it sputtering away, mad to be made into tea.

It is a good plan, too, if you are in a great hurry, to talk very loudly to each other about how you don't need any tea, and are not going to have any. You get near the kettle, so that it can overhear you, and then you shout out, 'I don't want any tea; do you, George?' to which George shouts back, 'Oh, no, I don't like tea; we'll have lemonade instead – tea's so indigestible.' Upon which the kettle boils over, and puts the stove out.

We adopted this harmless bit of trickery, and the result was that, by the time everything else was ready, the tea was waiting. Then we lit the lantern and squatted down to supper.

We wanted that supper.

For five-and-thirty minutes not a sound was heard through-out the length and breadth of that boat, save the clank of cutlery and crockery, and the steady grinding of four sets of molars. At the end of five-and-thirty minutes, Harris said, 'Ah!' and took his left leg out from under him and put his right one there instead.

Five minutes afterwards, George said, 'Ah!' too, and threw his plate out on the bank; and, three minutes later than that, Montmorency gave the first sign of contentment he had exhibited since we had started, and rolled over on his side, and spread his legs out; and then I said, 'Ah!' and bent my head back, and bumped it against one of the hoops, but I did not mind it. I did not even swear.

How good one feels when one is full – how satisfied with ourselves and with the world! People who have tried it, tell me that a clear conscience makes you very happy and contented; but a full stomach does the business quite as well, and is cheaper, and more easily obtained. One feels so forgiving and generous after a substantial and well-digested meal – so noble-minded, so kindly-hearted.

It is very strange, this domination of our intellect by our digestive organs. We cannot work, we cannot think, unless our stomach wills so. It dictates to us our emotions, our passions. After eggs and bacon, it says, 'Work!' After beefsteak and porter, it says, 'Sleep!' After a cup of tea (two spoonfuls for each cup, and don't let it stand more than three minutes), it says to the brain, 'Now, rise, and show your strength. Be eloquent, and deep, and tender; see, with a clear eye, into Nature and into life; spread your white wings of quivering thought, and soar, a god-like spirit, over the whirling world beneath you, up through long lanes of flaming stars to the gates of eternity!'

After hot muffins, it says, 'Be dull and soulless, like a beast of the field – a brainless animal with listless eye, unlit by any ray of fancy, or of hope, or fear, or love, or life.' And after brandy, taken in sufficient quantity, it says, 'Now, come, fool, grin and tumble, that your fellow-men may laugh – drivel in folly, and splutter in senseless sounds, and show what a helpless ninny is the poor man whose wit and will are drowned, like kittens, side by side, in half an inch of alcohol.'

We are but the veriest, sorriest slaves of our stomach. Reach not after morality and righteousness, my friends; watch vigilantly your stomach, and diet it with care and judgment. Then virtue and contentment will come and reign within your heart, unsought by any effort of your own; and you will be a good citizen, a loving husband, and a tender father – a noble, pious man.

Before our supper, Harris and George and I were quarrelsome and snappy and ill-tempered; after our supper, we sat and beamed on one another, and we beamed upon the dog, too. We loved each other, we loved everybody. Harris, in moving about, trod on George's corn. Had this happened before supper, George would have expressed wishes and desires concerning Harris's fate in this world and the next that would have made a thoughtful man shudder.

As it was, he said, 'Steady, old man; 'ware wheat.'

And Harris, instead of merely observing, in his most unpleasant tones, that a fellow could hardly help treading on some bit of George's foot, if he had to move about at all within ten yards of where George was sitting, suggesting that George never ought to come into an ordinary sized boat with feet that length, and advising him to hang them over the side, as he would have done before supper, now said: 'Oh, I'm sorry, old chap; I hope I haven't hurt you.'

And George said, 'Not at all'; that it was his fault; and Harris said no, it was his.

It was quite pretty to hear them.

We lit our pipes, and sat, looking out on the quiet night, and talked.

George said why could not we be always like this – away from the world, with its sins and temptation, leading sober, peaceful lives, and doing good. I said it was the sort of thing I had often longed for myself; and we discussed the possibility of our going away, we four, to some handy, well-fitted desert island, and living there in the woods.

Harris said that the danger about desert islands, as far as he had heard, was that they were so damp; but George said no, not if properly drained.

And then we got on to drains, and that put George in mind of a very funny thing that happened to his father once. He said his father was travelling with another fellow through Wales, and, one night, they stopped at a little inn, where there were some other fellows, and they joined the other fellows, and spent the evening with them.

They had a very jolly evening, and sat up late, and, by the

time they came to go to bed, they (this was when George's father was a very young man) were slightly jolly, too. They (George's father and George's father's friend) were to sleep in the same room, but in different beds. They took the candle, and went up. The candle lurched up against the wall when they got into the room, and went out, and they had to undress and grope into bed in the dark. This they did; but, instead of getting into separate beds, as they thought they were doing, they both climbed into the same one without knowing it – one getting in with his head at the top, and the other crawling in from the opposite side of the compass, and lying with his feet on the pillow.

There was silence for a moment, and then George's father said:

'Joe!'

'What's the matter, Tom?' replied Joe's voice from the other end of the bed.

'Why, there's a man in my bed,' said George's father, 'here's his feet on my pillow.'

'Well, it's an extraordinary thing, Tom,' answered the other; 'but I'm blest if there isn't a man in my bed, too!'

'What are you going to do?' asked George's father.

'Well, I'm going to chuck him out,' replied Joe.

'So am I,' said George's father, valiantly.

There was a brief struggle, followed by two heavy bumps on the floor, and then a rather doleful voice said:

'I say, Tom!'

'Yes!'

'How have you got on?'

'Well, to tell you the truth, my man's chucked *me* out.'

'So's mine! I say, I don't think much of this inn, do you?'

'What was the name of that inn?' said Harris.

'The "Pig and Whistle",' said George. Why?'

'Ah, no, then it isn't the same,' replied Harris.

'What do you mean?' queried George.

'Why it's so curious,' murmured Harris, 'but precisely that very same thing happened to *my* father once at a country inn. I've often heard him tell the tale. I thought it might have been the same inn.'

We turned in at ten that night, and I thought I should sleep well, being tired; but I didn't. As a rule, I undress and put my head on the pillow, and then somebody bangs at the door, and says it is half past eight; but, tonight, everything seemed against me; the novelty of it all, the hardness of the boat, the cramped position (I was lying with my feet under one seat, and my head on another), the sound of the lapping water round the boat, and the wind among the branches, kept me restless and disturbed.

I did get to sleep for a few hours, and then some part of the boat which seemed to have grown up in the night – for it certainly was not there when we started, and it had disappeared by the morning – kept digging into my spine. I slept through it for a while, dreaming that I had swallowed a sovereign, and that they were cutting a hole in my back with a gimlet, so as to try and get it out. I thought it very unkind of them, and I told them I would owe them the money, and they should have it at the end of the month. But they would not hear of that, and said it would be much better if they had it then, because otherwise the interest would accumulate so. I got quite cross with them after a bit, and told them what I thought of them, and then they gave the gimlet such an excruciating wrench that I woke up.

The boat seemed stuffy, and my head ached; so I thought I would step out into the cool night-air. I slipped on what clothes I could find about – some of my own, and some of George's and Harris's – and crept under the canvas on to the bank.

It was a glorious night. The moon had sunk and left the quiet earth alone with the stars. It seemed as if, in the silence and the hush, while we her children slept, they were talking with her, their sister – conversing of mighty mysteries in voices too vast and deep for childish human ears to catch the sound.

They awe us, these strange stars, so cold, so clear. We are as children whose small feet have strayed into some dim-lit temple of the god they have been taught to worship but know not; and, standing where the echoing dome spans the long vista of the shadowy light, glance up, half hoping, half afraid to see some awful vision hovering there.

And yet it seems so full of comfort and of strength, the night. In its great presence, our small sorrows creep away, ashamed. The day has been so full of fret and care, and our hearts have been so full of evil and of bitter thoughts, and the world has seemed so hard and wrong to us. Then Night, like some great loving mother, gently lays her hand upon our fevered head, and turns out little tear-stained face up to hers, and smiles, and, though she does not speak, we know what she would say, and lay our hot flushed cheek against her bosom, and the pain is gone.

Sometimes, our pain is very deep and real, and we stand before her very silent, because there is no language for our pain, only a moan. Night's heart is full of pity for us: she cannot ease our aching; she takes our hand in hers, and the little world grows very small and very far beneath us, and, borne on her dark wings, we pass for a moment into a mightier Presence than her own, and in the wondrous light of that great Presence, all human life lies like a book before us, and we know that Pain and Sorrow are but the angels of God.

Only those who have worn the crown of suffering can look upon that wondrous light; and they, when they return, may not speak of it, or tell the mystery they know.

Once upon a time, through a strange country, there rode some goodly knights, and their path lay by a deep wood, where tangled briers grew very thick and strong, and tore the flesh of them that lost their way therein. And the leaves of the trees that grew in the wood were very dark and thick, so that no ray of light came through the branches to lighten the gloom and sadness.

And, as they passed by that dark wood, one knight of those that rode, missing his comrades, wandered far away, and returned to them no more; and they, sorely grieving, rode on without him, mourning him as one dead.

Now, when they reached the fair castle towards which they had been journeying, they stayed there many days, and made merry; and one night, as they sat in a cheerful ease around the logs that burned in the great hall, and drank a loving measure, there came the comrade they had lost, and greeted them. His clothes were ragged, like a beggar's, and many sad wounds were on his sweet flesh, but upon his face there shone a great radiance of deep joy.

And they questioned him, asking him what had befallen him: and he told them how in the dark wood he had lost his way, and had wandered many days and nights, till, torn and bleeding, he had lain him down to die.

Then, when he was nigh unto death, lo! through the savage

gloom there came to him a stately maiden, and took him by the hand and led him on through devious paths, unknown to any man, until upon the darkness of the wood there dawned a light such as the light of day was unto but as a little lamp unto the sun; and, in that wondrous light, our wayworn knight saw as in a dream a vision, and so glorious, so fair the vision seemed, that of his bleeding wounds he thought no more, but stood as one entranced, whose joy is deep as is the sea, whereof no man can tell the depth.

And the vision faded, and the knight, kneeling upon the ground, thanked the good saint who into that sad wood had strayed his steps, so he had seen the vision that lay there hid.

And the name of the dark forest was Sorrow; but of the vision that the good knight saw therein we may not speak nor tell.

CHAPTER 11

How George, once upon a time, got up early in the morning – George, Harris, and Montmorency do not like the look of the cold water – Heroism and determination on the part of J. – George and his shirt: story with a moral – Harris as cook – Historical retrospect, specially inserted for the use of schools.

I woke at six the next morning; and found George awake too. We both turned round, and tried to go to sleep again, but we could not. Had there been any particular reason why we should *not* have gone to sleep again, but have got up and dressed then and there, we should have dropped off while we were looking at our watches, and have slept till ten. As there was no earthly necessity for our getting up under another two hours at the very least, and our getting up at that time was an utter absurdity, it was only in keeping with the natural cussedness of things in general that we should both feel that lying down for five minutes more would be death to us.

George said that the same kind of thing, only worse, had happened to him some eighteen months ago, when he was lodging by himself in the house of a certain Mrs Gippings. He said his watch went wrong one evening, and stopped at a quarter past eight. He did not know this at the time because, for some reason or other, he forgot to wind it up when he went to bed (an unusual occurrence with him), and hung it up over his pillow without ever looking at the thing.

It was in the winter when this happened, very near the shortest day, and a week of fog into the bargain, so the fact that it was still very dark when George woke in the morning was no guide to him as to the time. He reached up, and hauled down his watch. It was a quarter past eight.

'Angels and ministers of grace defend us!' exclaimed George; 'and here have I got to be in the City by nine. Why didn't somebody call me? Oh, this is a shame!' And he flung the watch down, and sprang out of bed, and had a cold bath, and washed himself, and dressed himself, and shaved himself in cold water because there was no time to wait for the hot, and then rushed and had another look at the watch.

Whether the shaking it had received in being thrown down on the bed had started it, or how it was, George could not say, but certain it was that from a quarter past eight it had begun to go, and now pointed to twenty minutes to nine.

George snatched it up, and rushed downstairs. In the sitting-room, all was dark and silent; there was no fire, no breakfast. George said it was a wicked shame of Mrs G., and he made up his mind to tell her what he thought of her when he came home in the evening. Then he dashed on his greatcoat and hat, and seizing his umbrella, made for the front door. The door was not even unbolted. George anathematized Mrs G. for a lazy old woman, and thought it was very strange that people could not get up at a decent, respectable time, unlocked and unbolted the door, and ran out.

He ran hard for a quarter of a mile, and at the end of that distance it began to be borne in upon him as a strange and curious thing that there were so few people about, and that there were no shops open. It was certainly a very dark and foggy morning, but still it seemed an unusual course to stop all business on that account. *He* had to go to business; why should other people stop in bed merely because it was dark and foggy?

At length he reached Holborn. Not a shutter was down! Not a bus was about! There were three men in sight, one of whom was a policeman; a market-cart full of cabbages, and a dilapidated-looking cab. George pulled out his watch and looked at it; it was five minutes to nine! He stood still and counted his pulse. He stooped down and felt his legs. Then, with his watch still in his hand, he went up to the policeman, and asked him if he knew what time it was.

'What's the time?' said the man, eyeing George up and down with evident suspicion; 'why, if you listen you will hear it strike.'

George listened, and a neighbouring clock immediately obliged.

'But it's only gone three!' said George in an injured tone, when it had finished.

'Well, how many did you want it to go?' replied the constable.

'Why, nine,' said George, showing his watch.

'Do you know where you live?' said the guardian of public order severely.

George thought, and gave the address.

'Oh! That's where it is, is it?' replied the man. 'Well, you take my advice and go there quietly, and take that watch of yours with you; and don't let's have any more of it.'

And George went home again, musing as he walked along, and let himself in.

At first, when he got in, he determined to undress and go to bed again; but when he thought of the re-dressing and re-washing, and the having of another bath, he determined he would not, but would sit up and go to sleep in the easy-chair.

But he could not get to sleep; he never felt more wakeful in his life; so he lit the lamp and got out the chess-board and played himself a game of chess. But even that did not enliven him: it seemed slow somehow; so he gave chess up and tried to read. He did not seem able to take any sort of interest in reading either, so he put on his coat again and went out for a walk.

It was horribly lonesome and dismal, and all the policemen he met regarded him with undisguised suspicion, and turned their lanterns on him and followed him about, and this had such an effect upon him at last that he began to feel as if he really had done something, and he got to slinking down the by-streets and hiding in dark doorways when he heard the regulation flip-flop approaching.

Of course, this conduct made the force only more distrustful of him than ever, and they would come and rout him out and ask him what he was doing there; and when he answered Nothing, he had merely come out for a stroll (it was then four o'clock in the morning), they looked as though they did not believe him, and two plain-clothes constables came home with him to see if he really did live where he had said he did. They saw him go in with his key, and then they took up a position opposite and watched his house.

He thought he would light a fire when he got inside, and make himself some breakfast, just to pass away the time; but he did not seem able to handle anything from a scuttleful of coals to a teaspoon without dropping it or falling over it, and making such a noise that he was in mortal fear that it would wake Mrs G. up, and that she would think it was burglars and open the window and call 'Police!' and then these two detectives would rush in and handcuff him, and march him off to the police-court.

He was in a morbidly nervous state by this time, and he pictured the trial, and his trying to explain the circumstances to the jury, and nobody believing him, and his being sentenced to twenty years' penal servitude, and his mother dying of a broken heart. So he gave up trying to get breakfast, and wrapped himself up in his overcoat, and sat in the easy-chair till Mrs G. came down at half past seven.

He said he had never got up too early since that morning; it had been such a warning to him.

We had been sitting huddled up in our rugs while George had been telling me this true story, and on his finishing it I set to work to wake up Harris with a scull. The third prod did it: and he turned over on the other side, and said he would be down in a minute, and that he would have his lace-up boots. We soon let him know where he was, however, by the aid of the hitcher, and he sat up suddenly, sending Montmorency, who had been sleeping the sleep of the just, right on the middle of his chest, sprawling across the boat.

Then we pulled up the canvas, and all four of us poked our head out over the offside, and looked down at the water and shivered. The idea, overnight, had been that we should get up early in the morning, fling off our rugs and shawls, and, throwing back the canvas, spring into the river with a joyous shout, and revel in a long delicious swim. Somehow, now the morning had come, the notion seemed less tempting. The water looked damp and chilly; the wind felt cold.

'Well, who's going to be first in?' said Harris at last.

There was no rush for precedence. George settled the matter so far as he was concerned by retiring into the boat and pulling on his socks. Montmorency gave vent to an involuntary howl, as if merely thinking of the thing had given him the horrors; and Harris said it would be so difficult to get into the boat again, and went back and sorted out his trousers.

I did not altogether like to give in, though I did not relish the plunge. There might be snags about, or weeds, I thought. I meant to compromise matters by going down to the edge and just throwing the water over myself; so I took a towel and crept out on the bank and wormed my way along on to the branch of a tree that dipped down into the water.

It was bitterly cold. The wind cut like a knife. I thought I would not throw the water over myself after all. I would go back into the boat and dress; and I turned to do so; and, as I turned, the silly branch gave way, and I and the towel went in together with a tremendous splash, and I was out midstream with a gallon of Thames water inside me before I knew what had happened.

'By Jove! old J.'s gone in,' I heard Harris say, as I came blowing to the surface. 'I didn't think he'd have the pluck to do it. Did you?'

'Is it all right?' sang out George.

'Lovely,' I spluttered back. 'You are duffers not to come in. I wouldn't have missed this for worlds. Why don't you try it? It only wants a little determination.'

But I could not persuade them.

Rather an amusing thing happened while dressing that morning. I was very cold when I got back into the boat, and, in my hurry to get my shirt on, I accidentally jerked it into the water. It made me awfully wild, especially as George burst out laughing. I could not see anything to laugh at, and I told George so, and he only laughed the more. I never saw a man laugh so much. I quite lost my temper with him at last, and I pointed out to him what a drivelling maniac of an imbecile idiot he was; but he only roared the louder. And then, just as I was landing the shirt, I noticed that it was not my shirt at all, but George's, which I had mistaken for mine; whereupon the humour of the thing struck me for the first time, and *I* began to laugh. And the more I looked from George's wet shirt to George, roaring with laughter, the more I was amused, and I laughed so much that I had to let the shirt fall back into the water again.

'Ar'n't you – you – going to get it out?' said George between his shrieks.

I could not answer him at all for a while, I was laughing so, but at last, between my peals I managed to jerk out:

'It isn't my shirt – it's *yours!*'

I never saw a man's face change from lively to severe so suddenly in all my life before.

'What!' he yelled, springing up. 'You silly cuckoo! Why can't you be more careful what you're doing? Why the deuce don't you go and dress on the bank? You're not fit to be in a boat, you're not. Gimme the hitcher.'

I tried to make him see the fun of the thing, but he could not. George is very dense at seeing a joke sometimes.

Harris proposed that we should have scrambled eggs for breakfast. He said he would cook them. It seemed, from his account, that he was very good at doing scrambled eggs. He often did them at picnics and when out on yachts. He was quite famous for them. People who had once tasted his scrambled eggs, so we gathered from his conversation, never cared for any other food afterwards, but pined away and died when they could not get them.

It made our mouths water to hear him talk about the things, and we handed him out the stove and the frying-pan and all the eggs that had not smashed and gone over everything in the hamper, and begged him to begin.

He had some trouble in breaking the eggs – or rather not so much trouble in breaking them exactly as in getting them into the frying-pan when broken, and keeping them off his trousers, and preventing them from running up his sleeve; but he fixed some half a dozen into the pan at last, and then squatted down by the side of the stove and chivvied them about with a fork.

It seemed harassing work, so far as George and I could judge. Whenever he went near the pan he burned himself, and then he would drop everything and dance round the stove, flicking his fingers about and cursing the things. Indeed, every time George and I looked round at him he was sure to be performing this feat. We thought at first that it was a necessary part of the culinary arrangements.

We did not know what scrambled eggs were, and we fancied that it must be some Red Indian or Sandwich Islands' sort of dish that required dances and incantations for its proper cooking. Montmorency went and put his nose over it once, and the fat spluttered up and scalded him, and then *he* began dancing and cursing. Altogether it was one of the most interesting and exciting operations I have ever witnessed. George and I were both quite sorry when it was over.

The result was not altogether the success that Harris had anticipated. There seemed so little to show for the business. Six eggs had gone into the frying-pan, and all that came out was a teaspoonful of burnt and unappetizing-looking mess.

Harris said it was the fault of the frying-pan, and thought it would have gone better if we had had a fish-kettle and a gas stove; and we decided not to attempt the dish again until we had those aids to housekeeping by us.

The sun had got more powerful by the time we had finished breakfast, and the wind had dropped, and it was as lovely a morning as one could desire. Little was in sight to remind us of the nineteenth century; and, as we looked out upon the river in the morning sunlight, we could almost fancy that the centuries between us and that ever-to-be-famous June morning of 1215 had been drawn aside, and that we, English yeomen's sons in homespun cloth, with dirk at belt, were waiting there to witness the writing of that stupendous page of history, the meaning whereof was to be translated to the common people some four hundred and odd years later by one Oliver Cromwell, who had deeply studied it.

It is a fine summer morning – sunny, soft, and still. But through the air there runs a thrill of coming stir. King John had slept at Duncroft Hall, and all the day before the little town of Staines has echoed to the clang of armed men, and the clatter of great horses over its rough stones, and the shouts of captains, and the grim oaths and surly jests of bearded bowmen, billmen, pikemen, and strange-speaking foreign spearmen.

Gay-cloaked companies of knights and squires have ridden in, all travel-stained and dusty. And all the evening long the timid townsmen's doors have had to be quick opened to let in rough groups of soldiers, for whom there must be found both board and lodging, and the best of both, or woe betide the house and all within; for the sword is judge and jury, plaintiff and executioner, in these tempestuous times, and pays for what it takes by sparing those from whom it takes it, if it pleases it to do so.

Round the camp-fire in the market-place gather still more of the Barons' troops, and eat and drink deep, and bellow forth roystering drinking songs, and gamble and quarrel as the evening grows and deepens into night. The firelight sheds quaint shadows on their piled-up arms and on their uncouth forms. The children of the town steal round to watch them, wondering; and brawny country wenches, laughing, draw near to bandy ale-house jest and jibe with the swaggering troopers so unlike the village swains, who, now despised, stand apart behind, with vacant grins upon their broad, peering faces. And out from the fields around, glitter the faint lights of more distant camps, as here some great lord's followers lie mustered, and there false John French's mercenaries hover like crouching wolves without the town.

And so, with sentinels in each dark street, and twinkling watch-fires on each height around, the night has worn away, and over this fair valley of old Thames has broken the morning of the great day that is to close so big with the fate of ages yet unborn.

Ever since grey dawn, in the lower of the two islands, just above where we are standing, there has been great clamour, and the sound of many workmen. The great pavilion brought there yester eve is being raised, and carpenters are busy nailing tiers of seats, while 'prentices from London town are there with many-coloured stuffs and silks and cloth of gold and silver.

And now, lo! down upon the road that winds along the river's bank from Staines there come towards us, laughing and talking together in deep guttural bass, a half a score of stalwart halbert-men – Barons' men, these – and halt at a hundred yards or so above us, on the other bank, and lean upon their arms, and wait.

And so, from hour to hour, march up along the road ever fresh groups and bands of armed men, their casques and breastplates flashing back along the long low lines of morning sunlight, until, as far as eye can reach, the way seems thick with glittering steel and prancing steeds. And shouting horsemen are galloping from group to group, and little banners are fluttering lazily in the warm breeze, and ever now and then there is a deeper stir as the ranks make way on either side, and some great Baron on his war-horse, with his guard of squires around him, passes along to take his station at the head of his serfs and vassals.

And up the slope of Cooper's Hill, just opposite, are gathered the wondering rustics and curious townsfolk, who have run from Staines, and none are quite sure what the bustle is about, but each one has a different version of the great event that they have come to see; and some say that much good to all the people will come from this day's work; but the old men shake their heads, for they have heard such tales before.

And all the river down to Staines is dotted with small craft
and boats and tiny coracles – which last are growing out of
favour now, and are used only by the poorer folk. Over the
rapids, where in after years trim Bell Weir lock will stand, they
have been forced or dragged by their sturdy rowers, and now
are crowding up as near as they dare come to the great covered
barges, which lie in readiness to bear King John to where the
fateful Charter waits his signing.

It is noon, and we and all the people have been waiting
patient for many an hour, and the rumour has run round that
slippery John has again escaped from the Baron's grasp, and
has stolen away from Duncroft Hall with his mercenaries at his
heels, and will soon be doing other work than signing charters
for his people's liberty.

Not so! This time the grip upon him has been one of iron, and
he has slid and wriggled in vain. Far down the road a little cloud
of dust has risen, and draws nearer and grows larger, and the
pattering of many hoofs grows louder, and in and out between
the scattered groups of drawn-up men, there pushes on its way a
brilliant cavalcade of gay-dressed lords and knights. And front
and rear, and either flank, there ride the yeomen of the Barons,
and in the midst King John.

He rides to where the barges lie in readiness, and the great
Barons step forth from their ranks to meet him. He greets them
with a smile and a laugh, and pleasant honeyed words, as
though it were some feast in his honour to which he had been
invited. But as he rises to dismount, he casts one hurried glance
from his own French mercenaries drawn up in the rear to the
grim ranks of the Barons's men that hem him in.

Is it too late? One fierce blow at the unsuspecting horseman
at his side, one cry to his French troops, one desperate charge
upon the unready lines before him, and these rebellious Barons
might rue the day they dared to thwart his plans! A bolder hand
might have turned the game even at that point. Had it been a
Richard there! the cup of liberty might have been dashed from
England's lips, and the taste of freedom held back for a hundred
years.

But the heart of King John sinks before the stern faces of the
English fighting men, and the arm of King John drops back on
to his rein, and he dismounts and takes his seat in the foremost

barge. And the Barons follow in, with each mailed hand upon the sword-hilt, and the word is given to let go.

Slowly the heavy, bright-decked barges leave the shore of Runnymede. Slowly against the swift current they work their ponderous way, till, with a low grumble, they grate against the bank of the little island that from this day will bear the name of Magna Charta Island. And King John has stepped upon the shore, and we wait in breathless silence till a great shout cleaves the air and the great cornerstone in England's temple of liberty has, now we know, been firmly laid.

CHAPTER 12

Henry VIII and Anne Boleyn – Disadvantages of living in same house with pair of lovers – A trying time for the English nation – A night search for the picturesque – Homeless and houseless – Harris prepares to die – An angel comes along – Effect of sudden joy on Harris – A little supper – Lunch – High price for mustard – A fearful battle – Maidenhead – Sailing – Three fishers – We are cursed.

I was sitting on the bank, conjuring up this scene to myself, when George remarked that when I was quite rested, perhaps I would not mind helping to wash up, and, thus recalled from the days of the glorious past to the prosaic present, with all its misery and sin, I slid down into the boat and cleaned out the frying-pan with a stick of wood and a tuft of grass, polishing it up finally with George's wet shirt.

We went over to Magna Charta Island, and had a look at the stone which stands in the cottage there and on which the greater Charter is said to have been signed; though, as to whether it really was signed there, or, as some say, on the other bank at Runnymede, I decline to commit myself. As far as my own personal opinion goes, however, I am inclined to give weight to the popular island theory. Certainly, had I been one of the Barons, at the time, I should have strongly urged upon my comrades the advisability of our getting such a slippery customer as King John on to the island, where there was less chance of surprises and tricks.

There are the ruins of an old priory in the grounds of Ankerwyke House, which is close to Picnic Point, and it was round about the grounds of this old priory that Henry VIII is said to have waited for and met Anne Boleyn. He also used to meet her at Hever Castle, in Kent, and also somewhere near St Albans. It must have been difficult for the people of England in those days to have found a spot where these thoughtless young folk were *not* spooning.

Have you ever been in a house where there are a couple courting? It is most trying. You think you will go and sit in the drawing-room, and you march off there. As you open the door, you hear a noise as if somebody had suddenly recollected something, and, when you get in, Emily is over by the window, full of interest in the opposite side of the road, and your friend, John Edward, is at the other end of the room with his whole soul held in thrall by photographs of other people's relatives.

'Oh!' you say, pausing at the door, 'I didn't know anybody was here.'

'Oh! didn't you?' says Emily, coldly, in a tone which implies that she does not believe you.

You hang about for a bit, then you say:

'It's very dark. Why don't you light the gas?'

John Edward says, Oh! he hadn't noticed it; and Emily says that papa does not like the gas lit in the afternoon.

You tell them one or two items of news, and give them your views and opinions on the Irish question; but this does not appear to interest them. All they remark on any subject is, 'Oh!' 'Is it?' 'Did he?' 'Yes', and 'You don't say so!' And, after ten minutes of such style of conversation, you edge up to the door, and slip out, and are surprised to find that the door immediately closes behind you, and shuts itself, without your having touched it.

Half an hour later, you think you will try a pipe in the conservatory. The only chair in the place is occupied by Emily; and John Edward, if the language of clothes can be relied upon, has evidently been sitting on the floor. They do not speak, but they give you a look that says all that can be said in a civilized community; and you back out promptly and shut the door behind you.

You are afraid to poke your nose into any room in the house now; so, after walking up and down the stairs for a while, you go and sit in your own bedroom. This becomes uninteresting, however, after a time, and so you put on your hat and stroll out into the garden. You walk down the path, and as you pass the summer-house you glance in, and there are those two young idiots, huddled up into one corner of it; and they see you, and are evidently under the idea that, for some wicked purpose of your own, you are following them about.

'Why don't they have a special room for this sort of thing, and make people keep to it?' you mutter; and you rush back to the hall and get your umbrella and go out.

It must have been much like this when that foolish boy Henry

VIII was courting his little Anne. People in Buckinghamshire would have come upon them unexpectedly when they were mooning round Windsor and Wraysbury, and have exclaimed, 'Oh! you here!' and Henry would have blushed and said, Yes, he'd just come over to see a man; and Anne would have said, 'Oh, I'm so glad to see you! Isn't it funny? I've just met Mr Henry VIII in the lane, and he's going the same way I am.'

Then those people would have gone away and said to themselves: 'Oh! we'd better get out of here while this billing and cooing is on. We'll go down to Kent.'

And they would go down to Kent, and the first thing they would see in Kent, when they got there, would be Henry and Anne fooling round Hever Castle.

'Oh, drat this!' they would have said. 'Here, let's go away. I can't stand any more of it. Let's go to St Albans – nice quiet place, St Albans.'

And when they reached St Albans, there would be that wretched couple, kissing under the Abbey walls. Then these folks would go and be pirates until the marriage was over.

From Picnic Point to Old Windsor lock is a delightful bit of the river. A shady road, dotted here and there with dainty little cottages, runs by the bank up to the 'Bells of Ouseley', a picturesque inn, as most up-river inns are, and a place where a very good glass of ale may be drunk – so Harris says; and on a matter of this kind you can take Harris's word. Old Windsor is a famous spot in its way. Edward the Confessor had a palace here, and here the great Earl Godwin was proved guilty by the justice of that age of having encompassed the death of the King's brother. Earl Godwin broke a piece of bread and held it in his hand.

'If I am guilty,' said the Earl, 'may this bread choke me when I eat it!'

Then he put the bread into his mouth and swallowed it, and it choked him, and he died.

After you pass Old Windsor, the river is somewhat uninteresting, and does not become itself again until you are nearing Boveney. George and I towed up past the Home Park, which stretches along the right bank from Albert to Victoria Bridge; and as we were passing Datchet, George asked me if I remembered our first trip up the river, and when we landed at

Datchet at ten o'clock at night, and wanted to go to bed.

I answered that I did remember it. It will be some time before I forget it.

It was the Saturday before the August Bank Holiday. We were tired and hungry, we same three, and when we got to Datchet we took out the hamper, the two bags, and the rugs and coats, and such like things and started off to look for diggings. We passed a very pretty little hotel, with clematis and creeper over the porch; but there was no honeysuckle about it, and, for some reason or other, I had got my mind fixed on honeysuckle, and I said:

'Oh, don't let's go in there! Let's go on a bit further, and see if there isn't one with honeysuckle over it.'

So we went on till we came to another hotel. That was a very nice hotel, too, and it had honeysuckle on it, round at the side; but Harris did not like the look of a man who was leaning against the front door. He said he didn't look a nice man at all, and he wore ugly boots: so we went on further. We went a goodish way without coming across any more hotels, and then we met a man, and asked him to direct us to a few.

He said:

'Why, you are coming away from them. You must turn right round and go back, and then you will come to the Stag.'

We said:

'Oh, we had been there, and didn't like it – no honeysuckle over it.'

'Well, then,' he said, 'there's the Manor House, just opposite. Have you tried that?'

Harris replied that we did not want to go there – didn't like the looks of a man who was stopping there – Harris did not like the colour of his hair, didn't like his boots, either.

'Well, I don't know what you'll do, I'm sure,' said our informant; 'because they are the only two inns in the place.'

'No other inns!' exclaimed Harris.

'None,' replied the man.

'What on earth are we to do?' cried Harris.

Then George spoke up. He said Harris and I could get an hotel built for us, if we liked, and have some people made to put in. For his part, he was going back to the Stag.

The greatest minds never realise their ideals in any matter;

[162]

and Harris and I sighed over the hollowness of all earthly desires, and followed George.

We took our traps into the Stag, and laid them down in the hall.

The landlord came up and said:

'Good evening, gentlemen.'

'Oh, good evening,' said George; 'we want three beds, please.'

'Very sorry, sir,' said the landlord; 'but I'm afraid we can't manage it.'

'Oh, well, never mind,' said George, 'two will do. Two of us can sleep in one bed, can't we?' he continued, turning to Harris and me.

Harris said, 'Oh, yes', he thought George and I could sleep in one bed very easily.

'Very sorry, sir,' again repeated the landlord; 'but we really haven't got a bed vacant in the whole house. In fact, we are putting two, and even three gentlemen in one bed, as it is.'

This staggered us for a bit.

But Harris, who is an old traveller, rose to the occasion, and, laughing cheerily, said:

'Oh, well, we can't help it. We must rough it. You must give us a shake-down in the billiard-room.'

'Very sorry, sir. Three gentlemen sleeping on the billiard-table already, and two in the coffee-room. Can't possibly take you in tonight.'

We picked up our things, and went over to the Manor House. It was a pretty little place. I said I thought I should like it better than the other house; and Harris said, 'Oh, yes,' it would be all right, and we needn't look at the man with the red hair; besides, the poor fellow couldn't help having red hair.

Harris spoke quite kindly and sensibly about it.

The people at the Manor House did not wait to hear us talk. The landlady met us on the doorstep with the greeting that we were the fourteenth party she had turned away within the last hour and a half. As for our meek suggestions of stables, billiard-room, or coal-cellars, she laughed them all to scorn; all these nooks had been snatched up long ago.

Did she know of any place in the whole village where we could get shelter for the night?

Well, if we didn't mind roughing it – she did not recommend it, mind – but there was a little beershop half a mile down the Eton road –

We waited to hear no more; we caught up the hamper and the bags, and the coats and rugs, and parcels, and ran. The distance seemed more like a mile than half a mile, but we reached the place at last, and rushed, panting, into the bar.

The people at the beershop were rude. They merely laughed at us. There were only three beds in the whole house, and they had seven single gentlemen and two married couples sleeping there already. A kind-hearted bargeman, however, who happened to be in the tap-room thought we might try the grocer's next door to the Stag, and we went back.

The grocer's was full. An old woman we met in the shop then kindly took us along with her for a quarter of a mile to a lady friend of hers who occasionally let rooms to gentlemen.

This old woman walked very slowly, and we were twenty minutes getting to her lady friend's. She enlivened the journey by describing to us, as we trailed along, the various pains she had in her back.

Her lady friend's rooms were let. From there we were recommended to No. 27. No. 27 was full, and sent us to No. 32, and No. 32 was full.

Then we went back into the high road, and Harris sat down on the hamper and said he would go no farther. He said it seemed a quite spot, and he would like to die there. He requested George and me to kiss his mother for him, and to tell all his relations that he forgave them and died happy.

At that moment an angel came by in the disguise of a small boy (and I cannot think of any more effective disguise an angel could have assumed), with a can of beer in one hand, and in the other something at the end of a string, which he let down on to every flat stone he came across, and then pulled up again, this producing a peculiarly unattractive sound, suggestive of suffering.

We asked this heavenly messenger (as we discovered him afterwards to be) if he knew of any lonely house, whose occupants were few and feeble (old ladies or paralysed gentlemen preferred), who could be easily frightened into giving up their beds for the night to three desperate men; or, if not this, could he recommend us to an empty pigsty, or a disused lime-kiln, or anything of that sort. He did not know of any such place – at least not one handy; but he said that, if we liked to come with him, his mother had a room to spare, and could put us up for the night.

We fell upon his neck there in the moonlight and blessed him, and it would have made a very beautiful picture if the boy himself had not been so overpowered by our emotion as to be unable to sustain himself under it, and sunk to the ground, letting us all down on top of him. Harris was so overcome with joy that he fainted, and had to seize the boy's beer-can and half empty it before he could recover consciousness, and then he started off at a run, and left George and me to bring on the luggage.

It was a little four-roomed cottage where the boy lived, and his mother – good soul! – gave us hot bacon for supper, and we ate it all – five pounds – and a jam tart afterwards, and two pots of tea, and then we went to bed. There were two beds in the room; one was a 2 ft 6 in. truckle bed, and George and I slept in that, and kept in by tying ourselves together with a sheet; and the other was the little boy's bed, and Harris had that all to himself, and we found him in the morning, with two feet of bare leg sticking out of the bottom, and George and I used it to hang the towels on while we bathed.

We were not so uppish about what sort of hotel we would have next time we went to Datchet.

To return to our present trip: nothing exciting happened, and we tugged steadily on a little below Monkey Island, where we drew up and lunched. We tackled the cold beef for lunch, and then we found that we had forgotten to bring any mustard. I don't think I ever in my life, before or since, felt I wanted mustard as badly as I felt I wanted it then. I don't care for mustard as a rule, and it is very seldom that I take it at all, but I would have given worlds for it then.

I don't know how many worlds there may be in the universe, but anyone who had brought me a spoonful of mustard at that precise moment could have had them all. I grow reckless like that when I want a thing and can't get it.

Harris said he would have given worlds for mustard, too. It would have been a good thing for anybody who had come up to that spot with a can of mustard then; he would have been set up in worlds for the rest of his life.

But there! I dare say both Harris and I would have tried to back out of the bargain after we had got the mustard. One makes these extravagant offers in moments of excitement, but, of course, when one comes to think of it, one sees how absurdly out of proportion they are with the value of the required article. I heard a man, going up a mountain in Switzerland, once say he would give worlds for a glass of beer, and when he came to a little shanty where they kept it, he kicked up a most fearful row because they charged him five francs for a bottle of Bass. He said it was a scandalous imposition, and he wrote to *The Times* about it.

It cast a gloom over the boat, there being no mustard. We ate our beef in silence. Existence seemed hollow and uninteresting. We thought of the happy days of childhood, and sighed. We brightened up a bit, however, over the apple-tart, and, when George drew out a tin of pineapple from the bottom of the hamper, and rolled it into the middle of the boat, we felt that life was worth living after all.

We are very fond of pineapple, all three of us. We looked at the picture on the tin; we thought of the juice. We smiled at one another, and Harris got a spoon ready.

Then we looked for the knife to open the tin with. We turned out everything in the hamper. We turned out the bags. We pulled up the boards at the bottom of the boat. We took everything out on the bank and shook it. There was no tin-opener to be found.

Then Harris tried to open the tin with a pocket-knife, and broke the knife and cut himself badly; and George tried a pair of scissors, and the scissors flew up, and nearly put his eye out. While they were dressing their wounds, I tried to make a hole in the thing with the spiky end of the hitcher, and the hitcher slipped and jerked me out between the boat and the bank into two feet of muddy water, and the tin rolled over, uninjured, and broke a teacup.

Then we all got mad. We took that tin out on the bank, and Harris went up into a field and got a big sharp stone, and I went back into the boat and brought out the mast, and George held the tin and Harris held the sharp end of his stone against the top

of it, and I took the mast and poised it high up in the air, and gathered up all my strength and brought it down.

It was George's straw hat that saved his life that day. He keeps that hat now (what is left of it), and, of a winter's evening, when the pipes are lit and the boys are telling stretchers about the dangers they have passed through, George brings it down and shows it round, and the stirring tale is told anew, with fresh exaggerations every time.

Harris got off with merely a flesh wound.

After that I took the tin off myself, and hammered at it with the mast till I was worn out and sick at heart, whereupon Harris took it in hand.

We beat it out flat; we beat it back square; we battered it into every form known to geometry – but we could not make a hole in it. Then George went at it, and knocked it into a shape, so strange, so weird, so unearthly in its wild hideousness, that he got frightened and threw away the mast. Then we all three sat round it on the grass and looked at it.

There was one great dent across the top that had the appearance of a mocking grin, and it drove us furious, so that Harris rushed at the thing, and caught it up, and flung it far into the middle of the river, and as it sank we hurled our curses at it, and we got into the boat and rowed away from the spot, and never paused till we reached Maidenhead.

Maidenhead itself is too snobby to be pleasant. It is the haunt of the river swell and his overdressed female companion. It is the town of showy hotels, patronized chiefly by dudes and ballet girls. It is the witch's kitchen from which go forth those demons of the river – steam-launches. The *London Journal* duke always has his 'little place' at Maidenhead; and the heroine of the three-volume novel always dines there when she goes out on the spree with somebody else's husband.

We went through Maidenhead quickly, and then eased up, and took leisurely that grand reach beyond Boulter's and Cookham locks. Cliveden Woods still wore their dainty dress of spring, and rose up, from the water's edge, in one long harmony of blended shades of fairy green. In its unbroken loveliness this is, perhaps, the sweetest stretch of all the river, and lingeringly we slowly drew our little boat away from its deep peace.

We pulled up in the backwater, just below Cookham, and

had tea; and, when we were through the lock, it was evening. A stiffish breeze had sprung up – in our favour, for a wonder; for, as a rule on the river, the wind is always dead against you whatever way you go. It is against you in the morning, when you start for a day's trip, and you pull a long distance, thinking how easy it will be to come back with the sail. Then, after tea, the wind veers round, and you have to pull hard in its teeth all the way home.

When you forget to take the sail at all, then the wind is consistently in your favour both ways. But there! this world is only a probation, and man was born to trouble as the sparks fly upward.

This evening, however, they had evidently made a mistake, and had put the wind round at our back instead of in our face. We kept very quiet about it, and got the sail up quickly before they found it out, and then we spread ourselves about the boat in thoughtful attitudes, and the sail bellied out, and strained, and grumbled at the mast, and the boat flew.

I steered.

There is no more thrilling sensation I know of than sailing. It comes as near to flying as man has got to yet – except in dreams. The wings of the rushing wind seem to be bearing you onward, you know not where. You are no longer the slow, plodding, puny thing of clay, creeping tortuously upon the ground; you are a part of Nature! Your heart is throbbing against hers. Her glorious arms are round you, raising you up against her heart! Your spirit is at one with hers; your limbs grow light! The voices of the air are singing to you. The earth seems far away and little; and the clouds so close above your head, are brothers, and you stretch your arms to them.

We had the river to ourselves, except that, far in the distance, we could see a fishing-punt, moored in midstream, on which three fishermen sat; and we skimmed over the water, and passed the wooden banks, and no one spoke.

I was steering.

As we drew nearer, we could see that the three men fishing seemed old and solemn-looking men. They sat on three chairs in the punt, and watched intently their lines. And the red sunset threw a mystic light upon the waters, and tinged with fire the towering woods, and made a golden glory of the piled-up clouds. It was an hour of deep enchantment, of ecstatic hope and longing. The little sail stood out against the purple sky, the gloaming lay around us, wrapping the world in rainbow shadows; and, behind us, crept the night.

We seemed like knights of some old legend, sailing across some mystic lake into the unknown realm of twilight, unto the great land of the sunset.

We did not go into the realm of twilight; we went slap into that punt, where those three old men were fishing. We did not know what had happened at first, because the sail shut out the view, but from the nature of the language that rose up upon the evening air, we gathered that we had come into the neighbourhood of human beings, and that they were vexed and discontented.

Harris let the sail down, and then we saw what had happened. We had knocked those three old gentlemen off their chairs into a general heap at the bottom of the boat, and they were now slowly and painfully sorting themselves out from each other, and picking fish off themselves; and as they worked, they cursed us – not with a common cursory curse, but with long, carefully-thought-out, comprehensive curses, that embraced the whole of our career, and went away into the distant future, and included all our relations, and covered everything connected with us – good, substantial curses.

Harris told them they ought to be grateful for a little excitement, sitting there fishing all day, and he also said that he was shocked and grieved to hear men their age give way to temper so.

But it did not do any good.

George said he would steer, after that. He said a mind like mine ought not to be expected to give itself away in steering boats – better let a mere commonplace human being see after that boat, before we jolly well all got drowned; and he took the lines, and brought us up to Marlow.

And at Marlow we left the boat by the bridge, and went and put up for the night at the 'Crown'.

CHAPTER 13

Marlow is one of the pleasantest river centres I know of. It is a bustling, lively little town; not very picturesque on the whole, it is true, but there are many quaint nooks and corners to be found in it, nevertheless – standing arches in the shattered bridge of Time, over which our fancy travels back to the days when Marlow Manor owned Saxon Algar for its lord, ere conquering William seized it to give to Queen Matilda, ere it passed to the Earls of Warwick or to worldly-wise Lord Paget, the councillor of four successive sovereigns.

There is lovely country round about it, too, if, after boating, you are fond of a walk, while the river itself is at its best here. Down to Cookham, past the Quarry Woods and the meadows, is a lovely reach. Dear old Quarry Woods! with your narrow, climbing paths, and little winding glades, how scented to this hour you seem with memories of sunny summer days! How haunted are your shadowy vistas with the ghosts of laughing faces! how from your whispering leaves there softly fall the voices of long ago!

From Marlow up to Sonning is even fairer yet. Grand old Bisham Abbey, whose stone walls have rung to the shouts of the Knights Templars, and which, at one time, was the home of Anne of Cleves and at another of Queen Elizabeth, is passed on the right bank just half a mile above Marlow Bridge. Bisham Abbey is rich in melodramatic properties. It contains a tapestry bed-chamber, and a secret room hid high up in the thick walls. The ghost of the Lady Hoby, who beat her little boy to death, still walks there at night, trying to wash its ghostly hands clean in a ghostly basin.

Warwick, the king-maker, rests there, careless now about such trivial things as earthly kings and earthly kingdoms; and

Salisbury, who did good service at Poitiers. Just before you come to the abbey, and right on the river's bank, is Bisham Church and, perhaps, if any tombs are worth inspecting, they are the tombs and monuments in Bisham Church. It was while floating in his boat under the Bisham beeches that Shelley, who was then living at Marlow (you can see his house now, in West Street), composed *The Revolt of Islam*.

By Hurley Weir, a little higher up, I have often thought that I could stay a month without having sufficient time to drink in all the beauty of the scene. The village of Hurley, five minutes' walk from the lock, is as old a little spot as there is on the river, dating, as it does, to quote the quaint phraseology of those dim days, 'from the time of King Sebert and King Offa'. Just past the weir (going up) is Danes' Field, where the invading Danes once encamped, during their march to Gloucestershire; and a little farther still, nestling by a sweet corner of the stream, is what is left of Medmenham Abbey.

The famous Medmenham monks, or 'Hell Fire Club', as they were commonly called, and of whom the notorious Wilkes was a member, were a fraternity whose motto was 'Do as you please', and that invitation still stands over the ruined doorway of the abbey. Many years before this bogus abbey, with its congregation of irreverent jesters, was founded, there stood upon this same spot a monastery of a sterner kind, whose monks were of a somewhat different type to the revellers that were to follow them, five hundred years afterwards.

The Cistercian monks, whose abbey stood there in the thirteenth-century, wore no clothes but rough tunics and cowls, and ate no flesh, nor fish, nor eggs. They lay upon straw, and they rose at midnight to mass. They spent the day in labour, reading, and prayer; and over all their lives there fell a silence, as of death, for no one spoke.

A grim fraternity, passing grim lives in that sweet spot, that God had made so bright! Strange that Nature's voices all around them – the soft singing of the waters, the whisperings of the river grass, the music of the rushing wind – should not have taught them a truer meaning of life than this. They listened there, through the long days, in silence, waiting for a voice from heaven; and all day long and through the solemn night it spoke to them in myriad tones, and they heard it not.

From Medmenham to sweet Hambledon Lock the river is full
of peaceful beauty, but, after it passes Greenlands, the rather
uninteresting-looking river residence of my newsagent – a quiet
unassuming old gentleman, who may often be met with about
these regions, during the summer months, sculling himself
along in easy vigorous style, or chatting genially to some old
lock-keeper, as he passes through – until well the other side of
Henley, it is somewhat bare and dull.

We got up tolerably early on the Monday morning at
Marlow, and went for a bathe before breakfast; and, coming
back, Montmorency made an awful ass of himself. The only
subject on which Montmorency and I have any serious
difference of opinion is cats. I like cats; Montmorency does not.

When I meet a cat, I say, 'Poor Pussy!' and stoop down and
tickle the side of its head; and the cat sticks up its tail in a rigid,
cast-iron manner, arches its back, and wipes its nose up against
my trousers; and all is gentleness and peace. When Montmorency meets a cat, the whole street knows about it; and there
is enough bad language wasted in ten seconds to last an
ordinary respectable man all his life, with care.

I do not blame the dog (contenting myself, as a rule, with
merely clouting his head or throwing stones at him), because I
take it that it is his nature. Fox-terriers are born with about four
times as much original sin in them as other dogs are, and it will
take years and years of patient effort on the part of us Christians
to bring about any appreciable reformation in the rowdiness of
the fox-terrier nature.

I remember being in the lobby of the Haymarket Stores one
day, and all round about me were dogs, waiting for the return of
their owners, who were shopping inside. There were a mastiff,
and one or two collies, and a St Bernard, a few retrievers and
Newfoundlands, a boar-hound, a French poodle, with plenty of
hair round its head, but mangy about the middle; a bulldog, a
few Lowther Arcade sort of animals, about the size of rats, and a
couple of Yorkshire tykes.

There they sat, patient, good, and thoughtful. A solemn
peacefulness seemed to reign in that lobby. An air of calmness
and resignation – of gentle sadness pervaded the room.

Then a sweet young lady entered, leading a meek-looking
little fox-terrier, and left him, chained up there, between the

bulldog and the poodle. He sat and looked about him for a minute. Then he cast up his eyes to the ceiling, and seemed, judging from his expression, to be thinking of his mother. Then he yawned. Then he looked round at the other dogs, all silent, grave, and dignified.

He looked at the bulldog, sleeping dreamlessly on his right. He looked at the poodle, erect and haughty, on his left. Then, without a word of warning, without the shadow of a provocation, he bit that poodle's near fore-leg, and a yelp of agony rang through the quiet shades of that lobby.

The result of his first experiment seemed highly satisfactory to him, and he determined to go on and make things lively all round. He sprang over the poodle and vigorously attacked a collie, and the collie woke up, and immediately commenced a fierce and noisy contest with the poodle. Then Foxey came back to his own place, and caught the bulldog by the ear, and tried to throw him away; and the bulldog, a curiously impartial animal, went for everything he could reach, including the hall-porter, which gave that dear little terrier the opportunity to enjoy an uninterrupted fight of his own with an equally willing Yorkshire tyke.

Anyone who knows canine nature need hardly be told that, by this time, all the other dogs in the place were fighting as if their hearths and homes depended on the fray. The big dogs fought each other indiscriminately; and the little dogs fought among themselves, and filled up their spare time by biting the legs of the big dogs.

The whole lobby was a perfect pandemonium, and the din was terrific. A crowd assembled outside in the Haymarket, and asked it if was a vestry meeting; or, if not, who was being murdered, and why? Men came with poles and ropes, and tried to separate the dogs, and the police were sent for.

And in the midst of the riot that sweet young lady returned, and snatched up that sweet little dog of hers (he had laid the tyke up for a month, and had on the expression, now, of a new-born lamb) into her arms, and kissed him, and asked him if he was killed, and what those great nasty brutes of dogs had been doing to him; and he nestled up against her, and gazed up into her face with a look that seemed to say: 'Oh, I'm so glad you've come to take me away from this disgraceful scene!'

She said that the people at the Stores had no right to allow great savage things like those other dogs to be put with respectable people's dogs, and that she had a great mind to summon somebody.

Such is the nature of fox-terriers; and, therefore, I do not blame Montmorency for his tendency to row with cats; but he wished he had not given way to it that morning.

We were, as I have said, returning from a dip, and halfway up the High Street a cat darted out from one of the houses in front of us, and began to trot across the road. Montmorency gave a cry of joy – the cry of a stern warrior who sees his enemy given over to his hands – the sort of cry Cromwell might have uttered when the Scots came down the hill – and flew after his prey.

His victim was a large black Tom. I never saw a larger cat, nor a more disreputable-looking cat. It had lost half its tail, one of its ears, and a fairly appreciable proportion of its nose. It was a long, sinewy-looking animal. It had a calm, contented air about it.

Montmorency went for that poor cat at the rate of twenty miles an hour; but the cat did not hurry up – did not seem to have grasped the idea that its life was in danger. It trotted quietly on until its would-be assassin was within a yard of it, and then it turned and sat down in the middle of the road, and looked at Montmorency with a gentle, inquiring expression, that said:

'Yes! You want me?'

Montmorency does not lack pluck; but there was some-thing about the look of that cat that might have chilled the heart of the boldest dog. He stopped abruptly, and looked back at Tom.

Neither spoke; but the conversation that one could imagine was clearly as follows:

THE CAT: 'Can I do anything for you?'
MONTMORENCY: 'No – no, thanks.'
THE CAT: 'Don't you mind speaking, if you really want anything, you know.'
MONTMORENCY (*backing down the High Street*): 'Oh, no – not at all – certainly – don't trouble. I – I am afraid I've made a mistake. I thought I knew you. Sorry I disturbed you.'

[175]

THE CAT: 'Not at all – quite a pleasure. Sure you don't want anything, now?'

MONTMORENCY (*still backing*): 'Not at all, thanks – not at all – very kind of you. Good morning.'

THE CAT: 'Good morning.'

Then the cat rose, and continued his trot; and Montmorency, fitting what he calls his tail carefully into its groove, came back to us, and took up an unimportant position in the rear.

To this day, if you say the word 'Cats!' to Montmorency, he will visibly shrink and look up piteously at you, as if to say: 'Please don't.'

We did our marketing after breakfast, and revictualled the boat for three days. George said we ought to take vegetables – that it was unhealthy not to eat vegetables. He said they were easy enough to cook, and that he would see to that; so we got ten pounds of potatoes, a bushel of peas, and a few cabbages. We got a beefsteak pie, a couple of gooseberry tarts, and a leg of mutton from the hotel; and fruit, and cakes, and bread and butter, and jam, and bacon and eggs, and other things we foraged round about the town for.

Our departure from Marlow I regard as one of our greatest successes. It was dignified and impressive, without being ostentatious. We had insisted at all the shops we had been to that the things should be sent with us then and there. None of your 'Yes, sir, I will send them off at once; the boy will be down there before you are, sir!' and then fooling about on the landing-stage, and going back to the shop twice to have a row about them, for us. We waited while the basket was packed, and took the boy with us.

We went to a good many shops, adopting this principle at each one; and the consequence was that, by the time we had finished, we had as fine a collection of boys with baskets following us around as heart could desire; and our final march down the middle of the High Street, to the river, must have been as imposing a spectacle as Marlow had seen for many a long day.

The order of the procession was as follows:

Montmorency, carrying a stick.

Two disreputable-looking curs, friends of Montmorency's.

George, carrying coats and rugs, and smoking a short pipe.
Harris, trying to walk with easy grace, while carrying a
bulged-out Gladstone bag in one hand and a bottle of
lime-juice in the other.
Greengrocer's boy and baker's boy, with baskets.
Boots from the hotel, carrying hamper.
Confectioner's boy, with basket.
Grocer's boy, with basket.
Long-haired dog.
Cheesemonger's boy, with basket.
Odd man, carrying a bag.
Bosom companion of odd man, with his hands in his pockets,
smoking a short clay.
Fruiterer's boy, with basket.
Myself, carrying three hats and a pair of boots, and trying to
look as if I didn't know it.
Six small boys, and four stray dogs.

When we got down to the landing-stage, the boatman said:

'Let me see, sir; was yours a steam-launch or a houseboat?'

On our informing him it was a double-sculling skiff, he seemed surprised.

We had a good deal of trouble with steam-launches that morning. It was just before the Henley week, and they were going up in large numbers; some by themselves, some towing house-boats. I do hate steam-launches; I suppose every rowing man does. I never see a steam-launch but I feel I should like to lure it to a lonely part of the river, and there, in the silence and the solitude, strangle it.

There is a blatant bumptiousness about a steam-launch, that has the knack of rousing every evil instinct in my nature, and I yearn for the good old days, when you could go about and tell people what you thought of them with a hatchet and a bow and arrows. The expression on the face of the man who, with his hands in his pockets, stands by the stern, smoking a cigar, is sufficient to excuse a breach of the peace by itself; and the lordly whistle for you to get out of the way would, I am confident, ensure a verdict of 'justifiable homicide', from any jury of river-men.

They used to *have* to whistle for us to get out of their way. If I may do so, without appearing boastful, I think I can honestly say that our one small boat, during that week, caused more annoyance and delay and aggravation to the steam-launches that we came across than all the other craft on the river put together.

'Steam-launch coming!' one of us would cry out, on sighting the enemy in the distance; and in an instant, everything was got ready to receive her. I would take the lines, and Harris and George would sit down beside me, all of us with our backs to the launch, and the boat would drift out quietly into midstream.

On would come the launch, whistling, and on we would go, drifting. At about a hundred yards off, she would start whistling like mad, and the people would come and lean over the side, and roar at us; but we never heard them! Harris would be telling us an anecdote about his mother, and George and I would not have missed a word of it for worlds.

Then that launch would give one final shriek of a whistle that would nearly burst the boiler, and she would reverse her engines, and blow off steam, and swing round and get aground; everyone on board of it would rush to the bow and yell at us, and the people on the bank would stand and shout at us, and all the other passing boats would stop and join in, till the whole river for miles up and down was in a state of frantic commotion. And then Harris would break off in the most interesting part of his narrative and look up with mild surprise, and say to George:

'Why, George, bless us, if here isn't a steam-launch!'

And George would answer:

'Well, do you know, I *thought* I heard something!'

Upon which we would get nervous and confused, and not know how to get the boat out of the way, and the people in the launch would crowd round and instruct us:

'Pull your right – you, you idiot! Back with your left. No, not *you* – the other one – leave the lines alone, can't you – now, both together. NOT *that* way. Oh, you – !'

Then they would lower a boat and come to our assistance; and, after a quarter of an hour's effort, would get us clean out of their way, so that they could go on; and we would thank them so much, and ask them to give us a tow. But they never would.

Another good way we discovered of irritating the aristocratic type of steam-launch, was to mistake them for a beanfeast, and ask them if they were Messrs Cubit's lot or the Bermondsey Good Templars, and could they lend us a saucepan.

Old ladies, not accustomed to the river, are always intensely nervous of steam-launches. I remember going up once from Staines to Windsor – a stretch of water peculiarly rich in these mechanical monstrosities – with a party containing three ladies of this description. It was very exciting. At the first glimpse of every steam-launch that came in view, they insisted on landing and sitting down on the bank until it was out of sight again. They said they were very sorry, but that they owed it to their families not to be foolhardy.

We found ourselves short of water at Hambledon lock; so we took our jar and went up to the lock-keeper's house to beg for some.

George was our spokesman. He put on a winning smile, and said:

'Oh, please could you spare us a little water?'

'Certainly,' replied the old gentleman; 'take as much as you want, and leave the rest.'

'Thank you so much,' murmured George, looking about him. 'Where – where do you keep it?'

'It's always in the same place, my boy,' was the stolid reply: 'just behind you.'

'I don't see it,' said George, turning round.

'Why, bless us, where's your eyes?' was the man's comment, as he twisted George round and pointed up and down the stream. 'There's enough of it to see, ain't there?'

'Oh!' exclaimed George, grasping the idea; 'but we can't drink the river, you know!'

'No; but you can drink *some* of it,' replied the old fellow. 'It's what *I've* drunk for the last fifteen years.'

George told him that his appearance, after the course, did not seem a sufficiently good advertisement for the brand; and that he would prefer it out of a pump.

We got some from a cottage a little higher up. I dare say *that* was only river water, if we had known. But we did not know, so it was all right. What the eye does not see, the stomach does not get upset over.

We tried river water once, later on in the season, but it was not a success. We were coming down-stream, and had pulled up to have tea in a backwater near Windsor. Our jar was empty, and it was a case of going without our tea or taking water from the river. Harris was for chancing it. He said it must be all right if we boiled the water. He said that the various germs of poison present in the water would be killed by the boiling. So we filled our kettle with Thames backwater, and boiled it; and very careful we were to see that it *did* boil.

We had made the tea, and were just settling down comfortably to drink it, when George, with his cup half-way to his lips, paused and exclaimed:

'What's that?'

'What's what?' asked Harris and I.

'Why that!' said George, looking westward.

Harris and I followed his gaze, and saw, coming down towards us on the sluggish current, a dog. It was one of the quietest and peacefullest dogs I have ever seen. I never met a dog who seemed more contented – more easy in its mind. It was floating dreamily on its back, with its four legs stuck up straight into the air. It was what I should call a full-bodied dog, with a well-developed chest. On he came, serene, dignified, and calm, until he was abreast of our boat, and there, among the rushes, he eased up, and settled down cosily for the evening.

George said he didn't want any tea, and emptied his cup into the water, Harris did not feel thirsty, either, and followed suit. I had drunk half mine, but I wished I had not.

I asked George if he thought I was likely to have typhoid.

He said: Oh no; he thought I had a very good chance indeed of escaping it. Anyhow, I should know in about a fortnight whether I had or had not.

We went up the backwater to Wargrave. It is a short cut, leading out of the right-hand bank about half a mile above Marsh lock, and is well worth taking, being a pretty, shady little piece of stream, besides saving nearly half a mile of distance.

Of course, its entrance is studded with posts and chains, and surrounded with notice-boards, menacing all kinds of torture, imprisonment, and death to everyone who dares set scull upon its waters – I wonder some of those riparian boors don't claim the air of the river and threaten everyone with forty shillings fine who breathes it – but the posts and chains a little skill will easily avoid; and as for the boards, you might, if you have five minutes to spare, and there is nobody about, take one or two of them down and throw them into the river.

Half-way up the backwater we got out and lunched; and it was during this lunch that George and I received rather a trying shock.

Harris received a shock, too; but I do not think Harris's shock could have been anything like so bad as the shock that George and I had over the business.

You see, it was in this way: we were sitting in a meadow. about ten yards from the water's edge, and we had just settled down comfortably to feed. Harris had the beefsteak pie between his knees, and was carving it, and George and I were waiting with our plates ready.

'Have you got a spoon there?' says Harris; 'I want a spoon to help the gravy with.'

The hamper was close behind us, and George and I both turned round to reach one out. We were not five seconds getting it. When we looked round again, Harris and the pie were gone!

It was a wide open field. There was not a tree or a bit of hedge for hundreds of yards. He could not have tumbled into the river, because we were on the water side of him, and he would have had to climb over us to do it.

George and I gazed all about. Then we gazed at each other.

'Has he been snatched up to heaven?' I queried.

'They'd hardly have taken the pie, too,' said George.

There seemed weight in this objection, and we discarded the heavenly theory.

'I suppose the truth of the matter is,' suggested George, descending to the commonplace and practicable, 'that there has been an earthquake.'

And then he added, with a touch of sadness in his voice: 'I wish he hadn't been carving that pie.'

With a sigh, we turned our eyes once more towards the spot where Harris and the pie had last been seen on earth; and there, as our blood froze in our veins and our hair stood up on end, we saw Harris's head – and nothing but his head – sticking bolt upright among the tall grass, the face very red, and bearing upon it an expression of great indignation!

George was the first to recover.

'Speak!' he cried, 'and tell us whether you are alive or dead –

and where is the rest of you?'

'Oh, don't be a stupid ass!' said Harris's head, 'I believe you did it on purpose.'

'Did what?' exclaimed George and I.

'Why, put me to sit here – darn silly trick! Here, catch hold of the pie.'

And out of the middle of the earth, as it seemed to us, rose the pie – very much mixed up and damaged; and after it scrambled Harris – tumbled, grubby, and wet.

He had been sitting, without knowing it, on the very verge of a small gully, the long grass hiding it from view; and in leaning a little back he had shot over, pie and all.

He said he had never felt so surprised in all his life, as when he first felt himself going, without being able to conjecture in the slightest what had happened. He thought at first that the end of the world had come.

Harris believes to this day that George and I planned it all beforehand. Thus does unjust suspicion follow even the most blameless; for, as the poet says, 'Who shall escape calumny?'

Who, indeed!

CHAPTER 14

We caught a breeze, after lunch, which took us gently up past Wargrave and Shiplake. Mellowed in the drowsy sunlight of a summer's afternoon, Wargrave, nestling where the river bends, makes a sweet old picture as you pass it, and one that lingers upon the retina of memory.

The 'George and Dragon' at Wargrave boasts a sign, painted on the one side by Leslie, R.A., and on the other by Hodgson of that ilk. Leslie has depicted the fight; Hodgson has imagined the scene 'After the Fight' – George, the work done, enjoying his pint of beer.

Day, the author of *Sandford and Merton*, lived and – more credit to the place still – was killed at Wargrave. In the church is a memorial to Mrs Sarah Hill, who bequeathed £1 annually, to be divided at Easter, between two boys and two girls who 'had never been undutiful to their parents; who had never been known to swear or to tell untruths, to steal, or to break windows'. Fancy giving up all that for five shillings a year! It is not worth it.

It is rumoured in the town that once, many years ago, a boy appeared who really never had done these things – or at all events, which was all that was required or could be expected, had never been *known* to do them – and thus won the crown of glory. He was exhibited for three weeks afterwards in the Town Hall, under a glass case.

What has become of the money since no one knows. They say it is always handed over to the nearest wax-works show.

Shiplake is a pretty village, but it cannot be seen from the river, being upon the hill. Tennyson was married in Shiplake Church.

The river up to Sonning winds in and out through many

islands and is very placid, hushed, and lonely. Few folk, except, at twilight, a pair or two of rustic lovers, walk along its banks. 'Arry and Lord Fitznoodle have been left behind at Henley, and dismal, dirty Reading is not yet reached. It is a part of the river in which to dream of bygone days, and vanished forms and faces, and things that might have been, but are not, confound them.

We got out at Sonning, and went for a walk round the village. It is the most fairy-tale little nook on the whole river. It is more like a stage village than one built of bricks and mortar. Every house is smothered in roses, and now, in early June, they were bursting forth in clouds of dainty splendour. If you stop at Sonning, put up at the 'Bull', behind the church. It is a veritable picture of an old country inn, with green, square courtyard in front, where, on seats beneath the trees, the old men group of an evening to drink their ale and gossip over village politics; with low, quaint rooms and latticed windows, and awkward stairs and winding passages.

We roamed about sweet Sonning for an hour or so, and then, it being too late to push on past Reading, we decided to go back to one of the Shiplake islands, and put up there for the night. It was still early when we got settled, and George said that, as we had plenty of time, it would be a splendid opportunity to try a good slap-up supper. He said he would show us what could be done up the river in the way of cooking, and suggested that, with the vegetables and the remains of the cold beef and general odds and ends, we should make an Irish stew.

It seemed a fascinating idea. George gathered wood and made a fire, and Harris and I started to peel the potatoes. I should never have thought that peeling potatoes was such an undertaking. The job turned out to be the biggest thing of its kind that I had ever been in. We began cheerfully, one might almost say skittishly, but our lightheartedness was gone by the time the first potato was finished. The more we peeled, the more peel there seemed to be left on; by the time we had got all the peel off and all the eyes out, there was no potato left – at least none worth speaking of. George came and had a look at it – it was about the size of a pea-nut. He said:

'Oh, that won't do! You're wasting them. You must scrape them.'

So we scraped them, and that was harder work than peeling. They are such an extraordinary shape, potatoes – all bumps and warts and hollows. We worked steadily for five-and-twenty minutes, and did four potatoes. Then we struck. We said we should require the rest of the evening for scraping ourselves.

I never saw such a thing as potato-scraping for making a fellow in a mess. It seemed difficult to believe that the potato-scrapings in which Harris and I stood half-smothered, could have come off four potatoes. It shows you what can be done with economy and care.

George said it was absurd to have only four potatoes in an Irish stew, so we washed half a dozen or so more, and put them in without peeling. We also put in a cabbage and about half a peck of peas. George stirred it all up, and then he said that there seemed to be a lot of room to spare, so we overhauled both the hampers, and picked out all the odds and ends and the remnants, and added them to the stew. There were half a pork pie and a bit of cold boiled bacon left, and we put them in. Then George found half a tin of potted salmon, and he emptied that into the pot.

He said that was the advantage of Irish stew: you got rid of such a lot of things. I fished out a couple of eggs that had got cracked, and we put those in. George said they would thicken the gravy.

I forget the other ingredients, but I know nothing was wasted; and I remember that, towards the end, Montmorency, who had evinced great interest in the proceedings throughout, strolled away with an earnest and thoughtful air, reappearing, a few minutes afterwards, with a dead water-rat in his mouth, which he evidently wished to present as his contribution to the dinner; whether in a sarcastic spirit, or with a genuine desire to assist, I cannot say.

We had a discussion as to whether the rat should go in or not. Harris said that he thought it would be all right, mixed up with the other things, and that every little helped; but George stood up for precedent. He said he had never heard of water-rats in Irish stew, and he would rather be on the safe side, and not try experiments.

Harris said:

'If you never try a new thing, how can you tell what it's like?

[185]

It's men such as you that hamper the world's progress. Think of the man who first tried German sausage!'

It was a great success, that Irish stew. I don't think I ever enjoyed a meal more. There was something so fresh and piquant about it. One's palate gets so tired of the old hackneyed things: here was a dish with a new flavour, with a taste like nothing else on earth.

And it was nourishing, too. As George said, there was good stuff in it. The peas and potatoes might have been a bit softer, but we all had good teeth, so that did not matter much; and as for the gravy, it was a poem – a little too rich, perhaps, for a weak stomach, but nutritious.

We finished up with tea and cherry tart. Montmorency had a fight with the kettle during tea-time, and came off a poor second.

Throughout the trip he had manifested great curiosity concerning the kettle. He would sit and watch it, as it boiled, with a puzzled expression, and would try and rouse it every now and then by growling at it. When it began to splutter and steam he regarded it as a challenge, and would want to fight it, only, at that precise moment, someone would always dash up and bear off his prey before he could get at it.

Today he determined he would be beforehand. At the first sound the kettle made, he rose, growling, and advanced towards it in a threatening attitude. It was only a little kettle, but it was full of pluck, and it up and spat at him.

'Ah! would ye!' growled Montmorency, showing his teeth; 'I'll teach ye to cheek a hard-working, respectable dog; ye miserable, long-nosed dirty-looking scoundrel, ye. Come on!'

And he rushed at that poor little kettle, and seized it by the spout.

Then, across the evening stillness, broke a blood-curdling yelp, and Montmorency left the boat, and did a constitutional three times round the island at the rate of thirty-five miles an hour, stopping every now and then to bury his nose in a bit of cool mud.

From that day Montmorency regarded the kettle with a mixture of awe, suspicion, and hate. Whenever he saw it he would growl and back at a rapid rate, with his tail shut down, and the moment it was put upon the stove he would promptly climb out of the boat, and sit on the bank, till the whole tea business was over.

George got out his banjo after supper, and wanted to play it, but Harris objected: he said he had got a headache, and did not feel strong enough to stand it. George thought the music might do him good – said music often soothed the nerves and took away a headache; and he twanged two or three notes, just to show Harris what it was like.

Harris said he would rather have the headache.

George has never learned to play the banjo to this day. He has had too much all-round discouragement to meet. He tried on two or three evenings, while we were up the river, to get a little practice, but it was never a success. Harris's language used to be enough to unnerve any man; added to which, Montmorency would sit and howl steadily, right through the performance. It was not giving the man a fair chance.

'What's he want to howl like that for when I'm playing?' George would exclaim indignantly, while taking aim at him with a boot.

'What do you want to play like that for when he is howling?' Harris would retort, catching the boot. 'You let him alone. He can't help howling. He's got a musical ear, and your playing *makes* him howl.'

So George determined to postpone study of the banjo until he reached home. But he did not get much opportunity even there. Mrs P. used to come up and say she was very sorry – for herself, she liked to hear him – but the lady upstairs was in a very delicate state, and the doctor was afraid it might injure the child.

Then George tried taking it out with him late at night and practising round the square. But the inhabitants complained to the police about it, and a watch was set for him one night, and he was captured. The evidence against him was very clear, and he was bound over to keep the peace for six months.

He seemed to lose heart in the business after that. He did make one or two feeble efforts to take up the work again when the six months had elapsed, but there was always the same coldness – the same want of sympathy on the part of the world to fight against; and, after a while, he despaired altogether, and advertised the instrument for sale at a great sacrifice – 'owner having no further use for same' – and took to learning card tricks instead.

It must be disheartening work learning a musical instrument. You would think that Society, for its own sake, would do all it could to assist a man to acquire the art of playing a musical instrument. But it doesn't!

I knew a young fellow once who was studying to play the bagpipes, and you would be surprised at the amount of opposition he had to contend with. Why, not even from the members of his own family did he receive what you call active encouragement. His father was dead against the business from the beginning, and spoke quite unfeelingly on the subject.

My friend used to get up early in the morning to practice, but he had to give that plan up, because of his sister. She was somewhat religiously inclined, and she said it seemed such an awful thing to begin the day like that.

So he sat up at night instead, and played after the family had gone to bed, but that did not do, as it got the house such a bad name. People, going home late, would stop outside to listen, and then put it about all over the town, and next morning, that a fearful murder had been committed at Mr Jefferson's the night before; and would describe how they had heard the victim's shrieks and the brutal oaths and curses of the murderer, followed by the prayer for mercy, and the last dying gurgle of the corpse.

So they let him practise in the day-time, in the back kitchen with all the doors shut; but his more successful passages could generally be heard in the sitting-room, in spite of these precautions, and would affect his mother almost to tears.

She said it put her in mind of her poor father (he had been swallowed by a shark, poor man, while bathing off the coast of New Guinea – where the connexion came in, she could not explain).

Then they knocked up a little place for him at the bottom of the garden, about a quarter of a mile from the house, and made him take the machine down there when he wanted to work it; and sometimes a visitor would come to the house who knew nothing of the matter, and they would forget to tell him all about it and caution him, and he would go out for a stroll round the garden and suddenly get within earshot of those bagpipes without being prepared for it, or knowing what it was. If he were a man of strong mind, it only gave him fits; but a person of mere average intellect is usually sent mad.

There is, it must be confessed, something very sad about the early efforts of an amateur in bagpipes. I have felt that myself when listening to my young friend. They appear to be a trying instrument to perform upon. You have to get enough breath for the whole tune before you start – at least, so I gathered from watching Jefferson.

He would begin magnificently with a wild, full, come-to-the-battle sort of note, that quite roused you. But he would get more and more piano as he went on, and the last verse generally collapsed in the middle with a splutter and a hiss.

You want to be in good health to play the bagpipes.

Young Jefferson only learnt to play one tune on those bagpipes: but I never heard any complaints about the insufficiency of his repertoire – none whatever. This tune was 'The Campbells are Coming, Hooray – Hooray!' so he said, though his father always held that it was 'The Blue Bells of Scotland'. Nobody seemed quite sure what it was exactly, but they all agreed that it sounded Scotch.

Strangers were allowed three guesses, and most of them guessed a different tune each time.

Harris was disagreeable after supper – I think it must have been the stew that had upset him: he is not used to high living – so George and I left him in the boat, and settled to go for a mooch round Henley. He said he should have a glass of whisky and a pipe, and fix things up for the night. We were to shout when we returned, and he would row over from the island and fetch us.

'Don't go to sleep, old man,' we said as we started.

'Not much fear of that while this stew is on,' he grunted, as he pulled back to the island.

Henley was getting ready for the regatta, and was full of bustle. We met a goodish number of men we knew about the town, and in their pleasant company the time slipped by somewhat quickly; so that it was nearly eleven o'clock before we set off on our four-mile walk home – as we had learned to call our little craft by this time.

It was a dismal night, coldish, with a thin rain falling; and as we trudged through the dark, silent fields, talking low to each other, and wondering if we were going right or not, we thought of the cosy boat, with the bright light streaming through the tight-drawn canvas; of Harris and Montmorency, and the whisky, and wished that we were there.

We conjured up the picture of ourselves inside, tired and a little hungry; of the gloomy river and the shapeless trees; and like a giant glow-worm underneath them, our dear old boat, so snug and warm and cheerful. We could see ourselves at supper there, pecking away at cold meat, and passing each other chunks of bread; we could hear the cheery clatter of our knives, the laughing voices, filling all the space, and over-flowing through the opening out into the night. And we hurried on to realize the vision.

We struck the tow-path at length, and that made us happy; because prior to this we had not been sure whether we were walking towards the river or away from it, and when you are tired and want to go to bed, uncertainties like that worry you. We passed Shiplake as the clock was striking the quarter to twelve; and then George said, thoughtfully:

'You don't happen to remember which of the islands it was, do you?'

'No,' I replied, beginning to grow thoughtful too, 'I don't. How many are there?'

'Only four,' answered George. 'It will be all right, if he's awake.'

'And if not?' I queried; but we dismissed that train of thought.

We shouted when we came opposite the first island, but there was no response; so we went to the second, and tried there, and obtained the same result.

'Oh! I remember now,' said George; 'it was the third one.'

And we ran on hopefully to the third one, and hallooed.

No answer!

The case was becoming serious. It was now past midnight. The hotels at Shiplake and Henley would be crammed; and we could not go round, knocking up cottages and householders in the middle of the night, to know if they let apartments! George suggested walking back to Henley and assaulting a policeman, and so getting a night's lodging in the station-house. But then there was the thought, 'Suppose he only hits us back and refuses to lock us up!'

We could not pass the whole night fighting policemen. Besides, we did not want to overdo the thing and get six months.

We despairingly tried what seemed in the darkness to be the fourth island, but met with no better success. The rain was coming down fast now, and evidently meant to last. We were wet to the skin, and cold and miserable. We began to wonder whether there were only four islands or more, or whether we were near the islands at all, or whether we were anywhere within a mile of where we ought to be, or in the wrong part of the river altogether; everything looked so strange and different in the darkness. We began to understand the sufferings of the Babes in the Wood.

Just when we had given up all hope – yes, I know that is always the time that things do happen in novels and tales; but I can't help it. I resolved when I began to write this book, that I would be strictly truthful in all things; and so I will be, even if I have to employ hackneyed phrases for the purpose.

It *was* just when we had given up all hope, and I must therefore say so. Just when we had given up all hope, then, I suddenly caught sight, a little way below us, of a strange, weird sort of glimmer flickering amongst the trees on the opposite bank. For an instant I thought of ghosts; it was such a shadowy, mysterious light. The next moment it flashed across me that it was our boat, and I sent up such a yell across the water that made the night seem to shake in its bed.

We waited breathless for a minute, and then – oh! divinest of music of the darkness! – we heard the answering bark of Montmorency. We shouted back loud enough to wake the Seven Sleepers – I never could understand myself why it should take more noise to waken seven sleepers than one – and, after what seemed an hour, but what was really, I suppose, about five minutes, we saw the lighted boat creeping slowly over the blackness, and heard Harris's sleepy voice asking where we were.

There was an unaccountable strangeness about Harris. It was something more than mere ordinary tiredness. He pulled the boat against a part of the bank from which it was quite impossible for us to get into it, and immediately went to sleep.

It took us an immense amount of screaming and roaring to wake him up again, and put some sense into him; but we succeeded at last, and got safely on board.

Harris had a sad expression on him, so we noticed, when we got into the boat. He gave you the idea of a man who had been through trouble. We asked him if anything had happened, and he said –

'Swans!'

It seemed we had moored close to a swan's nest, and soon after George and I had gone, the female swan came back and kicked up a row about it. Harris had chivvied her off, and she had gone away, and fetched up her old man. Harris said he had had quite a fight with these two swans; but courage and skill had prevailed in the end, and he had defeated them.

Half an hour afterwards they returned with eighteen other swans! It must have been a fearful battle, so far as we could understand Harris's account of it. The swans had tried to drag him and Montmorency out of the boat and drown them; and he had defended himself like a hero for four hours, and had killed the lot, and they had all paddled away to die.

'How many swans did you say there were?' asked George.

'Thirty-two,' replied Harris, sleepily.

'You said eighteen just now,' said George.

'No, I didn't,' grunted Harris; 'I said twelve. Think I can't count?'

What were the real facts about these swans we never found out. We questioned Harris on the subject in the morning, and he said, 'What swans?' and seemed to think that George and I had been dreaming.

Oh, how delightful it was to be safe in the boat, after our trials and fears! We ate a hearty supper, George and I, and we should have had some toddy after it, if we could have found the whisky, but we could not. We examined Harris as to what he had done with it; but he did not seem to know what we meant by 'whisky', or what we were talking about at all. Montmorency looked as if he knew something, but said nothing.

I slept well that night, and should have slept better if it had not been for Harris. I have a vague recollection of having been woken up at least a dozen times during the night by Harris wandering about the boat with the lantern, looking for his clothes. He seemed to be worrying about his clothes all night.

Twice he routed up George and myself to see if we were lying on his trousers. George got quite wild the second time.

'What the thunder do you want your trousers for, in the middle of the night?' he asked indignantly. 'Why don't you lie down, and go to sleep?'

I found him in trouble the next time I awoke because he could not find his socks; and my last hazy remembrance is of being rolled over on my side, and of hearing Harris muttering something about its being an extraordinary thing where his umbrella could have got to.

CHAPTER 15

We woke late the next morning, and, at Harris's earnest desire, partook of a plain breakfast, with 'non dainties'. Then we cleaned up, and put everything straight (a continual labour, which was beginning to afford me a pretty clear insight into a question that had often posed me – namely, how a woman with the work of only one house on her hands, manages to pass away her time), and, at about ten, set out on what we had determined should be a good day's journey.

We agreed that we would pull this morning, as a change from towing; and Harris thought the best arrangement would be that George and I should scull, and he steer. I did not chime in with this idea at all; I said I thought Harris would have been showing a more proper spirit if he had suggested that he and George should work, and let me rest a bit. It seemed to me that I was doing more than my fair share of the work on this trip, and I was beginning to feel strongly on the subject.

It always does seem to me that I am doing more work than I should do. It is not that I object to the work, mind you; I like work; it fascinates me. I can sit and look at it for hours. I love to keep it by me; the idea of getting rid of it nearly breaks my heart.

You cannot give me too much work; to accumulate work has almost become a passion with me; my study is so full of it now that there is hardly an inch of room for any more. I shall have to throw out a wing soon.

And I am careful of my work, too. Why, some of the work that I have by me now has been in my possession for years and years, and there isn't a finger-mark on it. I take a great pride in my work; I take it down now and then and dust it. No man keeps his work in a better state of preservation than I do.

But, though I crave for work, I still like to be fair. I do not ask for more than my proper share.

But I get it without asking for it – at least, so it appears to me – and this worries me.

George says he does not think I need trouble myself on the subject. He thinks it is only my over-scrupulous nature that makes me fear I am having more than my due; and that, as a matter of fact, I don't have half as much as I ought. But I expect he only says this to comfort me.

In a boat, I have always noticed that it is the fixed idea of each member of the crew that he is doing everything. Harris's notion was, that it was he alone who had been working, and that both George and I had been imposing upon him. George, on the other hand, ridiculed the idea of Harris's having done anything more than eat and sleep, and had a cast-iron opinion that it was he – George himself – who had done all the labour worth speaking of.

He said he had never been out with such a couple of lazy skulks as Harris and I.

That amused Harris.

'Fancy old George talking about work!' he laughed; 'why about half an hour of it would kill him. Have you ever seen George work?' he added, turning to me.

I agreed with Harris that I never had – most certainly not since we had started on this trip.

'Well, I don't see how *you* can know much about it, one way or the other,' George retorted to Harris; 'for I'm blest if you haven't been asleep half the time. Have you ever seen Harris fully awake, except at meal-times?' asked George, addressing me.

Truth compelled me to support George. Harris had been very little good in the boat, so far as helping was concerned, from the beginning.

'Well, hang it all, I've done more than old J., anyhow,' rejoined Harris.

'Well, you couldn't very well have done less,' added George.

'I suppose J. thinks he is the passenger,' continued Harris.

And that was their gratitude to me for having brought them and their wretched old boat all the way up from Kingston, and for having superintended and managed everything for them, and taken care of them, and slaved for them. It is the way of the world.

We settled the present difficulty by arranging that Harris and George should scull up past Reading, and that I should tow the boat on from there. Pulling a heavy boat against a strong stream has few attractions for me now. There was a time, long ago, when I used to clamour for the hard work: now I like to give the youngsters a chance.

I notice that most of the old river hands are similarly retiring, whenever there is any stiff pulling to be done. You can always tell the old river hand by the way in which he stretches himself out upon the cushions at the bottom of the boat, and encourages the rowers by telling them anecdotes about the marvellous feats he performed last season.

'Call what you're doing hard work?' he drawls, between his contented whiffs, addressing the two perspiring novices, who have been grinding away steadily up-stream for the last hour and a half; 'why, Jim Biffles and Jack and I, last season, pulled up from Marlow to Goring in one afternoon – never stopped once. Do you remember that, Jack?'

Jack, who has made himself a bed, in the prow, of all the rugs and coats he can collect, and who has been lying there asleep for the last two hours, partially wakes up on being thus appealed to, and recollects all about the matter, and also remembers that there was an unusually strong stream against them all the way – likewise a stiff wind.

'About thirty-four miles, I suppose, it must have been,' adds the first speaker, reaching down another cushion to put under his head.

'No – no; don't exaggerate, Tom,' murmurs Jack, reprovingly; 'thirty-three at the outside.'

And Jack and Tom, quite exhausted by this conversational effort, drop off to sleep once more. And the two simple-minded youngsters at the sculls feel quite proud of being allowed to row such wonderful oarsmen as Jack and Tom, and strain away harder than ever.

When I was a young man, I used to listen to these tales from my elders, and take them in, and swallow them, and digest every word of them, and then come up for more; but the new generation do not seem to have the simple faith of the old times.

We – George, Harris, and myself – took a 'raw 'un' up with us once last season, and we plied him with the customary stretchers about the wonderful things we had done all the way up.

We gave him all the regular ones – the time-honoured lies that have done duty up the river with every boating-man for years past – and added seven entirely original ones that we had invented for ourselves, including a really quite likely story, founded, to a certain extent, on an all but true episode, which had actually happened in a modified degree some years ago to friends of ours – a story that a mere child could have believed without injuring itself much.

And that young man mocked at them all, and wanted us to repeat the feats then and there, and to bet us ten to one that we didn't.

We got to chatting about our rowing experiences this morning, and to recounting stories of our first efforts in the art of oarsmanship. My own earliest boating recollection is of five of us contributing threepence each and taking out a curiously constructed craft on the Regent's Park lake, drying out subsequently in the park-keeper's lodge.

After that, having acquired a taste for the water, I did a good deal of rafting in various suburban brickfields – an exercise providing more interest and excitement than might be imagined, especially when you are in the middle of the pond and the proprietor of the materials of which the raft is constructed suddenly appears on the bank, with a big stick in his hand.

Your first sensation on seeing this gentleman is that, somehow or other, you don't feel equal to company and conversation, and that, if you could do so without appearing rude, you would rather avoid meeting him; and your object is, therefore, to get off on the opposite side of the pond to which he is and to go home quietly and quickly, pretending not to see him. He, on the contrary, is yearning to take you by the hand, and talk to you.

It appears that he knows your father, and is intimately acquainted with yourself, but this does not draw you towards him. He says he'll teach you to take his boards and make a raft of them; but, seeing that you know how to do this pretty well already, the offer, though doubtless kindly meant, seems a superfluous one on his part, and you are reluctant to put him to any trouble by accepting it.

His anxiety to meet you, however, is proof against all your coolness, and the energetic manner in which he dodges up and down the pond so as to be on the spot to greet you when you land is really quite flattering.

If he be of a stout, and short-winded build, you can easily avoid his advances; but, when he is of the youthful and long-legged type, a meeting is inevitable. The interview is, however, extremely brief, most of the conversation being on his part, your remarks being mostly of an exclamatory and monosyllabic order, and as soon as you can tear yourself away you do so.

I devoted some three months to rafting, and, being then as proficient as there was any need to be at that branch of the art, I determined to go in for rowing proper, and joined one of the Lea boating clubs.

Being out in a boat on the River Lea, especially on Saturday afternoons, soon makes you smart at handling a craft, and spry at escaping being run down by roughs or swamped by barges; and it also affords plenty of opportunity for acquiring the most prompt and graceful method of lying down flat at the bottom of the boat so as to avoid being chucked out into the river by passing tow-lines.

But it does not give you style. It was not till I came to the Thames that I got style. My style of rowing is very much admired now. People say it is so quaint.

George never went near the water until he was sixteen. Then he and eight other gentlemen of about the same age went down in a body to Kew one Saturday, with the idea of hiring a boat there, and pulling to Richmond and back; one of their number, a shock-headed youth, named Joskins, who had once or twice taken out a boat on the Serpentine, told them it was jolly fun, boating!

The tide was running out pretty rapidly when they reached the landing-stage, and there was a stiff breeze blowing across the river, but this did not trouble them at all, and they proceeded to select their boat.

There was an eight-oared racing outrigger drawn up on the stage; that was the one that took their fancy. They said they'd

have that one, please. The boatman was away, and only his boy
was in charge. The boy tried to damp their ardour for the
outrigger and showed them two or three very comfortable-
looking boats of the family-party build, but those would not do
at all; the outrigger was the boat they thought they would look
best in.

So the boy launched it, and they took off their coats and
prepared to take their seats. The boy suggested that George,
who, even in those days, was always the heavy man of any
party, should be number four. George said he should be happy
to be number four, and promptly stepped into bow's place and
sat down with his back to the stern. They got him into his proper
position at last, and then the others followed.

A particularly nervous boy was appointed cox, and the
steering principle explained to him by Joskins. Joskins himself
took stroke. He told the others that it was simple enough: all
they had to do was to follow him.

They said they were ready, and the boy on the landing-stage
took a boat-hook and shoved them off.

What then followed George is unable to describe in detail. He
has a confused recollection of having, immediately on starting,
received a violent blow in the small of the back from the
butt-end of number five's scull, at the same time that his own
seat seemed to disappear from under him by magic, and leave
him sitting on the boards. He also noticed, as a curious
circumstance, that number two was at the same instant lying on
his back at the bottom of the boat, with his legs in the air,
apparently in a fit.

They passed under Kew Bridge, broadside, at the rate of
eight miles an hour, Joskins being the only one who was rowing.
George, on recovering his seat, tried to help him, but, on
dipping his oar into the water, it immediately, to his intense
surprise, disappeared under the boat, and nearly took him with
it.

And the 'cox' threw both rudder lines overboard and burst
into tears.

How they got back George never knew, but it took them just
forty minutes. A dense crowd watched the entertainment from
Kew Bridge with much interest, and everybody shouted out to
them different directions. Three times they managed to get the

boat back through the arch, and three times they were carried
under it again, and every time 'cox' looked up and saw the
bridge above him he broke out into renewed sobs.

George said he little thought that afternoon that he should
ever come to really like boating.

Harris is more accustomed to sea rowing than to river work,
and says that, as an exercise, he prefers it. I don't. I remember
taking a small boat out at Eastbourne last summer: I used to do
a good deal of sea rowing years ago, and I thought I should be
all right; but I found I had forgotten the art entirely. When one
scull was deep down underneath the water, the other would be
flourishing wildly about in the air.

To get a grip of the water with both at the same time I had to
stand up. The parade was crowded with the nobility and
gentry, and I had to pull past them in this ridiculous fashion. I
landed half-way down the beach, and secured the services of an
old boatman to take me back.

I like to watch an old boatman rowing, especially one who
has been hired by the hour. There is something so beautifully
calm and restful about his method. It is so free from that fretful
haste, that vehement striving, that is every day becoming more
and more the bane of the nineteenth-century life. He is not for
ever straining himself to pass all the other boats. If another boat
overtakes him and passes him it does not annoy him; as a matter
of fact, they all do overtake him and pass him – all those that are
going his way. This would trouble and irritate some people; the
sublime equanimity of the hired boatman under the ordeal
affords us a beautiful lesson against ambition and uppishness.

Plain practical rowing of the get-the-boat-along order is not a
very difficult art to acquire, but it takes a good deal of practice
before a man feels comfortable when rowing past girls. It is the
'time' that worries a youngster. 'It's jolly funny,' he says, as for
the twentieth time within five minutes he disentangles his sculls
from yours; 'I can get on all right when I'm by myself!'

To see two novices try to keep time with one another is very
amusing. Bow finds it impossible to keep pace with stroke,
because stroke rows in such an extraordinary fashion. Stroke is
intensely indignant at this, and explains that what he has been
endeavouring to do for the last ten minutes is to adapt his
method to bow's limited capacity. Bow, in turn, then becomes

insulted, and requests stroke not to trouble his head about him (bow), but to devote his mind to getting a sensible stroke.

'Oh, shall *I* take stroke?' he adds, with the evident idea that that would at once put the whole matter right.

They splash along for another hundred yards with still moderate success, and then the whole secret of their trouble bursts upon stroke like a flash of inspiration.

'I tell you what it is: you've got my sculls,' he cries, turning to bow; 'pass yours over.'

'Well, do you know, I've been wondering how it was I couldn't get on with these,' answers bow, quite brightening up, and most willingly assisting in the exchange. '*Now* we shall be all right.'

But they are not – not even then. Stroke has to stretch his arms nearly out of their sockets to reach his sculls now; while bow's pair, at each recovery, hit him a violent blow in the chest. So they change back again, and come to the conclusion that the man has given them the wrong set altogether; and over their mutual abuse of this man they become quite friendly and sympathetic.

George said he had often longed to take to punting for a change. Punting is not as easy as it looks. As in rowing, you soon learn how to get along and handle the craft, but it takes long practice before you can do this with dignity and without getting the water all up your sleeve.

One young man I knew had a very sad accident happen to him the first time he went punting. He had been getting on so well that he had grown quite cheeky over the business, and was walking up and down the punt, working his pole with a careless grace that was quite fascinating to watch. Up he would march to the head of the punt, plant his pole, and then run along right to the other end, just like an old punter. Oh! it was grand.

And it would all have gone on being grand if he had not unfortunately, while looking round to enjoy the scenery, taken just one step more than there was any necessity for, and walked off the punt altogether. The pole was firmly fixed in the mud, and he was left clinging to it while the punt drifted away. It was an undignified position for him. A rude boy on the bank immediately yelled out to a lagging chum to 'hurry up and see a real monkey on a stick'.

I could not go to his assistance, because, as ill-luck would have it, we had not taken the proper precaution to bring out a spare pole with us. I could only sit and look at him. His expression as the pole slowly sank with him I shall never forget; there was so much thought in it.

I watched him gently let down into the water, and saw him scramble out, sad and wet. I could not help laughing, he looked such a ridiculous figure. I continued to chuckle to myself about it for some time, and then it was suddenly forced upon me that really I had got very little to laugh at when I came to think of it. Here was I, alone in a punt, without a pole, drifting helplessly down midstream – possibly towards a weir.

I began to feel very indignant with my friend for having stepped overboard and gone off in that way. He might, at all events, have left me the pole.

I drifted on for about a quarter of a mile, and then I came in sight of a fishing-punt moored in midstream, in which sat two old fishermen. They saw me bearing down upon them, and they called out to me to keep out of their way.

'I can't,' I shouted back.

'But you don't try,' they answered.

I explained the matter to them when I got nearer, and they caught me and lent me a pole. The weir was just fifty yards below. I am glad they happened to be there.

The first time I went punting was in company with three other fellows; they were going to show me how to do it. We could not all start together, so I said I would go down first and get out the punt, and then I could potter about and practise a bit until they came.

I could not get a punt out that afternoon, they were all engaged; so I had nothing else to do but to sit down on the bank, watching the river, and waiting for my friends.

I had not been sitting there long before my attention became attracted to a man in a punt who, I noticed with some surprise, wore a jacket and cap exactly like mine. He was evidently a novice at punting, and his performance was most interesting. You never knew what was going to happen when he put the pole in; he evidently did not know himself. Sometimes he shot up-stream and sometimes he shot down-stream, and at other times he simply spun round and came up the other side of the pole. And with every result he seemed equally surprised and annoyed.

The people about the river began to get quite absorbed in him after a while, and to make bets with one another as to what would be the outcome of his next push.

In the course of time my friends arrived on the opposite bank, and they stopped and watched him too. His back was towards them, and they only saw his jacket and cap. From this they immediately jumped to the conclusion that it was I, their beloved companion, who was making an exhibition of himself, and their delight knew no bounds. They commenced to chaff him unmercifully.

I did not grasp their mistake at first, and I thought, 'How rude of them to go on like that, with a perfect stranger, too!' But before I could call out and reprove them, the explanation of the matter occurred to me, and I withdrew behind a tree.

Oh, how they enjoyed themselves ridiculing that young man! For five good minutes they stood there, shouting ribaldry at him, deriding him, mocking him, jeering at him. They peppered him with stale jokes, they even made a few new ones and threw them at him. They hurled at him all the private family jokes belonging to our set, which must have been perfectly unintelligible to him. And then, unable to stand their brutal jibes any longer, he turned round on them, and they saw his face!

I was glad to notice that they had sufficient decency left in them to look very foolish. They explained to him that they had thought he was someone they knew. They said they hoped he would not deem them capable of so insulting anyone except a personal friend of their own.

Of course their having mistaken him for a friend excused it. I remember Harris telling me once of a bathing experience he had at Boulogne. He was swimming about there near the beach, when he felt himself suddenly seized by the neck from behind, and forcibly plunged under water. He struggled violently, but whoever had got hold of him seemed to be a perfect Hercules in strength, and all his efforts to escape were unavailing. He had given up kicking, and was trying to turn his thoughts upon solemn things, when his captor released him.

He regained his feet, and looked round for his would-be

murderer. The assassin was standing close by him, laughing heartily, but the moment he caught sight of Harris's face, as it emerged from the water, he started back and seemed quite concerned.

'I really beg your pardon,' he stammered confusedly, 'but I took you for a friend of mine!'

Harris thought it was lucky for him the man had not mistaken him for a relation, or he would probably have been drowned outright.

Sailing is a thing that wants knowledge and practice too – though, as a boy, I did not think so. I had an idea it came natural to a body, like rounders and touch. I knew another boy who held this view likewise, and so, one windy day, we thought we would try the sport. We were stopping down at Yarmouth, and we decided we would go for a trip up the Yare. We hired a sailing boat at the yard by the bridge, and started off.

'It's rather a rough day,' said the man to us, as we put off: 'better take in a reef and luff sharp when you get round the bend.'

We said we would make a point of it, and left him with a cheery 'Good morning', wondering to ourselves how you 'luffed', and where we were to get a 'reef' from, and what we were to do with it when we had got it.

We rowed until we were out of sight of the town, and then, with a wide stretch of water in front of us, and the wind blowing a perfect hurricane across it, we felt that the time had come to commence operations.

Hector – I think that was his name – went on pulling while I unrolled the sail. It seemed a complicated job, but I accomplished it at length, and then came the question, which was the top end?

By a sort of natural instinct, we, of course, eventually decided that the bottom was the top, and set to work to fix it upside-down. But it was a long time before we could get it up, either that way or any other way. The impression on the mind of the sail seemed to be that we were playing at funerals, and that I was the corpse and itself was the winding sheet.

When it found that this was not the idea, it hit me over the head with the boom, and refused to do anything.

'Wet it,' said Hector; 'drop it over and get it wet.'

He said people in ships always wetted the sails before they put them up. So I wetted it; but that only made matters worse than they were before. A dry sail clinging to your legs and wrapping itself round your head is not pleasant, but, when the sail is sopping wet, it becomes quite vexing.

We did get the thing up at last, the two of us together. We fixed it, not exactly upside-down – more sideways like – and we tied it up to the mast with the painter, which we cut off for the purpose.

That the boat did not upset I simply state as a fact. Why it did not upset I am unable to offer any reason. I have often thought about the matter since, but I have never succeeded in arriving at any satisfactory explanation of the phenomenon.

Possibly the result may have been brought about by the natural obstinacy of all things in this world. The boat may possibly have come to the conclusion, judging from a cursory view of our behaviour, that we had come out for a morning's suicide, and had thereupon determined to disappoint us. That is the only suggestion I can offer.

By clinging like grim death to the gunwale, we just managed to keep inside the boat, but it was exhausting work. Hector said that pirates and other seafaring people generally lashed the rudder to something or other, and hauled in the main top-jib, during severe squalls, and thought we ought to try to do something of the kind; but I was for letting her have her head to the wind.

As my advice was by far the easiest to follow, we ended by adopting it, and contrived to embrace the gunwale and give her her head.

The boat travelled up-stream for about a mile at a pace I have never sailed at since, and don't want to again. Then, at a bend, she heeled over till half her sail was under water. Then she righted herself by a miracle and flew for a long low bank of soft mud.

That mud-bank saved us. The boat ploughed its way into the middle of it and then stuck. Finding that we were once more able to move according to our ideas, instead of being pitched and thrown about like peas in a bladder, we crept forward, and cut down the sail.

We had had enough sailing. We did not want to overdo the

thing and get a surfeit of it. We had had a sail – a good all-round, exciting, interesting sail – and now we thought we would have a row, just for a change like.

We took the sculls and tried to push the boat off the mud, and, in doing so, we broke one of the sculls. After that we proceeded with great caution, but they were a wretched old pair, and the second one cracked almost easier than the first, and left us helpless.

The mud stretched out for about a hundred yards in front of us, and behind us was the water. The only thing to be done was to sit and wait until someone came by.

It was not the sort of day to attract people out on the river, and it was three hours before a soul came in sight. It was an old fisherman who, with immense difficulty, at last rescued us, and we were towed back in an ignominious fashion to the boatyard.

What between tipping the man who had brought us home, and paying for the broken sculls, and for having been out four hours and a half, it cost us a pretty considerable number of weeks' pocket-money, that sail. But we learned experience, and they say that it is always cheap at any price.

CHAPTER 16

We came in sight of Reading about eleven. The river is dirty and dismal here. One does not linger in the neighbourhood of Reading. The town itself is a famous old place, dating from the dim days of King Ethelred, when the Danes anchored their warships in the Kennet, and started from Reading to ravage all the land of Wessex; and here Ethelred and his brother Alfred fought and defeated them, Ethelred doing the praying and Alfred the fighting.

In later years, Reading seems to have been regarded as a handy place to run down to, when matters were becoming unpleasant in London. Parliament generally rushed off to Reading whenever there was a plague on at Westminster; and, in 1625, the Law followed suit, and all the courts were held at Reading. It must have been worth while having a mere ordinary plague now and then in London to get rid of both the lawyers and the Parliament.

During the Parliamentary struggle, Reading was besieged by the Earl of Essex, and, a quarter of a century later, the Prince of Orange routed King James's troops there.

Henry I lies buried at Reading, in the Benedictine abbey founded by him there, the ruins of which may still be seen; and, in this same abbey, great John of Gaunt was married to the Lady Blanche.

At Reading lock we came up with a steam-launch, belonging to some friends of mine, and they towed us up to within about a mile of Streatley. It is very delightful being towed up by a launch. I prefer it myself to rowing. The run would have been more delightful still, if it had not been for a lot of wretched small boats that were continually getting in the way of our launch, and, to avoid running down which, we had to be continually easing and stopping. It is really most annoying, the manner in which these rowing boats get in the way of one's launch up the river; something ought to be done to stop it.

And they are so confoundedly impertinent, too, over it. You can whistle till you nearly burst your boiler before they will trouble themselves to hurry. I would have one or two of them run down now and then, if I had my way, just to teach them all a lesson.

The river becomes very lovely from a little above Reading. The railway rather spoils it near Tilehurst, but from Maple-durham up to Streatley it is glorious. A little above Maple-durham lock you pass Hardwick house, where Charles I played bowls. The neighbourhood of Pangbourne, where the quaint little Swan Inn stands, must be as familiar to the *habitués* of the Art Exhibitions as it is to its own inhabitants.

My friends' launch cast us loose just below the grotto and then Harris wanted to make out that it was my turn to pull. This seemed to me most unreasonable. It had been arranged in the morning that I should bring the boat up to three miles above Reading. Well, here we were, ten miles above Reading! Surely it was now their turn again.

I could not get either George or Harris to see the matter in its proper light, however; so, to save argument, I took the sculls. I had not been pulling for more than a minute or so, when George noticed something black floating on the water, and we drew up to it. George leant over, as we neared it, and laid hold of it. And then he drew back with a cry, and a blanched face.

It was the dead body of a woman. It lay very lightly on the water, and the face was sweet and calm. It was not a beautiful face; it was too prematurely aged-looking, too thin and drawn, to be that; but it was a gentle, lovable face, in spite of its stamp of pinch and poverty, and upon it was that look of restful peace that comes to the faces of the sick sometimes when at last the pain has left them.

Fortunately for us – we having no desire to be kept hanging about coroners' courts – some men on the bank had seen the body too, and now took charge of it from us.

We found out the woman's story afterwards. Of course it was the old, old vulgar tragedy. She had loved and been deceived – or had deceived herself. Anyhow, she had sinned – some of us do now and then – and her family and friends, naturally shocked and indignant, had closed their doors against her.

Left to fight the world alone, with the millstone of her shame around her neck, she had sunk ever lower and lower. For a while she had kept both herself and the child on the twelve shillings a week that twelve hours' drudgery a day procured her, paying six shillings out of it for the child, and keeping her own body and soul together on the remainder.

Six shillings a week does not keep body and soul together very unitedly. They want to get away from each other when there is only such a very slight bond as that between them; and one day, I suppose, the pain and the dull monotony of it all had stood before her eyes plainer than usual, and the mocking spectre had frightened her. She had made one last appeal to friends, but, against the chill wall of their respectability, the voice of the erring outcast fell unheeded; and then she had gone to see her child – and held it in her arms and kissed it, in a weary, dull sort of way, and without betraying any particular emotion of any kind, and had left it, after putting into its hand a penny box of chocolate she had bought it, and afterwards, with her last few shillings, had taken a ticket and come down to Goring.

It seemed that the bitterest thoughts of her life must have centred about the wooded reaches and the bright green meadows around Goring; but women strangely hug the knife that stabs them, and, perhaps, amidst the gall, there may have mingled also sunny memories of sweetest hours, spent upon those shadowed deeps over which the great trees bend their branches down so low.

She had wandered about the woods by the river's brink all day, and then, when evening fell and the grey twilight spread its dusky robe upon the waters, she stretched her arms out to the silent river that had known her sorrow and her joy. And the old river had taken her into its gentle arms, and had laid her weary head upon its bosom, and had hushed away the pain.

Thus she had sinned in all things – sinned in living and in dying. God help her! and all other sinners, if any more there be.

Goring on the left bank and Streatley on the right are both or either charming places to stay at for a few days. The reaches down to Pangbourne woo one for a sunny sail or for a moonlight row, and the country round about is full of beauty. We had intended to push on to Wallingford that day, but the sweet smiling face of the river here lured us to linger for a while; and so we left our boat at the bridge, and went up into Streatley, and lunched at the 'Bull'; much to Montmorency's satisfaction.

They say that the hills on each side of the stream here once joined and formed a barrier across what is now the Thames, and that then the river ended there above Goring in one vast lake. I am not in a position either to contradict or affirm this statement, I simply offer it.

It is an ancient place, Streatley, dating back, like most riverside towns and villages, to British and Saxon times. Goring is not nearly so pretty a little spot to stop at as Streatley, if you have your choice; but it is passing fair enough in its way, and is nearer the railway in case you want to slip off without paying your hotel bill.

CHAPTER 17

We stayed two days at Streatley, and got our clothes washed. We had tried washing them ourselves, in the river, under George's superintendence, and it had been a failure. Indeed, it had been more than a failure, because we were worse off after we had washed our clothes than we were before. Before we had washed them, they had been very, very dirty, it is true; but they were just wearable. *After* we had washed them – well, the river between Reading and Henley was much cleaner, after we had washed our clothes in it, than it was before. All the dirt contained in the river between Reading and Henley we collected, during that wash, and worked it into our clothes.

The washerwoman at Streatley said she felt she owed it to herself to charge us just three times the usual price for that wash. She said it had not been like washing, it had been more in the nature of excavating.

We paid the bill without a murmur.

The neighbourhood of Streatley and Goring is a great fishing centre. There is some excellent fishing to be had here. The river abounds in pike, roach, dace, gudgeon, and eels, just here; and you can sit and fish for them all day.

Some people do. They never catch them. I never knew anybody catch anything up the Thames, except minnows and dead cats, but that has nothing to do, of course, with fishing! The local fisherman's guide doesn't say a word about catching anything. All it says is the place is 'a good station for fishing'; and from what I have seen of the district, I am quite prepared to bear out this statement.

There is no spot in the world where you can get more fishing, or where you can fish for a longer period. Some fishermen come here and fish for a day, and others stop and fish for a month.

You can hang on and fish for a year, if you want to: it will be all the same.

The *Angler's Guide to the Thames* says that 'jack and perch are also to be had about here', but there the *Angler's Guide* is wrong. Jack and perch may *be* about there. Indeed, I know for a fact that they are. You can *see* them there in shoals, when you are out for a walk along the banks; they come and stand half out of the water with their mouths open for biscuits. And, if you go for a bathe, they crowd round, and get in your way and irritate you. But they are not to be 'had' by a bit of worm on the end of a hook, nor anything like it – not they!

I am not a good fisherman myself. I devoted a considerable amount of attention to the subject at one time, and was getting on, as I thought, fairly well; but the old hands told me that I should never be any real good at it, and advised me to give it up. They said that I was an extremely neat thrower, and that I seemed to have plenty of gumption for the thing, and quite enough constitutional laziness. But they were sure I should never make anything of a fisherman. I had not got sufficient imagination.

They said that as a poet, or a shilling shocker, or a reporter, or anything of that kind, I might be satisfactory, but that, to gain any position as a Thames angler, would require more play of fancy, more power of invention than I appeared to possess.

Some people are under the impression that all that is required to make a good fisherman is the ability to tell lies easily and without blushing; but this is a mistake. Mere bald fabrication is useless; the veriest tyro can manage that. It is in the circumstantial detail, the embellishing touches of probability, the general air of scrupulous – almost of pedantic – veracity, that the experienced angler is seen.

Anybody can come in and say, 'Oh, I caught fifteen dozen perch yesterday evening'; or 'Last Monday I landed a gudgeon, weighing eighteen pounds, and measuring three feet from the tip of the tail'.

There is no art, no skill, required for that sort of thing. It shows pluck, but that is all.

No; your accomplished angler would scorn to tell a lie, that way. His method is a study in itself.

He comes in quietly with his hat on, appropriates the most

comfortable chair, lights his pipe, and commences to puff in silence. He lets the youngsters brag away for a while, and then, during a momentary lull, he removes the pipe from his mouth, and remarks, as he knocks the ashes out against the bars:

'Well, I had a haul on Tuesday evening that it's not much good my telling anybody about.'

'Oh! Why's that?' they ask.

'Because I don't expect anybody would believe me if I did,' replies the old fellow calmly, and without even a tinge of bitterness in his tone, as he refills his pipe, and requests the landlord to bring him three of Scotch, cold.

There is a pause after this, nobody feeling sufficiently sure of himself to contradict the old gentleman. So he has to go on by himself without any encouragement.

'No,' he continues thoughtfully; 'I shouldn't believe it myself if anybody told it to me, but it's a fact, for all that. I had been sitting there all the afternoon and had caught literally nothing – except a few dozen dace and a score of jack; and I was just about giving it up as a bad job when I suddenly felt a rather smart pull at the line. I thought it was another little one, and I went to jerk it up. Hang me, if I could move the rod! It took me half an hour – half an hour, sir! – to land that fish; and every moment I thought the line was going to snap! I reached him at last, and what do you think it was? A sturgeon! a forty-pound sturgeon! taken on a line, sir! Yes, you may well look surprised – I'll have another three of Scotch, landlord, please.'

And then he goes on to tell of the astonishment of everybody who saw it; and what his wife said, when he got home, and of what Joe Buggles thought about it.

I asked the landlord of an inn up the river once, if it did not injure him, sometimes, listening to the tales that the fishermen about there told him; and he said:

'Oh, no; not now, sir. It did used to knock me over a bit at first, but, lor love you! me and the missus we listen to 'em all day now. It's what you're used to, you know. It's what you're used to.'

I knew a young man once, he was a most conscientious fellow and, when he took to fly-fishing, he determined never to exaggerate his hauls by more than twenty-five per cent.

'When I have caught forty fish,' said he, 'then I will tell

people that I have caught fifty, and so on. But I will not lie any more than that, because it is sinful to lie.'

But the twenty-five per cent plan did not work well at all. He never was able to use it. The greatest number of fish he ever caught in one day was three, and you can't add twenty-five per cent to three – at least, not in fish.

So he increased his percentage to thirty-three and a third, but that, again, was awkward, when he had caught one or two; so, to simplify matters, he made up his mind to just double the quantity.

He stuck to this arrangement for a couple of months, and then he grew dissatisfied with it. Nobody believed him when he told them that he only doubled, and he, therefore, gained no credit that way whatever, while his moderation put him at a disadvantage among the other anglers. When he had really caught three small fish, and said he had caught six, it used to make him quite jealous to hear a man, whom he knew for a fact had only caught one, going about telling people he had landed two dozen.

So, eventually he made one final arrangement with himself, which he has religiously held to ever since, and that was to count each fish that he caught as ten, and to assume ten to begin with. For example, if he did not catch any fish at all, then he said he had caught ten fish – you could never catch less than ten fish by his system; that was the foundation of it. Then, if by any chance he really did catch one fish, he called it twenty, while two fish would count thirty, three forty, and so on.

It is a simple and easily worked plan, and there has been some talk lately of its being made use of by the angling fraternity in general. Indeed, the Committee of the Thames Anglers' Association did recommend its adoption about two years ago, but some of the older members opposed it. They said they would consider the idea if the number were doubled, and each fish counted as twenty.

If ever you have an evening to spare, up the river, I should advise you to drop into one of the little village inns, and take a seat in the tap-room. You will be nearly sure to meet one or two old rod-men, sipping their toddy there, and they will tell you enough fishy stories in half an hour to give you indigestion for a month.

George and I – I don't know what had become of Harris; he had gone out and had a shave, early in the afternoon, and had then come back and spent full forty minutes in pipe-claying his shoes, we had not seen him since – George and I, therefore, and the dog, left to ourselves, went for a walk to Wallingford on the second evening, and coming home, we called in at a little riverside inn, for a rest, and other things.

We went into the parlour and sat down. There was an old fellow there, smoking a long clay pipe, and we naturally began chatting.

He told us that it had been a fine day today and we told him that it had been a fine day yesterday, and then we all told each other that we thought it would be a fine day tomorrow; and George said the crops seemed to be coming up nicely.

After that it came out, somehow or other, that we were strangers in the neighbourhood, and that we were going away the next morning.

Then a pause ensued in the conversation, during which our eyes wandered round the room. They finally rested upon a dusty old glass-case, fixed very high up above the chimney-piece, and containing a trout. It rather fascinated me, that trout; it was such a monstrous fish. In fact, at first glance, I thought it was a cod.

'Ah!' said the old gentleman, following the direction of my gaze, 'fine fellow that, ain't he?'

'Quite uncommon,' I murmured; and George asked the old man how much he thought it weighed.

'Eighteen pounds six ounces,' said our friend, rising and taking down his coat. 'Yes,' he continued, 'it wur sixteen year ago, come the third o' next month, that I landed him. I caught him just below the bridge with a minnow. They told me he wur in the river, and I said I'd have him, and so I did. You don't see many fish that size about here now, I'm thinking. Good night, gentlemen, good night.'

And out he went, and left us alone.

We could not take our eyes off the fish after that. It really was a remarkably fine fish. We were still looking at it, when the local carrier, who had just stopped at the inn, came to the door of the room with a pot of beer in his hand, and he also looked at the fish.

'Good-sized trout, that,' said George, turning round to him.

'Ah! you may well say that, sir,' replied the man; and then, after a pull at his beer, he added, 'Maybe you wasn't here, sir, when that fish was caught?'

'No,' we told him. We were strangers in the neighbourhood.

'Ah!' said the carrier, 'then, of course, how should you? It was nearly five years ago that I caught that trout.'

'Oh! Was it you who caught it, then?' said I.

'Yes, sir,' replied the genial old fellow. 'I caught him just below the lock – leastways, what was the lock then – one Friday afternoon; and the remarkable thing about it is that I caught him with a fly. I'd gone out pike fishing, bless you, never thinking of a trout, and when I saw that whopper on the end of my line, blest if it didn't quite take me aback. Well, you see, he weighed twenty-six pound. Good night, gentlemen, good night.'

Five minutes afterwards a third man came in, and described how *he* had caught it early one morning, with bleak; and then he left, and a stolid, solemn-looking, middle-aged individual came in, and sat down over by the window.

None of us spoke for a while; but, at length, George turned to the new-corner, and said:

'I beg your pardon, I hope you will forgive the liberty that we – perfect strangers in the neighbourhood – are taking, but my friend here and myself would be so much obliged if you would tell us how you caught that trout up there.'

'Why, who told you I caught that trout!' was the surprised query.

We said that nobody had told us so, but somehow or other we felt instinctively that it was he who had done it.

'Well, it's a most remarkable thing – most remarkable,' answered the stolid stranger, laughing; 'because, as a matter of fact, you are quite right. I did catch it. But fancy your guessing it like that. Dear me, it's really a most remarkable thing.'

And then he went on, and told us how it had taken him half an hour to land it, and how it had broken his rod. He said he had weighed it carefully when he reached home, and it had turned the scale at thirty-four pounds.

He went in his turn, and when he was gone, the landlord came in to us. We told him the various histories we had heard

about his trout, and he was immensely amused, and we all laughed very heartily.

'Fancy Jim Bates and Joe Muggles and Mr Jones and old Billy Maunders all telling you that they had caught it. Ha! ha! ha! Well, that is good,' said the honest old fellow, laughing heartily. 'Yes, they are the sort to give it *me*, to put up in *my* parlour, if *they* had caught it, they are! Ha! ha! ha!'

And then he told us the real history of the fish. It seemed that he had caught it himself, years ago, when he was quite a lad; not by any art or skill, but by that unaccountable luck that appears to always wait upon a boy when he plays the wag from school, and goes out fishing on a sunny afternoon, with a bit of string tied on to the end of a tree.

He said that bringing home that trout had saved him from a whacking, and that even his schoolmaster had said it was worth the rule-of-three and practice put together.

He was called out of the room at this point, and George and I turned our gaze upon the fish.

It really was a most astonishing trout. The more we looked at it, the more we marvelled at it.

It excited George so much that he climbed up on the back of a chair to get a better view of it.

And then the chair slipped, and George clutched wildly at the trout-case to save himself, and down it came with a crash, George and the chair on top of it.

'You haven't injured the fish, have you?' I cried in alarm, rushing up.

'I hope not,' said George, rising cautiously and looking about.

But he had. That trout lay shattered into a thousand fragments – I say a thousand, but they may have only been nine hundred. I did not count them.

We thought it strange and unaccountable that a stuffed trout should break up into little pieces like that.

And so it would have been strange and unaccountable, if it had been a stuffed trout, but it was not.

That trout was plaster of Paris.

CHAPTER 18

We left Streatley early the next morning, and pulled up to Culham, and slept under the canvas, in the backwater there.

The river is not extraordinarily interesting between Streatley and Wallingford. From Cleeve you get a stretch of six and a half miles without a lock. I believe this is the longest uninterrupted stretch anywhere above Teddington, and the Oxford Club make use of it for their trial eights.

But however satisfactory this absence of locks may be to rowing men, it is to be regretted by the mere pleasure-seeker.

For myself, I am fond of locks. They pleasantly break the monotony of the pull. I like sitting in the boat and slowly rising out of the cool depths up into new reaches and fresh views; or sinking down, as it were, out of the world, and then waiting, while the gloomy gates creak, and the narrow strip of daylight between them widens till the fair smiling river lies full before you, and you push your little boat out from its brief prison on to the welcoming waters once again.

They are picturesque little spots, these locks. The stout old lock-keeper, or his cheerful-looking wife, or bright-eyed daughter, are pleasant folk to have a passing chat with.* You meet other boats there, and river gossip is exchanged. The Thames would not be the fairyland it is without its flower-decked locks.

Talking of locks reminds me of an accident George and I very nearly had one summer's morning at Hampton Court.

It was a glorious day, and the lock was crowded; and, as is a

---

*Or rather *were*. The Conservancy of late seems to have constituted itself into a society for the employment of idiots. A good many of the new lock-keepers, especially in the more crowded portions of the river, are excitable, nervous old men quite unfitted for their post.

common practice up the river, a speculative photographer was taking a picture of us all as we lay upon the rising waters.

I did not catch what was going on at first, and was, therefore, extremely surprised at noticing George hurriedly smooth out his trousers, ruffle his hair, and stick his cap on in a rakish manner at the back of his head, and then, assuming an expression of mingled affability and sadness, sit down in a graceful attitude, and try to hide his feet.

My first idea was that he had suddenly caught sight of some girl he knew, and I looked about to see who it was. Everybody in the lock seemed to have been suddenly struck wooden. They were all standing or sitting about in the most quaint and curious attitudes I have ever seen off a Japanese fan. All the girls were smiling. Oh, they did look so sweet! And all the fellows were frowning, and looking stern and noble.

And then, at last, the truth flashed across me, and I wondered if I should be in time. Ours was the first boat, and it would be unkind of me to spoil the man's picture, I thought.

So I faced round quickly, and took up a position in the prow, where I leant with careless grace upon the hitcher, in an attitude suggestive of agility and strength. I arranged my hair with a curl over the forehead, and threw an air of tender wistfulness into my expression, mingled with a touch of cynicism, which I am told suits me.

As we stood, waiting for the eventful moment, I heard someone behind call out:

'Hi! look at your nose.'

I could not turn round to see what was the matter, and whose nose it was that was to be looked at. I stole a sideglance at George's nose! It was all right – at all events, there was nothing wrong with it that could be altered. I squinted down at my own and that seemed all that could be expected also.

'Look at your nose, you stupid ass!' came the same voice again, louder.

And then another voice cried:

'Push your nose out, can't you, you – you two with the dog!'

Neither George nor I dared to turn round. The man's hand was on the cap and the picture might be taken any moment. Was it us they were calling to? What was the matter with our noses? Why were they to be pushed out!

But now the whole lock started yelling, and a stentorian voice from the back shouted:

'Look at your boat, sir; you in the red and black caps. It's your two corpses that will get taken in that photo, if you ain't quick.'

We looked then, and saw that the nose of our boat had got fixed under the woodwork of the lock, while the in-coming water was rising all around it, and tilting it up. In another moment we should be over. Quick as thought, we each seized an oar, and a vigorous blow against the side of the lock with the butt-ends released the boat, and sent us sprawling on our backs.

We did not come out well in that photograph, George and I. Of course, as was to be expected, our luck ordained it that the man should set his wretched machine in motion at the precise moment that we were both lying on our backs with a wild expression of 'Where am I? and what is it?' on our faces, and our feet waving madly in the air.

Our feet were undoubtedly the leading article in that photograph. Indeed, very little else was to be seen. They filled up the foreground entirely. Behind them, you caught glimpses of the other boats, and bits of the surrounding scenery; but everything and everybody else in the lock looked so utterly insignificant and paltry compared with our feet, that all the other people felt quite ashamed of themselves, and refused to subscribe to the picture.

The owner of one steam-launch, who had bespoke six copies, rescinded the order on seeing the negative. He said he would take them if anybody could show him his launch, but nobody could. It was somewhere behind George's right foot.

There was a good deal of unpleasantness over the business. The photographer thought we ought to take a dozen copies each, seeing that the photo was about nine-tenths us, but we declined. We said we had no objection to being photo'd full-length, but we preferred being taken the right way up.

Wallingford, six miles above Streatley, is a very ancient town, and has been an active centre for the making of English history. It was a rude, mud-built town in the time of the Britons, who squatted there, until the Roman legions evicted them; and replaced their clay-baked walls by mighty fortifications, the trace of which Time has not yet succeeded in sweeping away, so well those old-world masons knew how to build.

But Time, though he halted at Roman walls, soon crumbled Romans to dust; and on the ground, in later years, fought savage Saxons and huge Danes, until the Normans came.

It was a walled and fortified town up to the time of the Parliamentary war, when it suffered a long and bitter siege from Fairfax. It fell at last, and then the walls were razed.

From Wallingford up to Dorchester the neighbourhood of the river grows more hilly, varied and picturesque. Dorchester stands half a mile from the river. It can be reached by paddling up the Thames if you have a small boat; but the best way is to leave the river at Day's lock, and take a walk across the fields. Dorchester is a delightfully peaceful old place, nestling in stillness and silence and drowsiness.

Dorchester, like Wallingford, was a city in ancient British times; it was then called Caer Doren, 'the city on the water'. In more recent times the Romans formed a great camp here, the fortifications surrounding which now seem like low, even hills. In Saxon days it was the capital of Wessex. It is very old, and it was very strong and great once. Now it sits aside from the stirring world, and nods and dreams.

Round Clifton Hampden, itself a wonderfully pretty village, old-fashioned, peaceful and dainty with flowers, the river scenery is rich and beautiful. If you stay the night on land at Clifton, you cannot do better than put up at the 'Barley Mow'. It is, without exception, I should say, the quaintest, most old-world inn up the river. It stands on the right of the bridge, quite away from the village. Its low-pitched gables and thatched roof and latticed windows give it quite a story-book appearance, while inside it is even still more once-upon-timeyfied.

It would not be a good place for the heroine of a modern novel to stay at. The heroine of a modern novel is always 'divinely tall', and she is ever 'drawing herself up to her full height'. At the 'Barley Mow' she would bump her head against the ceiling each time she did this.

It would also be a bad house for a drunken man to put up at. There are too many surprises in the way of unexpected steps down into this room and up into that; and as for getting upstairs to his bedroom, or ever finding his bed when he got up, either operation would be an utter impossibility to him.

We were up early the next morning, as we wanted to be in
Oxford by the afternoon. It is surprising how early one *can* get
up, when camping out. One does not yearn for 'just another five
minutes' nearly so much, lying wrapped up in a rug on the
boards of a boat, with a Gladstone bag for a pillow, as one does
in a feather bed. We had finished breakfast, and were through
Clifton lock by half past eight.

From Clifton to Culham the river banks are flat, monoto-
nous, and uninteresting, but after you get through Culham lock
– the coldest and deepest lock on the river – the landscape
improves.

At Abingdon, the river passes by the streets. Abingdon is a
typical country town of the smaller order – quiet, eminently
respectable, clean, and desperately dull. It prides itself on being
old, but whether it can compare in this respect with Wallingford
and Dorchester seems doubtful. A famous abbey stood here
once, and within what is left of its sanctified walls they brew a
bitter ale nowadays.

In St Nicholas Church, at Abingdon, there is a monument to
John Blackwall and his wife Jane, who both, after leading a
happy married life, died on the very same day, August 21, 1625;
and in St Helen's Church it is recorded that W. Lee, who died in
1637, 'had in his lifetime issue from his loins two hundred
lacking but three'. If you work this out you will find that Mr W.
Lee's family numbered one hundred and ninety-seven. Mr W.
Lee – five times Mayor of Abingdon – was, no doubt, a
benefactor to his generation, but I hope there are not many of
his kind about in this overcrowded nineteenth-century.

From Abingdon to Nuneham Courtenay is a lovely stretch.
Nuneham Park is well worth a visit. It can be viewed on
Tuesdays and Thursdays. The house contains a fine collection
of pictures and curiosities, and the grounds are very beautiful.

The pool under Sandford lasher, just behind the lock, is a
very good place to drown yourself in. The undercurrent is
terribly strong, and if you once get down into it you are all right.
An obelisk marks the spot where two men have already been
drowned, while bathing there; and the steps of the obelisk are

generally used as a diving-board by young men now who wish to see if the place really *is* dangerous.

Iffley lock and mill, a mile before you reach Oxford, is a favourite subject with the river-loving brethren of the brush. The real article, however, is rather disappointing, after the pictures. Few things, I have noticed, come quite up to the pictures of them, in this world.

We passed through Iffley lock at about half past twelve, and then, having tidied up the boat and made all ready for landing, we set to work on our last mile.

Between Iffley and Oxford is the most difficult bit of the river I know. You want to be born on that bit of water, to understand it. I have been over it a fairish number of times, but I have never been able to get the hang of it. The man who could row a straight course from Oxford to Iffley ought to be able to live comfortably, under one roof, with his wife, his mother-in-law, his eldest sister, and the old servant who was in the family when he was a baby.

First the current drives you on to the right bank, and then on to the left, then it takes you out into the middle, turns you round three times, and carries you up-stream again, and always ends by trying to smash you up against a college barge.

Of course, as a consequence of this, we got in the way of a good many other boats, during the mile, and they in ours, and, of course, as a consequence of that, a good deal of bad language occurred.

I don't know why it should be, but everybody is always so exceptionally irritable on the river. Little mishaps, that you would hardly notice on dry land, drive you nearly frantic with rage, when they occur on the water. When Harris or George makes an ass of himself on dry land, I smile indulgently; when they behave in a chuckle-head way on the river, I use the most blood-curdling language to them. When another boat gets in my way, I feel I want to take an oar and kill all the people in it.

The mildest-tempered people, when on land, become violent and bloodthirsty when in a boat. I did a little boating once with a young lady. She was naturally of the sweetest and gentlest disposition imaginable, but on the river it was quite awful to hear her.

'Oh, drat the man!' she would exclaim, when some

unfortunate sculler would get in her way; 'why don't he look where he's going?'

And, 'Oh, bother the silly old thing!' she would say indignantly, when the sail would not go up properly. And she would catch hold of it, and shake it quite brutally.

Yet, as I have said, when on shore she was kind-hearted and amiable enough.

The air of the river has a demoralizing effect upon one's temper, and this it is, I suppose, which causes even bargemen to be sometimes rude to one another, and to use language which, no doubt, in their calmer moments they regret.

We spent two very pleasant days at Oxford. There are plenty of dogs in the town of Oxford. Montmorency had eleven fights on the first day, and fourteen on the second, and evidently thought he had got to Heaven.

Among folk too constitutionally weak, or too constitutionally lazy, whichever it may be, to relish up-stream work, it is a common practice to get a boat at Oxford, and row down. For the energetic, however, the up-stream journey is certainly to be preferred. It does not seem good to be always going with the current. There is more satisfaction in squaring one's back, and fighting against it, and winning one's way forward in spite of it – at least, so I feel, when Harris and George are sculling and I am steering.

To those who do contemplate making Oxford their starting-place, I would say, take your own boat – unless, of course, you can take someone else's without any possible danger of being found out. The boats that, as a rule, are let for hire on the Thames above Marlow, are very good boats. They are fairly water-tight; and so long as they are handled with care, they rarely come to pieces, or sink. There are places in them to sit down on, and they are complete with all the necessary arrangements – or nearly all – to enable you to row them and steer them.

But they are not ornamental. The boat you hire up the river above Marlow is not the sort of boat in which you can flash about and give yourself airs. The hired up-river boat very soon puts a stop to any nonsense of that sort on the part of its occupants. That is its chief – one may say – its only recommendation.

The man in the hired up-river boat is modest and retiring. He likes to keep on the shady side underneath the trees, and to do most of his travelling early in the morning or late at night, when there are not many people about on the river to look at him.

When the man in the hired up-river boat sees anyone he knows, he gets out on the bank, and hides behind a tree.

I was one of a party who hired an up-river boat one summer, for a few days' trip. We had none of us ever seen the hired up-river boat before; and we did not know what it was when we did see it.

We had written for a boat – a double sculling skiff; and when we went down with our bags to the yard, and gave our names, the man said:

'Oh, yes; you're the party that wrote for a double sculling skiff. It's all right. Jim, fetch round *The Pride of the Thames*.'

The boy went and reappeared five minutes afterwards, struggling with an antediluvian chunk of wood, that looked as though it had been recently dug out of somewhere and dug out carelessly, so as to have been unnecessarily damaged in the process.

My own idea, on first catching sight of the object, was that it was a Roman relic of some sort, – relic of *what* I do not know, possibly of a coffin.

The neighbourhood of the upper Thames is rich in Roman relics, and my surmise seemed to me a very probable one; but our serious young man, who is a bit of a geologist, pooh-poohed my Roman relic theory, and said it was clear to the meanest intellect (in which category he seemed to be grieved that he could not conscientiously include mine) that the thing the boy had found was the fossil of a whale; and he pointed out to us various evidences proving that it must have belonged to the pre-glacial period.

To settle the dispute, we appealed to the boy. We told him not to be afraid, but to speak the plain truth: Was it the fossil of a pre-Adamite whale, or was it an early Roman coffin?

The boy said it was *The Pride of the Thames*.

We thought this a very humorous answer on the part of the boy at first, and somebody gave him twopence as a reward for his ready wit; but when he persisted in keeping up the joke, as we thought, too long, we got vexed with him.

'Come, come, my lad!' said our captain sharply, 'don't let

us have any nonsense. You take your mother's washing-tub home again, and bring us a boat.'

The boat-builder himself came up then, and assured us, on his word as a practical man, that the thing really was a boat – was, in fact, the boat, the 'double sculling skiff' selected to take us on our trip down the river.

We grumbled a good deal. We thought he might, at least, have had it whitewashed or tarred – had *something* done to it to distinguish it from a bit of a wreck; but he could not see any fault in it.

He even seemed offended at our remarks. He said he had picked us out the best boat in all his stock, and he thought we might have been more grateful.

He said it, *The Pride of the Thames*, had been in use, just as it now stood (or rather as it now hung together), for the last forty years, to *his* knowledge, and nobody had complained of it before, and he did not see why we should be the first to begin.

We argued no more.

We fastened the so-called boat together with some pieces of string, got a bit of wall-paper and pasted over the shabbier places, said our prayers, and stepped on board.

They charged us thirty-five shillings for the loan of the remnant for six days; and we could have bought the thing out-and-out for four-and-sixpence at any sale of driftwood round the coast.

The weather changed on the third day – Oh! I am talking about our present trip now – and we started from Oxford upon our homeward journey in the midst of a steady drizzle.

The river – with the sunlight flashing from its dancing wavelets, gilding gold the grey-green beech-trunks, glinting through the dark, cool wood paths, chasing shadows o'er the shallows, flinging diamonds from the mill-wheels, throwing kisses to the lilies, wantoning with the weirs' white waters, silvering moss-grown walls and bridges, brightening every tiny townlet, making sweet each lane and meadow, lying tangled in the rushes, peeping, laughing, from each inlet, gleaming gay on many a far sail, making soft the air with glory – is a golden fairy stream.

But the river – chill and weary, with the ceaseless raindrops falling on its brown and sluggish waters, with the sound as of a woman, weeping low in some dark chamber, while the woods, all dark and silent, shrouded in their mists of vapour, stand like ghosts upon the margin; silent ghosts with eyes reproachful, like the ghosts of evil actions, like the ghosts of friends neglected – is a spirit-haunted water through the land of vain regrets.

Sunlight is the life-blood of Nature. Mother Earth looks at us with such dull, soulless eyes, when the sunlight has died away from out of her. It makes us sad to be with her then; she does not seem to know us or to care for us. She is as a widow who has lost the husband she loved, and her children touch her hand, and look up into her eyes, but gain no smile from her.

We rowed on all that day through the rain, and very melancholy work it was. We pretended, at first, that we enjoyed it. We said it was a change, and that we liked to see the river under all its different aspects. We said we could not expect to have it all sunshine, nor should we wish it. We told each other that Nature was beautiful, even in her tears.

Indeed, Harris and I were quite enthusiastic about the business, for the first few hours. And we sang a song about a gipsy's life, and how delightful a gipsy's existence was! free to storm and sunshine, and to every wind that blew! – and how he enjoyed the rain, and what a lot of good it did him; and how he laughed at people who didn't like it.

George took the fun more soberly, and stuck to the umbrella.

We hoisted the cover before we had lunch, and kept it up all the afternoon, just leaving a little space in the bow, from which one of us could paddle and keep a look-out. In this way we made nine miles, and pulled up for the night a little below Day's lock.

I cannot honestly say that we had a merry evening. The rain poured down with quiet persistency. Everything in the boat was damp and clammy. Supper was not a success. Cold veal pie, when you don't feel hungry, is apt to cloy. I felt I wanted whitebait and a cutlet; Harris babbled of soles and white-sauce, and passed the remains of his pie to Montmorency, who declined it, and apparently insulted by the offer, went and sat over at the other end of the boat by himself.

George requested that we would not talk about these things, at all events until he had finished his cold boiled beef without mustard.

We played penny nap after supper. We played for about an

hour and a half, by the end of which time George had won fourpence – George always is lucky at cards – and Harris and I had lost exactly twopence each.

We thought we would give up gambling then. As Harris said, it breeds an unhealthy excitement when carried too far. George offered to go on and give us our revenge; but Harris and I decided not to battle any further against Fate.

After that, we mixed ourselves some toddy, and sat round and talked. George told us about a man he had known, who had come up the river two years ago, and who had slept out in a damp boat on just such another night as that was, and it had given him rheumatic fever, and nothing was able to save him, and he had died in great agony ten days afterwards. George said he was quite a young man, and was engaged to be married. He said it was one of the saddest things he had ever known.

And that put Harris in mind of a friend of his, who had been in the Volunteers, and who had slept out under canvas one wet night down at Aldershot, 'on just such another night as this', said Harris; and he had woken up in the morning a cripple for life. Harris said he would introduce us both to the man when we got back to town; it would make our hearts bleed to see him.

This naturally led to some pleasant chat about sciatica, fevers, chills, lung diseases, and bronchitis; and Harris said how very awkward it would be if one of us were taken seriously ill in the night, seeing how far away we were from a doctor.

There seemed to be a desire for something frolicsome to follow up this conversation, and in a weak moment I suggested that George should get out his banjo, and see if he could not give us a comic song.

I will say for George that he did not want any pressing. There was no nonsense about having left his music at home, or anything of that sort. He at once fished out his instrument, and commenced to play *Two Lovely Black Eyes*.

I had always regarded *Two Lovely Black Eyes* as rather a commonplace tune until that evening. The rich vein of sadness that George extracted from it quite surprised me.

The desire that grew upon Harris and myself, as the mournful strains progressed, was to fall upon each other's necks and weep; but by great effort we kept back the rising tears, and listened to the wild yearnful melody in silence.

When the chorus came we even made a desperate effort to be merry. We refilled our glasses and joined in; Harris, in a voice trembling with emotion, leading, and George and I following a few words behind:

> Two lovely black eyes
> Oh! what a surprise!
> Only for telling a man he was wrong,
> Two –

There we broke down. The unutterable pathos of George's accompaniment to that 'two' we were, in our then state of depression, unable to bear. Harris sobbed like a little child, and the dog howled till I thought his heart or his jaw must surely break.

George wanted to go on with another verse. He thought that when he had got a little more into the tune, and could throw more 'abandon', as it were, into the rendering, it might not seem so sad. The feeling of the majority, however, was opposed to the experiment.

There being nothing else to do, we went to bed – that is, we undressed ourselves, and tossed about at the bottom of the boat for some three or four hours. After which, we managed to get some fitful slumber until five a.m., when we all got up and had breakfast.

The second day was exactly like the first. The rain continued to pour down, and we sat, wrapped up in our mackintoshes, underneath the canvas, and drifted slowly down.

One of us – I forget which one now, but I rather think it was myself – made a few feeble attempts during the course of the morning to work up the old gipsy foolishness about being children of Nature and enjoying the wet; but it did not go down well at all. That –

> I care not for the rain, not I!

was so painfully evident, as expressing the sentiments of each of us, that to sing it seemed unnecessary.

On one point we were all agreed, and that was that, come what might, we would go through with this job to the bitter end.

We had come out for a fortnight's enjoyment on the river, and a fortnight's enjoyment on the river we meant to have. If it killed us! – well, that would be a sad thing for our friends and relations, but it could not be helped. We felt that to give in to the weather in a climate such as ours would be a most disastrous precedent.

'It's only two days more,' said Harris, 'and we are young and strong. We may get over it all right, after all.'

At about four o'clock we began to discuss our arrangements for the evening. We were a little past Goring then, and we decided to paddle on to Pangbourne, and put up there for the night.

'Another jolly evening!' murmured George.

We sat and mused on the prospect. We should be in at Pangbourne by five. We should finish our dinner at, say, half past six. After that we could walk about the village in the pouring rain until bedtime; or we could sit in a dimly-lit bar-parlour and read the almanac.

'Why, the Alhambra would be almost more lively,' said Harris, venturing his head outside the cover for a moment and taking a survey of the sky.

'With a little supper at the –* to follow,' I added, half unconsciously.

'Yes, it's almost a pity we've made up our minds to stick to this boat,' answered Harris; and then there was silence for a while.

'If we *hadn't* made up our minds to contract our certain deaths in this bally old coffin,' observed George, casting a glance of intense malevolence over the boat, 'it might be worth while to mention that there's a train leaves Pangbourne, I know, soon after five, which would just land us in town in comfortable time to get a chop, and then go on to the place you mentioned afterwards.'

Nobody spoke. We looked at one another, and each one seemed to see his own mean and guilty thoughts reflected in the faces of the others. In silence, we dragged out and overhauled

* A capital little out-of-the-way restaurant in the neighbourhood of –, where you can get one of the best-cooked and cheapest little French dinners or suppers that I know of, with an excellent bottle of Beaune for three-and-six; and which I am not going to be idiot enough to advertise.

the Gladstone. We looked up the river and down the river; not a soul was in sight!

Twenty minutes later, three figures, followed by a shamed-looking dog, might have been seen creeping stealthily from the boat-house at the 'Swan', towards the railway station, dressed in the following neither neat nor gaudy costume:

Black leather shoes, dirty; suit of boating flannels, very dirty; brown felt hat, much battered; mackintosh, very wet; umbrella.

We had deceived the boatman at Pangbourne. We had not had the face to tell him that we were running away from the rain. We had left the boat, and all it contained, in his charge, with instructions that it was to be ready for us at nine the next morning. If, we said – *if* anything unforeseen should happen, preventing our return, we would write to him.

We reached Paddington at seven, and drove direct to the restaurant I have before described, where we partook of a light meal, left Montmorency, together with suggestions for a supper to be ready at half past ten, and then continued our way to Leicester Square.

We attracted a good deal of attention at the Alhambra. On our presenting ourselves at the pay-box we were gruffly directed to go round to Castle Street, and were informed that we were half an hour behind our time.

We convinced the man, with some difficulty, that we were *not* 'the world-renowned contortionists from the Himalaya Mountains', and he took our money and let us pass.

Inside we were a still greater success. Our fine bronzed countenances and picturesque clothes were followed round the place with admiring gaze. We were the cynosure of every eye.

It was a proud moment for us all.

We adjourned soon after the first ballet, and wended our way back to the restaurant, where supper was already awaiting us.

I must confess to enjoying that supper. For about ten days we seemed to have been living, more or less, on nothing but cold meat, cake, and bread and jam. It had been a simple, a nutritious diet; but there had been nothing exciting about it, and the odour of Burgundy, and the smell of French sauces, and the sight of clean napkins and long loaves, knocked as a very welcome visitor at the door of our inner man.

We pegged and quaffed away in silence for a while, until the

time came when, instead of sitting bolt upright, and grasping the knife and fork firmly, we leant back in our chairs and worked slowly and carelessly – when we stretched out our legs beneath the table, let our napkins fall, unheeded, to the floor, and found time to more critically examine the smoky ceiling than we had hitherto been able to do – when we rested our glasses at arm's length upon the table, and felt good, and thoughtful, and forgiving.

Then Harris, who was sitting next to the window, drew aside the curtain and looked out upon the street.

It glistened darkly in the wet, the dim lamps flickered with each gust, the rain splashed steadily into the puddles and trickled down the water-spouts into the running gutters. A few soaked wayfarers hurried past, crouching beneath their dripping umbrellas, the women holding up their skirts.

'Well,' said Harris, reaching his hand out for his glass, 'we have had a pleasant trip, and my hearty thanks for it to old Father Thames – but I think we did well to chuck it when we did. Here's to Three Men well out of a Boat!'

And Montmorency, standing on his hind legs, before the window, peering out into the night, gave a short bark of decided concurrence with the toast.

from Novel Notes

'Novel Notes' was begun by Jerome
as a light-hearted series in his magazine *The Idler* in 1892,
where himself and three 'fictional' friends
decided to write a novel together.
It was published as a book in 1893.
This chapter is picked for its description
of the joys of living on the river.

from NOVEL NOTES

We held our next business meeting on my houseboat. Brown was opposed at first to my going down to this houseboat at all. He thought that none of us should leave town while the novel was still on hand.

'Don't you agree with me, Jephson?' he added, turning to that ever-smoking philosopher. 'Don't you think it unwise for any of us to go away from London until this book is finished, and off our minds?'

'Well,' growled Jephson, without removing his pipe from his mouth, 'personally, I must confess I should like to see the dear old trees and fields once more before I die.'

Jephson never had been enthusiastic about this collaboration scheme. But then enthusiasm was not in his nature.

MacShaugnassy was of opinion that we should work better on a houseboat. He thought that, surrounded by the calm of nature, the literary spirit might descend upon us in greater quantities than had hitherto been the case. Speaking for himself, he said he never felt more like writing a really great work than when lying in a hammock among whispering leaves, with the deep blue sky above him, and a tumbler of iced claret cup within easy reach of his hand. Failing a hammock, he found a deck chair a great incentive to mental labour. In the interests of the novel, he strongly recommended me to take down with me at least one comfortable deck chair, and plenty of lemons.

I could not myself see any reason why we should not be able to think as well on a houseboat as anywhere else, and accordingly it was settled that I should go down and establish myself upon the thing, and that the others should visit me there from time to time, when we would sit round and toil.

This houseboat was Ethelbertha's idea. We had spent a day,

the summer before, on one belonging to a friend of mine, and she had been enraptured with the life. Everything was on such a delightfully tiny scale. You lived in a tiny little room; you slept on a tiny little bed, in a tiny, tiny little bedroom; and you cooked your little dinner by a tiny little fire, in the tiniest little kitchen that ever you did see. 'Oh, it must be lovely, living on a houseboat,' said Ethelbertha, with a gasp of ecstasy; 'it must be like living in a doll's house.'

Ethelbertha was very young – ridiculously young, as I think I have mentioned before – in these days of which I am writing, and the love of dolls, and of the gorgeous dresses that dolls wear, and of the many-windowed but inconveniently arranged houses that dolls inhabit – or are supposed to inhabit, for as a rule they seem to prefer sitting on the roof with their legs dangling down over the front door, which has always appeared to me to be unladylike. But then, of course, I am no authority on doll etiquette – had not yet, I think, quite departed from her. Nay, am I not sure that it had not? Do I not remember, years later, peeping into a certain room, the walls of which are covered with works of art of a character calculated to send any aesthetic person mad in less than half an hour, and seeing her, sitting on the floor, before a red brick mansion, containing two rooms and a kitchen; and are not her hands trembling with delight as she arranges the three real tin plates upon the dresser? And does she not knock at the real brass knocker upon the real front door until it comes off, and I have to sit down beside her on the floor and screw it on again?

Perhaps, however, it is unwise for me to recall these things, and bring them forward thus in evidence against her, for cannot she in turn laugh at me? Did not I also assist in the arrangement and appointment of that house beautiful? We differed on the matter of the drawing-room carpet, I recollect. Ethelbertha fancied a dark blue velvet, but I felt sure, taking the wall-paper into consideration, that some shade of terra-cotta would harmonise best. She agreed with me in the end, and we manufactured one out of an old chest protector, and laid it down. It had a really charming effect, and gave a delightfully warm tone to the room. The blue velvet we put in the kitchen. I deemed this extravagance myself, but Ethelbertha said that servants thought a lot of a good carpet, and that it paid to humour them in little things, when practicable.

The bedroom had one big bed and a cot in it; but I could not see where the girl was going to sleep. The architect had overlooked her altogether: that is so like an architect. The house also suffered from the inconvenience common to residences of its class, of possessing no stairs, so that to move from one room to another it was necessary to burst your way up through the ceiling, or else to come outside and climb in through a window; either of which methods must be fatiguing when you come to do it often.

Apart from these drawbacks, however, the house was one that any doll agent would have been justified in describing as a 'most desirable family residence'; and it had been furnished with a lavishness that bordered on positive ostentation. In the bedroom there was a washing-stand, and on the washing-stand there stood a jug and basin, and in the jug there was real water. But all this was as nothing. I have known mere ordinary, middle-class dolls houses in which you might find washing-stands and jugs and basins and real water – aye, and even soap, But in this abode of luxury there was a real towel; so that a body could not only wash himself, but wipe himself afterwards, and that is a sensation that, as all dolls know, can be enjoyed only in the very first-class houses.

Then, in the drawing-room, there was a clock, which would go on ticking so long as ever you continued to shake it (it never seemed to get tired); also a picture and a piano, and a book upon the table, and a vase of flowers that would tip over and upset the moment you touched it, just like a real vase of flowers. Oh, there was style about this room, I can tell you.

But the glory of the house was its kitchen. There were all things that heart could desire in this kitchen, saucepans with lids that took on and off, a flat-iron and a rolling-pin. A dinner service for three occupied about half the room, and what space was left was filled up by the stove – a *real* stove! Think of it, oh, ye owners of dolls' houses, a stove in which you could burn real bits of coal, and on which you could boil real bits of potato for dinner – except when people said you mustn't, because it was dangerous, and took the grate away from you, and blew out the fire, a thing that hampers a cook.

I never saw a house more complete in all its details. Nothing

[241]

had been overlooked, not even the family. There it lay on its back, just outside the front door, proud but calm, waiting to be put into possession. It was not an extensive family. It consisted of four – papa, and mamma, and baby, and the hired girl; just the family for a beginner.

It was a well-dressed family too – not merely with grand clothes outside, covering a shameful condition of things beneath, such as alas! is too often the case in doll society, but with every article necessary and proper to a lady or gentleman, down to items that I could not mention. And all these garments, you must know, could be unfastened and taken off. I have known dolls – stylish enough dolls, to look at, some of them – who have been content to go about with their clothes gummed on to them, and, in some cases, nailed on with tin-tacks, which I take to be a slovenly and unhealthy habit. But this family could be undressed in five minutes without the aid of either hot water or a chisel.

Not that it was advisable from an artistic point of view that any of them should be undressed. They had not the figure that looks well in its natural state – none of them. There was a want of fullness about them all. Besides, without their clothes, it might have been difficult to distinguish the baby from the papa, or the maid from the mistress, and thus domestic complications might have arisen.

When all was ready for their reception we established them in their home. We put as much of the baby to bed as the cot would hold, and made the papa and mamma comfortable in the drawing-room, where they sat on the floor and stared thoughtfully at each other across the table. (They had to sit on the floor because the chairs were not big enough.) The girl we placed in the kitchen, where she leant against the dresser in an attitude suggestive of drink, embracing the broom we had given her with maudlin affection. Then we lifted up the house with care and carried it cautiously into another room, and with the deftness of experienced conspirators, placed it at the foot of a small bed, on the south-west corner of which an absurdly small somebody had hung an absurdly small stocking.

To return to our own doll's house, Ethelbertha and I, discussing the subject during our return journey in the train, resolved that, next year, we ourselves would possess a houseboat, a smaller houseboat, if possible, than even the one we had just seen. It should have art-muslin curtains and a flag, and the flowers about it should be wild roses and forget-me-nots. I could work all the morning on the roof, with an awning over me to keep off the sun, while Ethelbertha trimmed the roses and made cakes for tea; and in the evenings we would sit out on the little deck, and Ethelbertha would play the guitar (she would begin learning it at once), or we could sit quiet and listen to the nightingales.

For, when you are very, very young, you dream that the summer is all sunny days and moonlight nights, that the wind blows always softly from the west, and that roses will thrive anywhere. But, as you grow older, you grow tired of waiting for the dull grey sky to break. So you close the door and come in, and crouch over the fire, wondering why the winds blow ever from the east: and you have given up trying to rear roses.

I knew a little cottage girl who saved up her money for months and months so as to buy a new frock to go to a flower show in. But the day of the flower show was a nasty wet day, so she wore an old frock instead. And all the fête days for quite a long while were nasty wet days, and she feared she would never have a chance of wearing her pretty white dress. But at last there came a fête day morning that was bright and sunny, and then that little cottage girl clapped her hands and ran upstairs, and took her new frock (which had been her 'new frock' for so long a time that it was now the oldest frock she had) from the box where it lay neatly folded between lavender and thyme, and held it up, and laughed to think how nice she would look in it.

But when she went to put it on, she found that she had outgrown it, and that it was too small for her every way. So she had to wear a common old frock after all.

Things happen that way, you know, in this world. There were a boy and girl once who loved each other very dearly. But they were both poor, so they agreed to wait till he had made enough money for them to live comfortably upon, and then they would marry and be happy. It took him a long while to do, because making money is very slow work, and he wanted, while he was about it, to make enough for them to be very happy upon indeed. He accomplished the task eventually, however, and came back home a wealthy man.

Then they met again in the same poorly-furnished parlour where they had parted. But they did not sit as near to each other as they had sat then. For she had lived alone so long that she had grown prim and old-maidish, and she was feeling vexed with him for having dirtied the carpet with his muddy boots. And he had worked so long earning money that he had grown hard and cold like the money itself, and was trying to think of something affectionate to say to her.

So for a while they sat, one each side of the paper 'fire-stove ornament,' both wondering why they had shed such scalding tears on that day they had kissed each other good-bye; then said 'good-bye' again, and were glad.

There is another tale with much the same moral and I learnt at school out of a copybook. If I remember rightly, it runs somewhat like this:

Once upon a time there lived a wise grasshopper and a foolish ant. All through the pleasant summer weather, the grasshopper sported and played, gambolling with his fellows in and out among the sunbeams, dining sumptuously each day on leaves and dewdrops, never troubling about the morrow, singing ever his one peaceful, droning song.

Then there came the cruel winter, and the grasshopper, looking round, saw that his friends, the flowers, lay dead, and knew thereby that his own little span was drawing near its close.

Then he felt glad that he had been so happy, and had not wasted his life. 'It has been very short,' said he to himself; 'but it has been very pleasant, and I think I have made the best use of it. I have drunk in the sunshine, I have lain on the soft, warm air, I have tasted the juice of the sweet green leaves. I have done what I could. I have spread my wings, I have sung my song. Now I will thank God for the sunny days that are passed, and die.'

Saying which, he crawled under a brown leaf and met his fate in the way that all brave grasshoppers should; and a little bird that was passing by picked him up tenderly and buried him.

Now when the foolish ant saw this, she was greatly puffed up with Pharisaical conceit. 'How thankful I ought to be,' said she, 'that I am industrious and prudent, and not like this poor grasshopper. While he was flitting about from flower to flower, and enjoying himself, I was hard at work, putting by against the winter. Now he is dead, while I am about to make myself cosy in my warm home, and eat all the good things that I have been saving up.'

But, as she spoke, the gardener came along with his spade, and levelled the hill where she dwelt to the ground, and left her lying dead amidst the ruins.

Then the same kind little bird that had buried the grasshopper came and picked her out and buried her also; and afterwards he composed and sang a song, the burthen of which was 'Gather ye rosebuds while ye may.' It was a very pretty song, and a very wise song, and a man who lived in those days, and to whom the birds, loving him and feeling that he was almost one of themselves, had taught their language, fortunately overheard it and wrote it down, so that all may read it to this day.

Unhappily for us, however, Fate is a harsh governess, who has no sympathy with our desire for rosebuds. 'Don't stop to pick flowers now, my dear,' she cries, in her sharp, cross tones, as she seizes our arm and jerks us back into the roadway; 'we haven't time to-day. We will come back again to-morrow, and you shall pick them then.'

And we have to follow her, knowing, if we are experienced children, that the chances are that we shall never come that way again; or that, if we do, it will be when the roses are dead.

Fate would not hear of our having a houseboat that summer – which was an exceptionally fine summer – but promised us that if we were good and saved up our money we should have one next year; and Ethelbertha and I, being simple-minded, inexperienced children, were content with the promise, and had faith in its satisfactory fulfilment.

As soon as we reached home, we informed Amenda of our plan. The moment the girl opened the door, Ethelbertha burst out with:

'Oh! can you swim, Amenda?'

'No, mum,' answered Amenda, with entire absence of curiosity as to why such a question had been addressed to her, 'I never knew but one girl as could, and she got drowned.'

'Well, you'll have to make haste and learn, then,' continued Ethelbertha, 'because you won't be able to walk out with your young man, you'll have to swim out. We're not going to live in a

[245]

house any more. We're going to live on a little boat in the middle of the river.'

Ethelbertha' chief object in life at this period was to surprise and shock Amenda, and her chief sorrow, that she had never succeeded in doing so. She had hoped great things from this announcement, but the girl remained unmoved. 'Oh, are you mum,' she replied; and then went on to speak of other matters.

I believe the result would have been precisely the same if we had told her we were going to live in a balloon.

I do not know how it was, I am sure. Amenda was always most respectful in her manner. But she had a knack of making me feel, when in her presence, that Ethelbertha and I were a couple of children, playing at being grown up and married, and that she was humouring us.

Amenda stayed with us for nearly five years – until the milkman, having saved up sufficient to buy a 'walk' of his own, had become practicable – but her attitude towards us never changed. Even when we came to be really important married people, the proprietors of a 'family,' it was evident that she only considered that we had gone a step further in the game, and were playing now at being fathers and mothers.

By some subtle process, she contrived to imbue the Baby also with this idea. The child never seemed to me to take either of us quite seriously. She would play with us, or join with us in light, frivolous conversation; but when it came to the serious affairs of life, such as bathing or feeding, she preferred her nurse.

Ethelbertha attempted to take her out in the perambulator one morning, but the child would not hear of it for a moment.

'It's all right, Baby dear,' explained Ethelbertha, soothingly. 'Baby's going out with mumma this morning.'

'Oh, no, Baby ain't,' was Baby's rejoinder, in effect if not in words. 'Baby don't take a hand in experiments – not this baby. I don't want to be upset or run over.'

Poor Ethel! I shall never forget how heartbroken she was. It was the want of confidence that hurt her so.

But these are reminiscences of other days, having no connection with the days of which I am – or should be – writing; and to wander from one matter to another is, in a teller of tales, a grievous sin, and a growing custom much to be condemned. Therefore, I will close my eyes to all other memories, and endeavour to see only that little white and green houseboat by the ferry, which was the scene of our future collaborations.

Houseboats then were not built to the scale of Mississippi steamers, but this boat was a small one, even for that primitive age. The man from whom we hired it described it as 'compact.' The man to whom, at the end of the first month, we tried to sub-let it, characterized it as 'poky.' In our letters, we traversed this definition. In our hearts, we agreed with it.

At first, however, its size – or, rather, its lack of size – was one of its chief charms in Ethelbertha's eyes. The fact that if you rose up out of your bed carelessly you were certain to knock your head against the ceiling, and that it was utterly impossible for any man to put on his trousers except in the saloon, she regarded as a capital joke.

That she herself had to take a looking-glass and go upon the roof to do her back hair, she considered less amusing.

Amenda accepted her new surroundings with philosophic indifference. On being informed that what she had mistaken for a linen press was her bedroom, she remarked that there was one advantage about it, and that was, that she could not tumble out of bed, seeing there was nowhere to tumble; and, on being shown the kitchen, she remarked that she should like it for two things – one was that she could sit in the middle and reach everything without getting up; the other, that nobody else could come into the apartment while she was there.

'You see, Amenda,' explained Ethelbertha, apologetically, 'we shall really live outside.'

'Yes, mum,' answered Amenda, 'I should say that would be the best place to do it.'

If only we could have lived more outside, the life might have been pleasant enough, but the weather rendered it impossible, six days out of the seven, for us to do more than look out of the window and feel thankful that we had got a roof over our heads.

I have known wet summers before and since. I have learnt by many bitter experiences the danger and foolishness of leaving the shelter of London during any time between the first of May and the thirty-first of October. Indeed, the country is always associated in my mind with recollections of long, weary days passed in the pitiless rain, and sad, dreary evenings spent in other people's clothes. But never have I known, and never, I

pray night and morning, may I know again, such a summer as
the one we lived through (though none of us expected to) on that
confounded houseboat.

At about five o'clock in the morning, we would be awakened
by the rain's forcing its way in through the window and wetting
the bed and would get up and mop out the saloon. After
breakfast, I would try to work, but the beating of the hail upon
the roof just over my head would drive every idea out of my
brain, and, after a wasted hour or two, I would fling down my
pen and hunt up Ethelbertha, and we would put on our
mackintoshes and take our umbrellas and go out for a row or a
walk. At mid-day, we would return and put on some dry
clothes, and sit down to dinner.

In the afternoon the storm generally freshened up a bit, and
we were kept pretty busy rushing about with towels and cloths,
trying to prevent the water from coming into the rooms and
swamping us. During tea-time, the saloon was usually
illuminated by forked lightning. The evenings we spent in
baling out the boat, after which we took it in turns to go into the
kitchen and warm ourselves. At eight we supped, and from then
until it was time to go to bed we sat wrapped up in rugs,
listening to the roaring of the thunder and the howling of the
wind, and the lashing of the waves, and wondering whether the
boat would hold out through the night.

Friends would come down to spend the day with us – elderly,
irritable people, fond of warmth and comfort; people who did
not, as a rule, hanker after jaunts, even under the most
favourable conditions; but who had been persuaded by our silly
talk that a day on the river would be to them like a Saturday to
Monday in Paradise. Poor creatures! They would generally
return home, looking as if they had had a day *in* the river.

They would arrive early in the morning, soaked; and we
would shut them up in different bunks, and leave them to strip
themselves and put on things of Ethelbertha's or of mine. But
Ethel and I, in those days, were slim so that stout, middle-aged
people in our clothes neither looked well nor felt happy.

Upon their emerging, we would take them into the saloon
and try to entertain them by telling them what we had intended
to do with them had the day been fine. But their answers were
short, and occasionally snappy, and after a while the

conversation would flag, and we would sit round reading last week's newspapers and coughing.

The moment their own clothes were dry (we lived in a perpetual atmosphere of steaming clothes) they would insist upon leaving us, which seemed to me discourteous after all that we had done for them, and would dress themselves once more and start off home, and get wet again before they got there.

We would generally receive a letter a few days afterwards, written by some relative, informing us that both patients were doing as well as could be expected, and promising to send us a card for the funeral in case of a relapse.

Our chief recreation, our sole consolation, during the long weeks of our imprisonment, was to watch from our windows the pleasure-seekers passing by in their small, open boats, and to reflect what an awful day they had had, or were going to have, as the case might be.

In the morning, they would head up stream – young men with their sweethearts; nephews taking out their rich old aunts; husbands and wives (some of them pairs, some of them odd ones); stylish-looking girls with cousins; energetic-looking men with dogs; high-class silent parties; low-class noisy parties; quarrelsome family parties – boatload after boatload they went by, wet, but still hopeful, pointing out bits of blue sky to one another.

In the evening, they would return, drenched and gloomy, saying disagreeable things to one another.

That summer, I am convinced, was responsible for the breaking off of many an engagement, and the abandonment, maybe, of one or two elopements. A wet day on the river affords lovers an insight into each other's character that is not otherwise easily obtainable. Angelina learns that Edwin's language is not so limited as she had imagined, and Edwin perceives that Angelina's smile is not the fixture he had thought it.

One couple, and one couple only, out of the many hundreds that passed under our review, came back from the ordeal with pleasant faces. He was rowing hard and singing, with a handkerchief tied round his head to keep his hat on, and she was laughing at him, while trying to hold up an umbrella with one hand and steer with the other.

There are but two explanations to account for people being jolly on the river in the rain. The one I dismissed as being both uncharitable and improbable. The other was creditable to the human race, and adopting it, I took off my cap to this damp but cheerful pair as they went by. They answered with a wave of the hand, and I stood looking after them till they disappeared in the mist.

I am inclined to think that those young people, if they be still alive, are very happy. Maybe, fortune has been kind to them, or maybe she has not, but in either event they are, I am inclined to think, happier than are most people.

Now and again, the daily tornado would rage with such fury as to defeat its own purpose by prematurely exhausting itself, and thus being unable, towards evening, to come up to time; and, on these rare occasions, we would sit out on the deck, and enjoy the unwonted luxury of a little fresh air.

I remember well those few pleasant evenings: the river, luminous with the drowned light, the dark banks where the night lurked, the storm-tossed sky, jewelled here and there with stars.

It was delightful not to hear for an hour or so the sullen thrashing of the rain; but to sit and listen to the leaping of the fishes, or the soft swirl raised by the water-rat, swimming stealthily among the rushes, or the restless twitterings of the few still wakeful birds.

There was an old corncrake lived near us, and the way he used to disturb all the other birds, and keep them from going to sleep, was shameful. Amenda, who was town-bred, mistook him at first for one of those cheap alarm clocks, and wondered who was winding him up, and why they went on doing it all night; and, above all, why they didn't oil him.

He would begin his unhallowed performance about dusk, just as every respectable bird was preparing to settle down for the night. A family of thrushes had their nest a few yards from his stand, and they used to get perfectly furious with him.

'There's that fool at it again,' the female thrush would say; 'why can't he do it in the day-time if he must do it at all?' (She spoke, of course, in twitters, but I am confident the above is a correct translation.)

After a while, the young thrushes would wake up and begin

chirping, and then the mother would get madder than ever.

'Can't you say something to him?' she would cry indignantly to her husband. 'How do you think the children can get to sleep, poor things, with that hideous row going on all night? Might just as well be living in a saw-mill.'

Thus adjured, the male thrush would put his head over the nest, and call out in a nervous, apologetic manner:

'I say, you know, you there, I wish you wouldn't mind being quiet a bit. My wife says she can't get the children to sleep. It's too bad, you know, 'pon my word it is.'

'Gor on,' the corncrake would answer, surlily. 'You keep your wife herself quiet; that's enough for you to do.' And on he would go again worse than before.

Then a mother blackbird, from a little further off, would join in the fray.

'Ah, it's a good hiding he wants, not a talking to. And if I was a cock, I'd give it him.' (This remark would be made in a tone of withering contempt, and would appear to bear reference to some previous discussion.)

'You're quite right, ma'am,' Mrs Thrush would reply. 'That's what I tell my husband, but' (with rising inflection, so that every lady in the plantation might hear) '*he* wouldn't move himself, bless you – no, not if I and the children were to die before his eyes for want of sleep.'

'Ah, he ain't the only one, my dear,' the blackbird would pipe back, 'they're all alike.' Then, in a voice more of sorrow than of anger, 'But there, it ain't their fault, I suppose, poor things. If you ain't got the spirit of a bird you can't help yourself.'

I would strain my ears at this point to hear if the male blackbird was moved at all by these taunts, but the only sound I could ever detect coming from his neighbourhood was that of palpably exaggerated snoring.

By this time, the whole district would be awake, expressing views concerning that corncrake that might have wounded a less callous nature.

'Blow me tight, Bill,' some vulgar little hedge-sparrow would chirp out, in the midst of the hubbub, 'if I don't believe the gent thinks 'e's a-singing.'

' 'Tain't 'is fault,' Bill would reply, with mock sympathy. 'Somebody's put a penny in the slot, and 'e can't stop 'isself.'

Irritated by the laugh that this would call forth from the younger birds, the corncrake would exert himself to be more objectionable than ever, and as a means to this end, would commence giving his marvellous imitation of the sharpening of a rusty saw by a steel file.

But at this an old crow, not to be trifled with, would cry out, angrily:

'Stop that, now. If I come down to you I'll peck your cranky head off, I will.'

And then would follow silence for a quarter of an hour, after which the whole thing would begin again.

from The Passing of the Third Floor Back

'Mrs Korner Sins Her Mercies' is a short story
from a collection called *The Passing of the Third Floor Back*,
published in 1907, the title story of which
became Jerome's best remembered play.

Mrs Korner Sins Her Mercies

'I do mean it,' declared Mrs Korner, 'I like a man to be a man.'

'But you would not like Christopher – I mean Mr Korner – to be that sort of man,' suggested her bosom friend.

'I don't mean that I should like it if he did if often. But I should like to feel that he was able to be that sort of man – Have you told your master that breakfast is ready?' demanded Mrs Korner of the domestic staff, entering at the moment with three boiled eggs and a teapot.

'Yus, I've told 'im,' replied the staff indignantly.

The domestic staff of Acacia Villa, Ravenscourt Park, lived in a state of indignation. It could be heard of mornings and evenings saying its prayers indignantly.

'What did he say?'

'Said 'e'll be down the moment 'e's dressed.'

'Nobody wants him to come before,' commented Mrs Korner. 'Answered me that he was putting on his collar when I called up to him five minutes ago.'

'Answer yer the same thing now, if yer called up to 'im agen, I 'spect,' was the opinion of the staff. 'Was on 'is 'ands and knees when I looked in, scooping round under the bed for 'is collar stud.'

Mrs Korner paused with teapot in her hand. 'Was he talking?'

'Talkin'? Nobody there to talk to; I 'adn't got no time to stop and chatter.'

'I mean to himself,' explained Mrs Korner. 'He – he wasn't swearing?' There was a note of eagerness, almost of hope, in Mrs Korner's voice.

'Swearin'! 'E! Why, 'e don't know any.'

'Thank you,' said Mrs Korner. 'That will do, Harriet; you may go.'

Mrs Korner put down the teapot with a bang. 'The very girl,' said Mrs Korner bitterly, 'the very girl despises him.'

'Perhaps,' suggested Miss Greene, 'he had been swearing and had finished.'

But Mrs Korner was not to be comforted. 'Finished! Any other man would have been swearing all the time.'

'Perhaps,' suggested the kindly bosom friend, ever the one to plead the cause of the transgressor, 'perhaps he was swearing, and she did not hear him. You see, if he had his head well underneath the bed – '

The door opened.

'Sorry I am late,' said Mr Korner, bursting cheerfully into the room. It was a point with Mr Korner always to be cheerful in the morning. 'Greet the day with a smile and it will leave you with a blessing,' was the motto Mrs Korner, this day a married woman of six months and three weeks standing, had heard her husband murmur before getting out of bed on precisely two hundred and two occasions. The Motto entered largely into the scheme of Mr Korner's life. Written in fine copper-plate upon cards all of the same size, a choice selection counselled him each morning from the rim of his shaving-glass.

'Did you find it?' asked Mrs Korner.

'It is most extraordinary,' replied Mr Korner, as he seated himself at the breakfast table. 'I saw it go under the bed with my own eyes. Perhaps – '

'Don't ask me to look for it,' interrupted Mrs Korner. 'Crawling about on their hands and knees, knocking their heads against iron bedsteads, would be enough to make some people swear.' The emphasis was on the 'some.'

'It is not bad training for the character,' hinted Mr Korner, 'occasionally to force one's self to perform patiently tasks calculated – '

'If you get tied up in one of those long sentences of yours you will never get out in time to eat your breakfast,' was the fear of Mrs Korner.

'I should be sorry for anything to happen to it,' remarked Mr Korner, 'its intrinsic value may perhaps – '

'I will look for it after breakfast,' volunteered the amiable Miss Greene. 'I am good at finding things.'

'I can well believe it,' the gallant Mr Korner assured her, as

[256]

with the handle of his spoon he peeled his egg. 'From such bright eyes as yours, few – '

'You've only got ten minutes,' his wife reminded him. 'Do get on with your breakfast.'

'I should like,' said Mr Korner, 'to finish a speech occasionally.'

'You never would,' asserted Mrs Korner.

'I should like to try,' sighed Mr Korner, 'one of these days – '

'How did you sleep, dear? I forgot to ask you,' questioned Mrs Korner of the bosom friend.

'I am always restless in a strange bed the first night,' explained Miss Greene. 'I daresay, too, I was a little excited.'

'I could have wished,' said Mr Korner, 'it had been a better example of the delightful art of the dramatist. When one goes but seldom to the theatre – '

'One wants to enjoy one's self,' interrupted Mrs Korner.

'I really do not think,' said the bosom friend, 'that I have ever laughed so much in all my life.'

'It was amusing. I laughed myself,' admitted Mr Korner. 'At the same time I cannot help thinking that to treat drunkenness as a theme – '

'He wasn't drunk,' argued Mrs Korner, 'he was just jovial.'

'My dear!' Mr Korner corrected her, 'he simply couldn't stand.'

'He was much more amusing than some people who can,' retorted Mrs Korner.

'It is possible, my dear Aimée,' her husband pointed out to her, 'for a man to be amusing without being drunk; also for a man to be drunk without – '

'Oh, a man is all the better,' declared Mrs Korner, 'for letting himself go occasionally.'

'My dear – '

'You, Christopher, would be all the better for letting yourself go – occasionally.'

'I wish,' said Mr Korner, as he passed his empty cup, 'you would not say things you do not mean. Any one hearing you – '

'If there's one thing makes me more angry than another,' said Mrs Korner, 'it is being told I say things that I do not mean.'

'Why say them then?' suggested Mr Korner.

'I don't. I do – I mean I do mean them,' explained Mrs Korner.

'You can hardly mean, my dear,' persisted her husband, 'that you really think I should be all the better for getting drunk – even occasionally.'

'I didn't say drunk; I said "going it." '

'But I do "got it" in moderation,' pleaded Mr Korner. "Moderation in all things," that is my motto.'

'I know it,' returned Mrs Korner.

'A little of everything and nothing – ' this time Mr Korner interrupted himself. 'I fear,' said Mr Korner, rising, 'we must postpone the further discussion of this interesting topic. If you would not mind stepping out with me into the passage, dear, there are one or two little matters connected with the house – '

Host and hostess squeezed past the visitor and closed the door behind them. The visitor continued eating.

'I do mean it,' repeated Mrs Korner, for the third time, reseating herself a minute later at the table. 'I would give anything – anything,' reiterated the lady recklessly, 'to see Christopher more like the ordinary sort of man.'

'But he has always been the sort – the sort of man he is,' her bosom friend reminded her.

'Oh, during the engagement, of course, one expects a man to be perfect. I didn't think he was going to keep it up.'

'He seems to me,' said Miss Greene, 'a dear, good fellow. You are one of those people who never know when they are well off.'

'I know he is a good fellow,' agreed Mrs Korner, 'and I am very fond of him. It is just because I am fond of him that I hate feeling ashamed of him. I want him to be a manly man, to do the things that other men do.'

'Do all the ordinary sort of men swear and get occasionally drunk?'

'Of course they do,' asserted Mrs Korner, in a tone of authority. 'One does not want a man to be a milksop.'

'Have you ever seen a drunken man?' inquired the bosom friend, who was nibbling sugar.

'Heaps,' replied Mrs Korner, who was sucking marmalade off her fingers.

By which Mrs Korner meant that some half a dozen times in her life she had visited the play, choosing by preference the lighter form of British drama. The first time she witnessed the real thing, which happened just precisely a month later, long after the conversation here recorded had been forgotten by the parties most concerned, no one could have been more utterly astonished than was Mrs Korner.

How it came about Mr Korner was never able to fully satisfy himself. Mr Korner was not the type that serves the purpose of the temperance lecturer. His 'first glass' he had drunk more years ago than he could recollect, and since had tasted the varied contents of many others. But never before had Mr Korner exceeded, nor been tempted to exceed, the limits of his favourite virtue, moderation.

'We had one bottle of claret between us,' Mr Korner would often recall to his mind, 'of which he drank the greater part. And then he brought out the little green flask. He said it was made from pears – that in Peru they kept it specially for children's parties. Of course, that may have been his joke; but in any case I cannot see how just one glass – I wonder could I have taken more than one glass while he was talking.' It was a point that worried Mr Korner.

The 'he' who had talked, possibly, to such bad effect was a distant cousin of Mr Korner's, one Bill Damon, chief mate of the steamship *La Fortuna*. Until their chance meeting that afternoon in Leadenhall Street, they had not seen each other since they were boys together. The *Fortuna* was leaving St Katherine's Docks early the next morning bound for South America, and it might be years before they met again. As Mr Damon pointed out, Fate, by thus throwing them into each other's arms, clearly intended they should have a cosy dinner together that very evening in the captain's cabin of the *Fortuna*. Mr Korner, returning to the office, despatched to Ravenscourt Park an express letter, announcing the strange news that he might not be home that evening much before ten, and at half-past six, for the first time since his marriage, directed his steps away from home and Mrs Korner.

The two friends talked of many things. And later on they spoke of sweethearts and of wives. Mate Damon's experiences had apparently been wide and varied. They talked – or, rather, the mate talked, and Mr Korner listened – of the olive-tinted beauties of the Spanish Main, of the dark-eyed passionate creoles, of the blond Junos of the Californian valleys. The mate had theories concerning the care and management of women: theories that, if the mate's word could be relied upon, had stood the test of studied application. A new world opened out to Mr Korner; a world where lovely women worshipped with doglike devotion men who, though loving them in return, knew how to be their masters. Mr Korner, warmed gradually from cold disapproval to bubbling appreciation, sat entranced. Time alone set a limit to the recital of the mate's adventures. At eleven o'clock the cook reminded them that the captain and the pilot might be aboard at any moment. Mr Korner, surprised at the lateness of the hour, took a long and tender farewell of his cousin, and found St Katherine's Docks one of the most bewildering places out of which he had ever tried to escape. Under a lamp-post in the Minories, it suddenly occurred to Mr Korner that he was an unappreciated man. Mrs Korner never said and did the sort of things by means of which the beauties of the Southern Main endeavoured feebly to express their consuming passion for gentlemen superior in no way – as far as he could see – to Mr Korner himself. Thinking over the sort of things Mrs Korner did say and did do, tears sprung into Mr Korner's eyes. Noticing that a policeman was eyeing him with curiosity, he dashed them aside and hurried on. Pacing the platform of the Mansion House Station, where it is always draughty, the thought of his wrongs returned to him with renewed force. Why was there no trace of doglike devotion about Mrs Korner? The fault – so he bitterly told himself– the fault was his. 'A woman loves her master; it is her instinct,' mused Mr Korner to himself. 'Damme,' thought Mr Korner, 'I don't believe that half her time she knows I am her master.'

'Go away,' said Mr Korner to a youth of pasty appearance who, with open mouth, had stopped immediately in front of him.

'I'm fond o' listening,' explained the pasty youth.

'Who's talking?' demanded Mr Korner.

'You are,' replied the pasty youth.

It is a long journey from the city to Ravenscourt Park, but the task of planning out the future life of Mrs Korner and himself kept Mr Korner wide awake and interested. When he got out of the train the thing chiefly troubling him was the three-quarters of a mile of muddy road stretching between him and his determination to make things clear to Mrs Korner then and there.

The sight of Acacia Villa, suggesting that everybody was in bed and asleep, served to further irritate him. A doglike wife would have been sitting up to see if there was anything he wanted. Mr Korner, acting on the advice of his own brass plate, not only knocked but also rang. As the door did not immediately fly open, he continued to knock and ring. The window of the best bedroom on the first floor opened.

'Is that you?' said the voice of Mrs Korner. There was, as it happened, distinct suggestion of passion in Mrs Korner's voice, but not of the passion Mr Korner was wishful to inspire. It made him a little more angry than he was before.

'Don't you talk to me with your head out of the window as if this were a gallanty show. You come down and open the door,' commanded Mr Korner.

'Haven't you got your latchkey?' demanded Mrs Korner.

For answer Mr Korner attacked the door again. The window closed. The next moment but six or seven, the door was opened with such suddenness that Mr Korner, still gripping the knocker, was borne inward in a flying attitude. Mrs Korner had descended the stairs ready with a few remarks. She had not anticipated that Mr Korner, usually slow of speech, could be even readier.

'Where's my supper?' indignantly demanded Mr Korner, still supported by the knocker.

Mrs Korner, too astonished for words, simply stared.

'Where's my supper?' repeated Mr Korner, by this time worked up into genuine astonishment that it was not ready for him. 'What's everybody mean, going off to bed, when the masterororous hasn't had his supper?'

'Is anything the matter, dear?' was heard the voice of Miss Greene, speaking from the neighbourhood of the first landing.

'Come in, Christopher,' pleaded Mrs Korner, 'please come in, and let me shut the door.'

Mrs Korner was the type of young lady fond of domineering with a not ungraceful hauteur over those accustomed to yield readily to her; it is a type that is easily frightened.

'I wan' grilled kinneys-on-toast,' explained Mr Korner,

exchanging the knocker for the hat-stand, and wishing the next moment that he had not. 'Don't let's 'avareytalk about it. Unnerstan'? I dowan' any talk about it.'

'What on earth am I to do?' whispered the terrified Mrs Korner to her bosom friend, 'there isn't a kidney in the house.'

'I should poach him a couple of eggs,' suggested the helpful bosom friend; 'put plenty of Cayenne pepper on them. Very likely he won't remember.'

Mr Korner allowed himself to be persuaded into the dining-room, which was also the breakfast parlour and the library. The two ladies, joined by the hastily clad staff, whose chronic indignation seemed to have vanished in face of the first excuse for it that Acacia Villa had afforded her, made haste to light the kitchen fire.

'I should never have believed it,' whispered the white-faced Mrs Korner, 'never.'

'Makes yer know there's a man about the 'ouse, don't it?' chirped the delighted staff. Mrs Korner, for answer, boxed the girl's ears; it relieved her feelings to a slight extent.

The staff retained its equanimity, but the operations of Mrs Korner and her bosom friend were retarded rather than assisted by the voice of Mr Korner, heard every quarter of a minute, roaring out fresh directions.

'I dare not go in alone,' said Mrs Korner, when all things were in order on the tray. So the bosom friend followed her, and the staff brought up the rear.

'What's this?' frowned Mr Korner. 'I told you chops.'

'I'm so sorry, dear,' faltered Mrs Korner, 'but there weren't any in the house.'

'In a perfectly organizedouse such as for the future I meanterave,' continued Mr Korner, helping himself to beer, 'there should always be chopanteak. Unnerstanme? chopanteak!'

'I'll try and remember, dear,' said Mrs Korner.

'Pearsterme,' said Mr Korner, between mouthfuls, 'you're norrer sort of housekeeper I want.'

'I'll try to be, dear,' pleaded Mrs Korner.

'Where's your books?' Mr Korner suddenly demanded.

'My books?' repeated Mrs Korner, in astonishment.

Mr Korner struck the corner of the table with his fist, which made most things in the room, including Mrs Korner, jump.

'Don't you defy me, my girl,' said Mr Korner. 'You know whatermean, your housekeepin' books.'

They happened to be in the drawer of the chiffonier. Mrs Korner produced them, and passed them to her husband with a trembling hand. Mr Korner, opening one by hazard, bent over it with knitted brows.

'Pearsterme, my girl, you can't add,' said Mr Korner.

'I – I was always considered rather good at arithmetic, as a girl,' stammered Mrs Korner.

'What you mayabeen as a girl, and what – twenner-seven and nine?' fiercely questioned Mr Korner.

'Thirty-eight-seven,' commenced to blunder the terrified Mrs Korner.

'Know your nine tables or don't you?' thundered Mr Korner.

'I used to,' sobbed Mrs Korner.

'Say it,' commanded Mr Korner.

'Nine times one are nine,' sobbed the poor little woman, 'nine times two – '

'Goron,' said Mr Korner sternly.

She went on steadily, in a low monotone, broken by stifled sobs. The dreary rhythm of the repetition may possibly have assisted. As she mentioned fearfully that nine times eleven were ninety-nine, Miss Greene pointed stealthily toward the table. Mrs Korner, glancing up fearfully, saw that the eyes of her lord and master were closed; heard the rising snore that issued from his head, resting between the empty beer-jug and the cruet stand.

'He will be all right,' counselled Miss Greene. 'You go to bed and lock yourself in. Harriet and I will see to his breakfast in the morning. It will be just as well for you to be out of the way.'

And Mrs Korner, only too thankful for some one to tell her what to do, obeyed in all things.

Toward seven o'clock the sunlight streaming into the room caused Mr Korner first to blink, then yawn, then open half an eye.

'Greet the day with a smile,' murmured Mr Korner, sleepily, 'and it will – '

Mr Korner sat up suddenly and looked about him. This was not bed. The fragments of a jug and glass lay scattered round his feet. To the table cloth an overturned cruet-stand mingled with egg gave colour. A tingling sensation about his head called for investigation. Mr Korner was forced to the conclusion that somebody had been trying to make a salad of him – somebody with an exceptionally heavy hand for mustard. A sound directed Mr Korner's attention to the door.

The face of Miss Greene, portentously grave, was peeping through the jar.

Mr Korner rose. Miss Greene entered stealthily, and closing the door, stood with her back against it.

'I suppose you know what – what you've done?' suggested Miss Greene.

She spoke in a sepulchral tone; it chilled poor Mr Korner to the bone.

'It is beginning to come back to me, but not – not very clearly,' admitted Mr Korner.

'You came home drunk – very drunk,' Miss Greene informed him, 'at two o'clock in the morning. The noise you made must have awakened half the street.'

A groan escaped from his parched lips.

'You insisted upon Aimée cooking you a hot supper.'

'I insisted!' Mr Korner glanced down upon the table. 'And – and she did it!'

'You were very violent,' explained Miss Greene; 'we were terrified at you, all three of us.' Regarding the pathetic object in front of her, Miss Greene found it difficult to recollect that a few hours before she really had been frightened of it. Sense of duty alone restrained her present inclination to laugh.

'While you sat there, eating your supper,' continued Miss Greene remorselessly, 'You made her bring you her books.'

Mr Korner had passed the stage when anything could astonish him.

'You lectured her about her housekeeping.' There was a twinkle in the eye of Mrs Korner's bosom friend. But lightning could have flashed before Mr Korner's eyes without his noticing it just then.

'You told her that she could not add, and you made her say her tables.'

'I made her – ' Mr Korner spoke in the emotionless tones of one merely desiring information. 'I made Aimée say her tables?'

[264]

'Her nine times,' nodded Miss Greene.

Mr Korner sat down upon his chair and stared with stony eyes into the future.

'What's to be done?' said Mr Korner, 'she'll never forgive me; I know her. You are not chaffing me?' he cried with a momentary gleam of hope. 'I really did it?'

'You sat in that very chair where you are sitting now and ate poached eggs, while she stood opposite to you and said her nine times table. At the end of it, seeing you had gone to sleep yourself, I persuaded her to go to bed. It was three o'clock, and we thought you would not mind.' Miss Greene drew up a chair, and, with her elbows on the table, looked across at Mr Korner. Decidedly there was a twinkle in the eyes of Mrs Korner's bosom friend.

'You'll never do it again,' suggested Miss Greene.

'Do you think it possible,' cried Mr Korner, 'that she may forgive me?'

'No, I don't,' replied Miss Greene. At which Mr Korner's face fell back to zero. 'I think the best way out will be for you to forgive her.'

The idea did not even amuse him. Miss Greene glanced round to satisfy herself that the door was still closed, and listened a moment to assure herself of the silence.

'Don't you remember,' Miss Greene took the extra precaution to whisper it, 'the talk we had at breakfast time the first morning of my visit, when Aimée said you would be all the better for "going it" occasionally?'

Yes, slowly it came back to Mr Korner. But she only said 'going it,' Mr Korner recollected to his dismay.

'Well, you've been "going it," ' persisted Miss Greene. 'Besides, she did not mean "going it." She meant the real thing, only she did not like to say the word. We talked about it after you had gone. She said she would give anything to see you more like the ordinary man. And that is her idea of the ordinary man.'

Mr Korner's sluggishness of comprehension irritated Miss Greene. She leaned across the table and shook him. 'Don't you understand? You have done it on purpose to teach her a lesson. It is she who has got to ask you to forgive her.'

'You think – ?'

'I think, if you manage it properly, it will be the best day's

[265]

work you have ever done. Get out of the house before she wakes. I shall say nothing to her. Indeed, I shall not have the time; I must catch the ten o'clock from Paddington. When you come home this evening, you talk first; that's what you've got to do.' And Mr Korner, in his excitement, kissed the bosom friend before he knew what he had done.

Mrs Korner sat waiting for her husband that evening in the drawing-room. She was dressed as for a journey, and about the corners of her mouth were lines familiar to Christopher, the sight of which sent his heart into his boots. Fortunately, he recovered himself in time to greet her with a smile. It was not the smile he had been rehearsing half the day, but that it was a smile of any sort astonished the words away from Mrs Korner's lips, and gave him the inestimable advantage of first speech.

'Well,' said Mr Korner cheerily, 'and how did you like it?'

For the moment Mrs Korner feared her husband's new complaint had already reached the chronic stage, but his still smiling face reassured her – to that extent at all events.

'When would you like me to "go it" again? Oh, come,' continued Mr Korner in response to his wife's bewilderment, 'you surely have not forgotten the talk we had at breakfast time – the first morning of Mildred's visit. You hinted how much more attractive I should be for occasionally "letting myself go!" '

Mr Korner, watching intently, perceived that upon Mrs Korner recollection was slowly forcing itself.

'I was unable to oblige you before,' explained Mr Korner, 'having to keep my head clear for business, and not knowing what the effect upon me might be. Yesterday I did my best, and I hope you are pleased with me. Though, if you could see your way to being content – just for the present and until I get more used to it – with a similar performance not oftener than once a fortnight say, I should be grateful,' added Mr Korner.

'You mean – ' said Mrs Korner, rising.

'I mean, my dear,' said Mr Korner, 'that almost from the day of our marriage you have made it clear that you regard me as a milksop. You have got your notion of men from silly books and sillier plays, and your trouble is that I am not like them. Well, I've shown you that, if you insist upon it, I can be like them.'

'But you weren't,' argued Mrs Korner, 'not a bit like them.'

[266]

'I did my best,' repeated Mr Korner; 'we are not all made alike. That was *my* drunk.'

'I didn't say "drunk." '

'But you meant it,' interrupted Mr Korner. 'We were talking about drunken men. The man in the play was drunk. You thought him amusing.'

'He was amusing,' persisted Mrs Korner, now in tears. 'I meant that sort of drunk.'

'His wife,' Mr Korner reminded her, 'didn't find him amusing. In the third act she was threatening to return home to her mother, which, if I may judge from finding you here with all your clothes on, is also the idea that has occurred to you.'

'But you – you were so awful,' whimpered Mrs Korner.'

'What did I do?' questioned Mr Korner.

'You came hammering at the door – '

'Yes, yes, I remember that, I wanted my supper, and you poached me a couple of eggs. What happened after that?'

The recollection of that crowning indignity lent to her voice the true note of tragedy.

'You made me say my tables – my nine times!'

Mr Korner looked at Mrs Korner, and Mrs Korner looked at Mr Korner, and for a while there was silence.

'Were you – were you really a little bit on,' faltered Mrs Korner, 'or only pretending?'

'Really,' confessed Mr Korner. 'For the first time in my life. If you are content, for the last time also.'

'I am sorry,' said Mrs Korner, 'I have been very silly. Please forgive me.'

from They and I

This extract from *They and I*,
an otherwise pedestrian semi-autobiographical memoir
disguised as a novel, and published in 1909,
is selected for its sheer delight
in the absurdity of a domestic quarrel.

from THEY AND I

It has always struck me how much more satisfactorily people quarrel on the stage than in real life. On the stage the man, having made up his mind to have it out, enters and closes the door. He lights a cigarette; if not a teetotaller mixes himself a brandy and soda. His wife all this time is careful to remain silent. Quite evident it is that he is preparing for her benefit something unpleasant, and chatter might disturb him. To fill up the time she toys with a novel or touches softly the keys of the piano until he is quite comfortable and ready to begin. He glides into his subject with the studied calm of one with all the afternoon before him. She listens to him in rapt attention. She does not dream of interrupting him; would scorn the suggestion of chipping in with any little notion of her own likely to disarrange his train of thought. All she does when he pauses, as occasionally he has to for the purpose of taking breath, is to come to his assistance with short encouraging remarks, such, for instance, as: 'Well.' 'You think that.' 'And if I did?' Her object seems to be to help him on. 'Go on,' she says from time to time, bitterly. And he goes on easing up, she puts it to him as one sportsman to another: Is he quite finished? Is that all? Sometimes it isn't. As often as not he has been saving the pick of the basket for the last.

'No,' he says, 'that is not all. There is something else!'

That is quite enough for her. That is all she wanted to know. She merely asked in case there might be. As it appears there is, she re-settles herself in her chair and is again all ears.

When it does come – when he is quite sure there is nothing he has forgotten, no little point that he has overlooked, she rises.

'I have listened patiently,' she begins, 'to all that you have said.' (The devil himself could not deny this. 'Patience' hardly seems the word. 'Enthusiastically' she might almost have said.) 'Now' – with rising inflection – 'you listen to me.'

The stage husband – always the gentleman – bows; stiffly maybe, but quite politely; and prepares in his turn to occupy the rôle of dumb but dignified defendant. To emphasise the coming change in their positions, the lady most probably crosses over to what has hitherto been his side of the stage; while he, starting at the same moment, and passing her about the centre, settles himself down in what must be regarded as the listener's end of the room. We then have the whole story over again from her point of view; and this time it is the gentleman who would bite off his tongue rather than make a retort calculated to put the lady off.

In the end it is the party who is in the right that conquers. Off the stage this is more or less of a toss-up; on the stage, never. If justice be with the husband, then it is his voice that, gradually growing louder and louder, rings at last triumphant through the house. The lady sees herself that she has been to blame, and wonders why it did not occur to her before – is grateful for the revelation, and asks to be forgiven. If, on the other hand, it was the husband who was at fault, then it is the lady who will be found eventually occupying the centre of the stage; the miserable husband who, morally speaking, will be trying to get under the table.

Now, in real life things don't happen quite like this. What the quarrel in real life suffers from is want of system. There is no order, no settled plan. There is much too much go-as-you-please about the quarrel in real life, and the result is naturally pure muddle. The man, turning things over in the morning while shaving, makes up his mind to have this matter out and have done with it. He knows exactly what he is going to say. He repeats it to himself at intervals during the day. He will first say This, and then he will go on to That; while he is about it he will perhaps mention the Other. He reckons it will take him a quarter of an hour. Which will just give him time to dress for dinner.

After it is over, and he looks at his watch, he finds it has taken him longer than that. Added to which he has said next to nothing – next to nothing, that is, of what he meant to say. It went wrong from the very start. As a matter of fact there wasn't

any start. He entered the room and closed the door. That is as
far as he got. The cigarette he never even lighted. There ought
to have been a box of matches on the mantelpiece behind the
photo-frame. And of course there were none there. For her to fly
into a temper merely because he reminded her that he had
spoken about this very matter at least a hundred times before,
and accuse him of going about his own house 'stealing' his own
matches was positively laughable. They had quarrelled for
about five minutes over those wretched matches, and then for
another ten because he said that women had no sense of
humour, and she wanted to know how he knew. After that there
had cropped up the last quarter's gas-bill, and that by a process
still mysterious to him had led him them into the subject of his
behaviour on the night of the Hockey Club dance. By an effort of
almost supernatural self-control he had contrived at length to
introduce the subject he had come home half an hour earlier
than usual on purpose to discuss. It didn't interest her in the
least. What she was full of by this time was a girl named
Arabella Jones. She got in quite a lot while he was vainly trying
to remember where he had last seen the damned girl. He had
just succeeded in getting back to his own topic when the
Cuddiford girl from next door dashed in without a hat to borrow
a tuning-fork. It had been quite a business finding the
tuning-fork, and when she was gone they had to begin all over
again. They had quarrelled about the drawing-room carpet;
about her sister Florrie's birthday present; and the way he
drove the motor-car. It had taken them over an hour and a half,
and rather than waste the tickets for the theatre, they had gone
without their dinner. The matter of the cold chisel still
remained to be thrashed out.

It had occurred to me that through the medium of the drama
I might show how the domestic quarrel could so easily be
improved. Adolphus Goodbody, a worthy young man deeply
attached to his wife, feels nevertheless that the dinners she is
inflicting upon him are threatening with permanent damage his
digestive system. He determines, come what may, to insist upon
a change. Elvira Goodbody, a charming girl, admiring and
devoted to her husband, is notwithstanding a trifle *en tête*,
especially when her domestic arrangements happen to be the
theme of discussion. Adolphus, his courage screwed to the

sticking-point, broaches the difficult subject; and for the first half of the act my aim was to picture the progress of the human quarrel, not as it should be, but as it is. They never reach the cook. The first mention of the word 'dinner' reminds Elvira (quick to perceive that argument is brewing, and alive to the advantage of getting in first) that twice the month before he had dined out, not returning till the small hours of the morning. What she wants to know is where this sort of thing is going to end? If the purpose of Freemasonry is the ruin of the home and the desertion of women, then all she has to say – it turns out to be quite a good deal. Adolphus, when able to get in a word, suggests that eleven o'clock at the latest can hardly be described as the 'small hours of the morning': the fault with women is that they never will confine themselves to the simple truth. From that point onwards, as can be imagined, the scene almost wrote itself. They have passed through all the customary stages, and are planning, with exaggerated calm, arrangements for the separation which each now feels to be inevitable, when a knock comes to the front door, and there enters a mutual friend.

Their hasty attempts to cover up the traces of mental disorder with which the atmosphere is strewed do not deceive him. There has been, let us say, a ripple on the water of perfect agreement. Come! What was it all about?

'About!' They look from one to the other. Surely it would be simpler to tell him what it had *not* been about. It had been about the parrot, her want of punctuality, about his using the butter-knife for the marmalade, about a pair of slippers he had lost at Christmas, about the education question, and her dressmaker's bill, and his friend George, and the next-door dog –

The mutual friend cuts short the catalogue. Clearly there is nothing for it but to begin the quarrel all over again; and this time, if they will put themselves into his hands, he feels sure he can promise victory to whichever one is in the right.

Elvira – she has a sweet, impulsive nature – throws her arms around him: that is all she wants. If only Adolphus could be brought to see! Adolphus grips him by the hand. If only Elvira would listen to sense!

The mutual friend – he is an old stage-manager – arranges the scene: Elvira in easy-chair by fire with crochet. Enter

Adolphus. He lights a cigarette; flings the match on the floor; with his hands in his pockets paces up and down the room; kicks a footstool out of his way.

'Tell me when I am to begin,' says Elvira.

The mutual friend promises to give her the right cue.

Adolphus comes to a halt in the centre of the room.

'I am sorry, my dear,' he says, 'but there is something I must say to you – something that may not be altogether pleasant for you to hear.'

To which Elvira, still crocheting, replies, 'Oh, indeed. And pray what may that be?'

This was not Elvira's own idea. Springing from her chair, she had got as far as: 'Look here. If you have come home early merely for the purpose of making a row – ' before the mutual friend could stop her. The mutual friend was firm. Only by exacting strict obedience could he guarantee a successful issue. What she had got to say was, 'Oh, indeed. Etcetera.' The mutual friend had need of all his tact to prevent its becoming a quarrel of three.

Adolphus, allowed to proceed, explained that the subject about which he wished to speak was the subject of dinner. The mutual friend this time was beforehand. Elvira's retort to that was: 'Dinner! You complain of the dinners I provide for you?' enabling him to reply, 'Yes, madam, I do complain,' and to give reasons. It seemed to Elvira that the mutual friend had lost his senses. To tell her to 'wait'; that 'her time would come'; of what use was that! Half of what she wanted to say would be gone out of her head. Adolphus brought to a conclusion his criticism of Elvira's kitchen; and then Elvira, incapable of restraining herself further, rose majestically.

The mutual friend was saved the trouble of suppressing Adolphus. Until Elvira had finished Adolphus never got an opening. He grumbled at their dinners. He! who can dine night after night with his precious Freemasons. Does he think she likes them any better? She, doomed to stay at home and eat them. What does he take her for? An ostrich? Whose fault is it that they keep an incompetent cook too old to learn and too obstinate to want to? Whose old family servant was she? Not Elvira's. It has been to please Adolphus that she has suffered the woman. And this is her reward. This! She breaks down.

Adolphus is astonished and troubled. Personally he never liked the woman. Faithful she may have been, but a cook never. His own idea, had he been consulted, would have been a small pension. Elvira falls upon his neck. Why did he not say so before? Adolphus presses her to his bosom. If only he had known! They promise the mutual friend never to quarrel again without his assistance.

from My Life and Times

'The Wheels of Change' is one of the more amusing
and inconsequential chapters from
Jerome's *My Life and Times* (1926),
an excellent autobiography he had the good fortune
to live to see published at the end
of a busy and happy life.

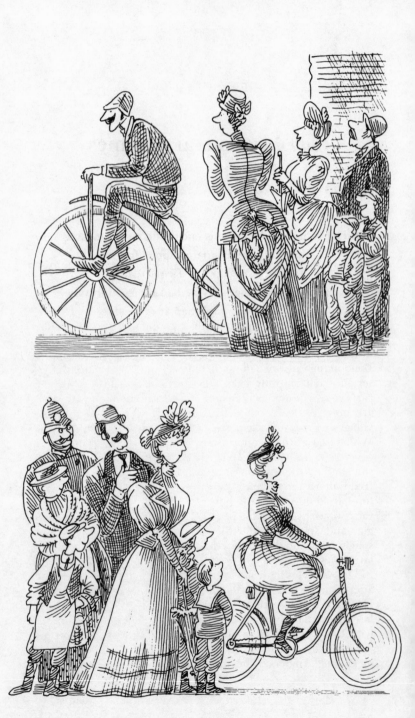

CHAPTER V

The Wheels of Change

When I was a boy, a stage-coach started each morning (Sundays excepted) from an old inn off the Minories. Not the shining band-box of the coloured print, with its dancing horses, its jolly coachman, and its dandy guard, but a heavy lumbering vehicle drawn by four shambling horses, all of a different size, driven by a rheumaticky old curmudgeon, who had to be hoisted on to his seat, and his whip handed up to him afterwards. It went through Ongar and Epping, but its final destination I forget. To many of the smaller towns round London the railway had not then penetrated; and similar relics set out each morning from other ancient hostelries. Carriers' carts were common everywhere, connecting London with what are now its nearer suburbs, but which were then outlying villages. A row of them stood always in the middle of the Whitechapel Road, opposite St Mary's church. They were covered with a hood, and had a bench for passengers along each side, and a little window at the back. For those in a hurry who could afford the price, postchaises were still to be hired, with top-hatted postilions and horses, with bells, that galloped over the cobbles. Respectable people – especially publicans – kept a gig; and sporting old ladies, on visits to their bankers or solicitors, would drive themselves into the city behind their own fat ponies.

The bicycle had not yet arrived: though nearly every afternoon an odd old fellow used to ride down Mare Street, Hackney, on a tricycle he had made for himself. In wet weather, he carried an umbrella over his head with one hand, and steered with the other. He was quite a public character, and people used to wait about to see him pass. The first bicycles were nicknamed 'spiders.' The front wheel was anything from fifty to

sixty inches in diameter and was joined to a diminutive back
wheel by a curved steel bar, shaped like a note of interrogation.
Their riders had to be youths of skill and courage, or woe betide
them. They wore tight-fitting breeches and short jackets that
ended at the waist. Your modern youngster on his grimy
'jig-pig' with his padded legs, his bulging mackintosh, his
skull-cap and his goggles, goes further and faster, I admit; but
his slim grandfather, towering above the traffic on his flashing
wheel, was a braver sight for Gods and girls.

It was my nephew, Frank Shorland, who first rode a safety
bicycle in London. A little chap named Lawson claimed to have
invented it. He became a company promoter, and later retired
to Devonshire. A cute little chap. The luck ran against him. It
was he who first foresaw the coming of the motor, and organized
that first joy ride from the Hotel Metropole to Brighton in 1896.
Young Frank was well known as an amateur racer. He believed
in the thing the moment he saw it, and agreed to ride his next
race on one. He was unmercifully chaffed by the crowd. His
competitors, on their tall, graceful 'spiders,' looked down upon
him, wondering and amazed. But he won easily, and from that
day 'spiders' went out of fashion; till they came to be used only
by real spiders for the spinning of their webs.

The coming of the 'safety' made bicycling universally
popular. Till then, it had been confined to the young men. I
remember the bitter controversy that arose over the argument:
'Should a lady ride a bicycle?' It was some while before the
dropped bar was thought of, and so, in consequence, she had to
ride in knickerbockers: very fetching they looked in them, too,
the few who dared. But in those days a woman's leg was
supposed to be a thing known only to herself and God. 'Would
you like it, if your sister showed her legs? Yes, or no?' was always
the formula employed to silence you, did you venture a defence.
Before that, it had been: 'Could a real lady ride outside an
omnibus?' or 'Might a virtuous female ride alone in a hansom
cab?' The woman question would seem to have been always
with us. The landlady of an hotel on the Ripley Road, much
frequented then by cyclists, went to the length of refusing to
serve any rider who, on close inspection, turned out to be of the
feminine gender; and the Surrey magistrates supported her.
The contention was that a good woman would not – nay, could

not – wear knickerbockers, 'Bloomers' they were termed: that, consequently, any woman who did wear bloomers must be a bad citizeness: in legal language, a disorderly person, and an innkeeper was not bound to serve 'disorderly characters.' The decision turned out a blessing in disguise to the cycling trade. It stirred them to invention. To a bright young mechanical genius occurred the 'dropped bar.' A Bishop's wife, clothed in seemly skirts, rode on a bicycle through Leamington.

Bicycling became the rage. In Battersea Park, any morning between eleven and one, all the best blood in England could be seen, solemnly peddling up and down the half-mile drive that runs between the river and the refreshment kiosk. But these were the experts – the finished article. In shady bypaths, elderly countesses, perspiring peers, still in the wobbly stage, battled bravely with the laws of equilibrium; occasionally defeated, would fling their arms round the necks of hefty young hooligans who were reaping a rich harvest as cycling instructors: 'Proficiency guaranteed in twelve lessons.' Cabinet Ministers, daughters of a hundred Earls might be recognized by the initiated, seated on the gravel, smiling feebly and rubbing their heads. Into quiet roads and side-streets, one ventured at the peril of one's limbs. All the world seemed to be learning bicycling: sighting an anxious pedestrian, they would be drawn, as by some irresistible magnetic influence, to avoid all other pitfalls and make straight for him. One takes it that, nowadays, the human race learns bicycling at an age when the muscles are more supple, the fear of falling less paralyzing to the nerves. Still occasionally, of an early morning, one encounters the ubiquitous small boy, pursuing an erratic course upon a wheel far and away too high for him – borrowed without permission, one assumes, from some still sleeping relative. With each revolution, his whole body rises and falls. He seems to be climbing some Sisyphean staircase. But one feels no anxiety. One knows that by some miracle he will, at the last moment, succeed in swerving round one; will shave the old lady with the newspapers by a hair's breadth; will all but run over the dog; and disappear round the corner. Providence is helpful to youth. To the middle aged it can be spiteful. The bicycle took my generation unprepared.

In times of strike, there emerges the old hansom. Its bony

horse must be twenty years older, but looks much the same. Its driver has grown grey and harmless; thanks you for a shilling over his fare, and trots away. Once, he was both the terror and the pride of London town. Nervous old ladies and gentlemen, on their way home to genteel suburbs, would ride in fear and trembling, wondering what he would say – or do – to them if they failed immediately to satisfy his exorbitant demand. Young men, with sweethearts, would furtively count their change, trying to guess how much it would cost them to silence his loud-mouthed sarcasm. Myself, I discovered that there was but one way of teaching him Christian behaviour; and that was by knowing more bad language than he had ever learnt, and getting it in first. How could he know that I had slept in doss-houses, shared hay-ricks with tramps? I had the further advantage over him of being able to add vituperation both in French and German. Outclassed, he would whip up his horse, glad to escape. But not all had my gift of tongues. The late Weedon Grossmith had recourse to guile. He had found a charming place called 'The Old House' at Canonbury. But it was far from theatre-land; and Weedon's difficulty was getting home at nights. From the Strand to Canonbury was what the drivers used to call 'collar work.' The horse had the work. The driver had the extra tip. Weedon was willing to pay in reason, but the old hansom-cab driver was a born bully: especially when dealing with a smallish gentleman in a lonely *cul-de-sac*. So instead of giving the address of his own front gate, Weedon always gave the address of a house near by that happened to be next to a police station. The constable on duty – not perhaps entirely forgotten on his birthday and other anniversaries – would stroll up as Weedon Grossmith jumped out. The cabman would accept his fare, plus a respectable addition, with a pleasant 'Thank you, sir'; and wishing Weedon and the constable good-night, drive off. And all was peace.

It was a picturesque vehicle, the old hansom: there was that to be said for it. George Augustus Sala, a bright young journalist, on the staff of *The Daily Telegraph*, called it the London gondola. And the bright young journalists of Venice wrote of their own gondola, I doubt not, as the Venetian hansom. But to ride in, they were the most uncomfortable contrivances ever invented. To get into them, you grabbed at two handles, one jutting out from the splash-board and the other just over the wheel, and hauled yourself up on to a small iron step. If the horse made a start before you got further, you were carried down the street in this position, looking like a monkey on a stick. If you had not secured a firm hold, you were jerked back into the gutter, and the cab went on without you: which was safer, but even less dignified. Getting out was more difficult. A false step landed you on all fours, and your aunt or your sister, or whatever it might happen to be, stepped on you. To enter or alight without getting your hat knocked off by the reins was an art in itself. The seat was just big enough for two. It was high, and only long ladies could reach the floor. The others bobbed up and down with their feet dangling. The world always thought the worst, but as often as not, one put one's arm round her purely to prevent her from slipping off. There was a trap door in the roof. Along dim-lit roads, one noticed the cabman holding it open, and driving with his head bent down. A folded window could be let down by the driver to protect you from the rain. It was called the guillotine. That was another thing that always knocked your hat off: and then it hit you on the head. Most people chose the rain. If by any chance the horse slipped – and he was the sort of horse that made one wonder how it was that he stood up – then the 'apron' doors would fly open and you would be shot out into the road – minus, of course, your hat. Another experience that could happen to you in a hansom was the breaking of the belly-band; and then the whole thing tilted up; and you lay on your back with your legs in the air and no possibility, if you were a lady, of getting at your skirts. As they had fallen, so they must abide; her only hope being that all such things as had now become visible were seemly. There was nothing to catch hold of, nothing by which one could regain one's feet. There one had to lie till the driver had extricated himself, and, with the help of the hilarious crowd, had brought the cab back to the horizontal. Then you crawled out, and distributed shillings; and walked home, without your hat.

I have no regrets for the passing of the hansom.

The old two-horse 'bus, one is glad has disappeared, if only for the sake of the horses. It had straw inside and a little oil lamp that made up in smell what it lacked in illuminating power. It carried twelve inside, and fourteen out – ten on the knife-board,

and two each side of the driver. The seats by the driver were
reserved for acrobats. You caught a swinging strap and sprang
on to the hub of the front wheel, leapt from there on to the
trace-pin and then with a final bound gained the foot-board.
The 'knife-board' was easier of attainment. You climbed up a
fixed ladder, the rungs a foot apart. The only real danger was
from the man above you. If he kicked out you were done. There
was no bell. Passengers stopped the 'bus by prodding the
conductor with their umbrellas. The driver wore a mighty coat
with flapping capes, and wrapped a rug round his legs before
strapping himself to his seat. He was a genial soul, not above
accepting a cigar, and had a tongue as clever as his hands. Wit
and sarcasm dropped from him as he drove. The motor has
silenced the humour of the streets.

I cannot help fancying that London was a cosier place to
dwell in, when I was a young man. For one thing, it was less
crowded. Life was not one everlasting scrimmage. There was
time for self-respect, for courtesy. For another thing, one got out
of it quicker. On summer afternoons, four-horse brakes would
set out for Barnet, Esher Woods, Chingford and Hampton
Court. One takes now the motor 'bus, and goes further; but it is
through endless miles of brick and mortar. And at the end, one
is but in another crowd. Forty years ago, one passed by fields
and leafy ways, and came to pleasant tea gardens, with bowling
greens, and birds, and lovers' lanes.

Of a night time, threepenny 'buses took us to Cremorne
Gardens, where bands played, and we danced and supped
under a thousand twinkling lights. Or one walked there through
the village of Chelsea, past the old wooden bridge. Battersea
Park was in the making, and farm lands came down to the
water's edge. The ladies may not all have been as good as they
were beautiful; but somehow the open sky and the flowing river
took the sordidness away. Under the trees and down the
flower-bordered paths, it was possible to imagine the shadow of
Romance. The Argyll Rooms, Evans' and others were more
commonplace. But even so, they were more human – less brutal
than our present orgy of the streets. Fashion sipped its tea, and
stayed to dinner, at the lordly 'Star & Garter,' and drove home
in phaeton or high dog-cart across Richmond Park and Putney
Heath. The river was a crowded highway. One went by steamer

to 'The Ship' at Greenwich, for its famous fish dinner, with
Mouton Rothschild at eight and six the bottle. Or further on, to
'The Falcon' at Gravesend, where the long dining-room looked
out upon the river, and one watched the ships passing silently
upon the evening tide. On Sundays, for half a crown, one
travelled to Southend and back. Unlimited tea was served on
board, with shrimps and watercress, for ninepence. We lads
had not spent much money on our lunch, but the fat stewardess
would only laugh as she brought us another pile of thick-cut
bread and butter. I was on the 'Princess Alice' on her last
completed voyage. She went down the following Sunday, and
nearly every soul on board was drowned. So, also, I was on the
last complete voyage the 'Lusitania' made from New York.
They would not let us land at Liverpool, but made us anchor at
the mouth of the Mersey, and took us off in tugs. We were
loaded up to the water line with ammunition. 'Agricultural
Machinery,' I think it was labelled. Penny gaffs were common.
They were the Repertory Theatre of the period. One sat on
benches and ate whelks and fried potatoes and drank beer.
Sweeney Todd, the Barber of Fleet Street, was always a great draw,
though *Maria Martin, or The Murder in the Red Barn*, ran it close.
Hamlet, cut down to three-quarters of an hour, and consisting
chiefly of broad-sword combats, was also popular. Prize fights
took place on Hackney marshes, generally on Sunday morning;
and foot-pads lurked on Hampstead Heath. Theatre patrons
had no cause to complain of scanty measure. The programme
lasted generally from six till twelve. It began with a farce,
included a drama and an opera, and ended up with a burlesque.
After nine o'clock, half prices were charged for admission. At
most of the bridges one paid toll. Waterloo was the cheapest.
Foot passengers there were charged only a halfpenny. It came
to be known as the Scotchman's bridge. The traditional
Scotchman, on a visit to a friend in London, was supposed to
have been taken everywhere and treated. Coming to Waterloo
Bridge, his host put his hand in his pocket, as usual, to draw out
the required penny. The Scotchman with a fine gesture stepped
in front of him. 'My turn,' said the Scotchman. Before the
Aerated Bread Company came along, there were only three
places in London, so far as I can remember, where a cup of tea
could be obtained: one in St Paul's Churchyard, another in the

Strand called the Bun Shop, and the third in Regent Street at
the end of the Quadrant. It was the same in New York when I
first went there. I offered to make Charles Frohman's fortune
for him. My idea was that he should put down five thousand
dollars, and that we should start tea shops, beginning in Fifth
Avenue. I reckon I missed being a millionaire. Gatti's in the
Strand first introduced ices into London. Children were
brought up from the country during the holidays to have a
twopenny ice at Gatti's. It was at the old Holborn Restaurant
that first one dined to music. It was held to be Continental and
therefore immoral; and the everlasting woman question rose
again to the surface: could a good woman dine to the
accompaniment of a string band?

As a matter of fact, it didn't really matter in those days. A
giddy old aunt from the country would sometimes clamour to be
taken out, but 'nice' women fed at home. At public dinners, a
gallery was set aside for them. They came in – like the children –
with the dessert; and were allowed to listen to the speeches.
Sometimes they were noticed, and their health drunk. The toast
was always entrusted to the comic man, and responded to by
the youngest bachelor: supposed to be the nearest thing to a
lady capable of speech. In all the best houses there was a
'smoking-room' into which the master of the house, together
with his friends, when he had any, would retire to smoke their
pipes or their cigars. Cigarettes were deemed effeminate. A
popular writer in 1870 explained the victory of Germany over
France by pointing out that the Germans were a pipe-smoking
people, while the French smoked cigarettes. If there wasn't any
smoking-room he smoked in the back kitchen. After smoking,
and before rejoining the ladies, one sucked a clove. It was said to
purify the breath. I remember, soon after the Savoy Hotel was
opened, a woman being asked to leave the supper-room for
smoking a cigarette. She offered to put it out; but the feelings of
the other guests had been too deeply outraged; forgiveness, it
was felt, would be mere weakness. A gentleman, seen in
company with a woman who smoked, lost his reputation.

Only mansions boasted bathrooms. The middle classes
bathed on Saturdays. It was a tremendous performance,
necessitating the carrying of many buckets of water from the
basement to the second floor. The practical-minded, arguing

that it was easier for Mohammed to go to the mountain, took
their bath in the kitchen. There were Spartans who professed
themselves unhappy unless they had a cold 'tub' every
morning. The servants hated them. It was kept under the bed,
and at night time was hauled out, and left ready for him with a
can of water. It was shaped like a wide shallow basin, and the
water just covered your toes. You sat in it with your legs tucked
up and soused yourself with the sponge. The difficulty with
emptying it. You lifted it up and staggered about with it,
waiting for the moment when the waters should grow calm and
cease from wobbling. Sometimes you succeeded in pouring it
into the pail without spilling half of it on to the floor, and
sometimes you didn't. It was the Americans who introduced
baths into England. Till the year of Jubilee, no respectable
young lady went out after dusk unless followed by the
housemaid. For years the stock joke in *Punch* was ankles. If a
lady, crossing the road, lifted her dress sufficiently high to show
her ankles, traffic became disorganized. Crowds would collect
upon the curb to watch her. The high-minded turned their eyes
the other way. But the shameless – like Miss Tincklepot's parrot
– would make no bones about 'having a damn good look.' There
came a season when Fashion decreed that skirts should be two
inches from the ground; and *The Daily Telegraph* had a leader
warning the nation of the danger of unchecked small begin-
nings. Things went from bad to worse. A women's club was
launched called 'The Pioneers.' All the most desperate women
in London enrolled themselves as members. Shaw, assumed to
be a feminist, was invited to address them. He had chosen for
his text Ephesians, fifth chapter, twenty-second verse, and had
been torn limb from limb, according to the earlier reports. And
The Times had a leader warning the nation of the danger, should
woman cease to recognize that the sphere of her true
development lay in the home circle. Hardly a year later, female
suffrage for unmarried women householders in their own right
was mooted in the House of Commons, and London rocked
with laughter. It was the typewriter that led to the discovery of
woman. Before then, a woman in the city had been a rare and
pleasing sight. The tidings flew from tongue to tongue, and way
was made for her. The right of a married woman to go shopping
by herself, provided she got back in time for tea, had long been

recognized; and when Irving startled London by giving
performances on Saturday afternoons ('*matinées*' they came to
be called) women, unattended by any male protector, were
frequently to be noticed in the pit.

The telephone was hailed as a tremendous advance towards
the millennium. The idea then current was that, one by one, the
world's troubles were disappearing. But for a long while, it
saved time and temper to take a cab and go round and see the
man. Electric lighting was still in the experimental stage; and
for some reason got itself mixed up with Bradlaugh and
atheism: maybe, because it used to go out suddenly, a
phenomenon attributed by many to the wrath of God. A judge
of the High Court was much applauded for denouncing it from
the Bench, and calling for tallow candles. A wave of
intellectuality passed over England in the later 'eighties. A
popular form of entertainment was the Spelling-Bee. The
competitors sat in rows upon the platform, while the body of the
hall would be filled with an excited audience, armed with
dictionaries. Every suburb had its amateur Parliament, with
real Liberals and Conservatives. At Chelsea, where we met over
a coffee shop in Flood Street, we had an Irish party, which was
always being 'suspended': when it would depart, cursing us, to
sing the 'Marseillaise,' and 'The Wearin' of the Green,' in the
room below. Rowdy young men and women – of the sort that
nowadays go in for night clubs and jazz dancing – filled the
ranks of the Fabian Society; and revelled in evenings at Essex
Hall. They argued with the Webbs, and interrupted Shaw.
Wells had always plenty to say, but was not an orator. He would
lose his hair if contradicted, and wave his arms about. Shaw's
plays always led to scenes on the first night. At 'Widowers'
Houses,' there was a free fight in the gallery. Shaw made a
speech that had the effect of reconciling both his friends and
enemies in a united desire to lynch him. The Salvation Army
came as a great shock to the Press. It was the Salvation Army's
'vulgarity,' its 'cheap sentiment' that wounded the fine feelings
of Fleet Street. Squire Bancroft was the first citizen of credit and
renown to champion the Salvation Army. Fleet Street rubbed
its eyes. It had always thought the Bancrofts so respectable. But
gradually the abuse died down.

Soho, when I was a young man, was the haunt of

revolutionaries. I came to know a few of them. When the revolutionary is not revolutionizing, he loves a sentimental song, or a pathetic recitation: will accept the proffered cigar and grow reminiscent over a tenpenny bottle of *vin ordinaire*. What I admired about them was their scorn of all pretences. Fourpence laid out at any barber's in the neighbourhood might have put the police off the scent. They despised such subterfuge. Their very trousers were revolutionary. Except on the legs of the conspirators' chorus in 'Madame Angot,' one never saw the like. I thought, at times, of suggesting to them that they should wear masks and carry dark lanterns. I believe, if I had done so, it would have appealed to them. It could have made no practical difference; and would have added a final touch of picturesqueness.

A little while before the war, I renewed acquaintance with the Russian revolutionary, this time at the house of Prince Kropotkin, in Brighton. Prince Kropotkin himself was a kindly, dapper little gentleman of aristocratic appearance, but his compatriots, who came to visit him, there was no mistaking. The sight of them, as they passed by, struck terror to the stoutest hearts of Kemp Town. There was one gentleman with a beard down to his waist and a voice that shook the ornaments upon the mantelpiece. He belonged to a new religious sect that held it wrong, among other things, to destroy house flies; but was less scrupulous, I gathered, regarding the existence of the *petite bourgeoisie*. Alas! even the best of us are not always consistent. During the war, I have listened to members of humanitarian societies chortling over the thought that German babies were being starved to death.

I fancy the At Home has died out. Anyhow one hopes so. It was a tiresome institution. Good women had a special afternoon: 'At Home every Thursday.' Sometimes it was every other Thursday, or every first Friday, or third Monday. One's brain used to reel, trying to remember them. Most often, one turned up on the wrong day. Poor ladies would remain in all the afternoon, sitting in the drawing-room in all their best clothes, surrounded by expensive refreshments; and not a soul to speak to. In my mother's day, the morning was the fashionable time for calls. There were always cake and biscuits in a silver basket, and port and sherry on the sideboard. They used to talk about the servants, and how things were going from bad to worse.

Douglas Sladen was the most successful At Home giver that I ever knew. Half *Who's Who* must have come to his receptions at Addison Mansions from ten-thirty to the dawn. He had a wonderful way when he introduced you of summarizing your career, opinions, and general character in half a dozen sentences, giving you like information concerning the other fellow – or fellowess. You knew what crimes and follies to avoid discussing, what talents and virtues it would be kind to drag into the conversation.

Science informs us that another Glacial period is on the way – that sooner or later the now temperate zone will again be buried under ice. But, for the moment, we would seem to be heading the other way. Snow drifts in the London streets were common in my early winters. Often the bridges were impassable, till an army of sweepers had cleared a passage. I have watched the sleighs, with their jingling bells, racing along the Embankment. One year, we had six weeks of continuous skating. There was quite a fair on the Serpentine, and a man with a dog crossed the Thames on foot at Lambeth. Fogs were something like fogs in those days. One, I remember, lasted exactly a week. Gas flares roared at Charing Cross and Hyde Park Corner. From the other side of the road they looked like distant lighthouses. Link-boys, waving their burning torches, plied for hire; and religious fanatics went to and fro, invisible, hoarsely proclaiming the end of the world.

On a morning in 1896, a line of weird-shaped vehicles, the like of which London had never seen before, stood drawn up in Northumberland Avenue outside the Hotel Metropole. They were the new horseless carriages, called automobiles, about which we had heard much talk. Lawson, a company promoter, who claimed to have invented the safety bicycle, had got them together. The law, insisting that every mechanically propelled vehicle should be preceded by a man carrying a red flag, had expired the day before; and at nine o'clock we started for Brighton. I shared a high two-seater with the editor of a financial journal, a gentleman named Duguid. We were fifth in the procession. Our driver, a large man, sat perched up on a dicky just in front of us, and our fear throughout the journey was, lest he should fall backwards, and bury us. An immense crowd had gathered, and until we were the other side of Croydon it was necessary for mounted police to clear a way for us. At Purley the Brighton coach overtook us, and raced us into Reigate. By the time we reached Crawley, half our number had fallen out for repairs and alterations. We were to have been received at Brighton by the Mayor and Corporation and lunched at the Grand Hotel. The idea had been that somewhere between twelve and one the whole twenty-five of us would come sweeping down the Preston road amid enthusiastic cheers. It was half-past three before the first of us appeared. At lengthening intervals some half-a-dozen others straggled in (Duguid and myself were, I think, the last), to be received with sarcasm and jeers. We washed ourselves – a tedious operation – and sat down to an early dinner. Little Lawson made a witty speech. All the Vested Interests of the period – railway companies; livery stable keepers, and horse dealers; the Grand Junction Canal; the Amalgamated Society of Bathchair Proprietors, and so forth, were, of course, all up in arms against him. One petition, praying Parliament to put its foot down upon the threatened spoiling of the countryside, was signed 'Friends of the Horse.' It turned out to be from the Worshipful Company of Whipmakers. Some credit is due to the motorists of those days. It was rarely that one reached one's destination. As a matter of fact, only the incurable optimist ever tried to. The common formula was: 'Oh, let's start off, and see what happens.' Generally, one returned in a hired fly. Everywhere along the country roads, one came across disabled cars: some drawn up against the grass, others helplessly blocking the way. Beside them, dejected females sitting on a rug. Underneath, a grimy man, blaspheming: another running round and treading on him. Experienced wives took their knitting and a camp stool. Very young men with a mechanical turn of mind get enjoyment out of them, apparently. At the slightest sign of trouble, they would take the whole thing to pieces, and spread it out upon the roadside. Some cheerful old lady, an aunt presumably, would be grovelling on her hands and knees, with her mouth full of screws, looking for more. Passing later in the evening, one would notice the remains piled up against the hedge with a lantern hung on them. At first, we wore masks and coloured goggles. Horses were terrified when they met us. We had to stop

[291]

the engine and wait. I remember one old farmer with a very restive filly. Of course we were all watching him. 'If you ladies and gentlemen,' he said, 'wouldn't mind turning your faces the other way, maybe I'd get her past.'

Motors were of strange and awful shapes, at the beginning. There was one design supposed to resemble a swan; but, owing to the neck being short, it looked more like a duck: that is, if it looked like anything. To fill the radiator, you unscrewed its head and poured the water down its neck; and as you drove the screw would work loose, and the thing would turn round and look at you out of one eye. Others were shaped like canoes and gondolas. One firm brought out a dragon. It had a red tongue, and you hung the spare wheel on its tail.

Flying-machines, properly speaking, came in with the war. We used to have balloon ascents from the Crystal Palace on fine Thursdays. You paid a guinea to go up and took your chance as to where you would come down. Most of them came home the next morning with a cold. Now the journey from London to Paris takes two hours. Thus the wheels go round; and to quote from a once popular poet: 'Ever the right comes uppermost, and ever is justice done.'

Monty Python Books
in Methuen Paperbacks

Other Silly Books
in Methuen Paperbacks

Cartoon Books
in Methuen Paperbacks

Simon Bond
101 USES OF A DEAD CAT
101 MORE USES OF A DEAD CAT
UNSPEAKABLE ACTS
ODD VISIONS AND BIZARRE SIGHTS
SUCCESS AND HOW TO BE ONE

Mel Calman
BUT IT'S MY TURN TO LEAVE YOU
HOW ABOUT A LITTLE QUARREL BEFORE BED?
HELP! AND OTHER RUMINATIONS
CALMAN REVISITED
THE BIG NOVEL
IT'S ONLY YOU THAT'S INCOMPATIBLE

Steve Bell
THE IF . . . CHRONICLES
IF . . . ONLY AGAIN

Claire Bretécher
FRUSTRATION
MORE FRUSTRATION

B. Kliban
CAT
NEVER EAT ANYTHING BIGGER THAN YOUR HEAD
WHACK YOUR PORCUPINE
TINY FOOTPRINTS AND OTHER DRAWINGS
TWO GUYS FOOLING AROUND WITH THE MOON

Sempé
DISPLAYS OF AFFECTION

Claude Serre
MEN IN WHITE COATS
THE CAR
SPORT
STUFFING

Bill Tidy

FOSDYKE SAGA: TWELVE

Thelwell

ANGELS ON HORSEBACK

THELWELL'S GYMKHANA

PENELOPE

THELWELL COUNTRY

A LEG AT EACH CORNER

THELWELL'S RIDING ACADEMY

UP THE GARDEN PATH

THE COMPLEAT TANGLER

THELWELL'S BOOK OF LEISURE

THIS DESIRABLE PLOT

TOP DOG

THREE SHEETS IN THE WIND

BELT UP

THE EFFLUENT SOCIETY

THELWELL GOES WEST

THELWELL'S BRAT RACE

SOME DAMN FOOL'S SIGNED THE RUBENS AGAIN

Other humorous and diverting books in Methuen Paperbacks

Kenneth Baker (editor)

I HAVE NO GUN BUT I CAN SPIT

Lisa Birnbach

THE OFFICIAL PREPPY HANDBOOK

Arthur Bloch

MURPHY'S LAW VOL I

MURPHY'S LAW VOL II

MORE MURPHY'S LAW

Eleanor Bron

LIFE AND OTHER PUNCTURES

Sandra Boynton
CHOCOLATE: THE CONSUMING PASSION

Jilly Cooper
SUPER MEN AND SUPER WOMEN
WORK AND WEDLOCK

Graeme Garden
THE SEVENTH MAN

Frank Muir and Patrick Campbell
CALL MY BLUFF

Bill Oddie
BILL ODDIE'S LITTLE BLACK BIRD BOOK

Katharine Whitehorn
WHITEHORN'S SOCIAL SURVIVAL
HOW TO SURVIVE IN HOSPITAL
HOW TO SURVIVE CHILDREN
HOW TO SURVIVE IN THE KITCHEN